D1540006

Social Science in Latin America

JOINT COMMITTEE ON LATIN AMERICAN STUDIES
OF THE AMERICAN COUNCIL OF LEARNED SOCIETIES
AND THE SOCIAL SCIENCE RESEARCH COUNCIL

Members 1965–66

JOSEPH GRUNWALD, The Brookings Institution, CHAIRMAN

CHARLES W. ANDERSON, University of Wisconsin

DAVID E. APTER, University of California, Berkeley

JOHN P. AUGELLI, University of Kansas

ROBERT N. BURR, University of California, Los Angeles

FRED P. ELLISON, University of Texas

ORLANDO FALS BORDA, National University of Colombia

ALLAN R. HOLMBERG, Cornell University

Staff: BRYCE WOOD, Social Science Research Council

Social Science
in Latin America

*Papers Presented at the Conference
on Latin American Studies
Held at Rio de Janeiro,
March 29–31, 1965*

EDITED BY
MANUEL DIÉGUES JÚNIOR
and BRYCE WOOD

*Columbia University Press
New York & London   1967*

The Conference on Latin American Studies was sponsored by the Joint Committee on Latin American Studies of the American Council of Learned Societies and the Social Science Research Council with the collaboration of the Latin American Center for Research in the Social Sciences, Rio de Janeiro.

Library
I.U.P.
Indiana, Pa.

300.98   C76a
C. 1

Copyright © 1967 Columbia University Press
Library of Congress Catalog Card Number: 67-15255
Printed in the United States of America

Foreword

Since its appointment in 1959, the Joint Committee on Latin American Studies of the American Council of Learned Societies and the Social Science Research Council has sought to advance research on Latin America through grants to individual scholars in the United States and Canada, and by improving communication among social scientists and humanists throughout the Americas. In this effort the Committee has also been concerned with providing perspective on the state of the social sciences in the region.

In order to further these objectives, the Committee sponsored a series of conferences of Latin American and North American educators which dealt primarily with training and research in the social science disciplines. A meeting in 1961 at Stanford, California, was concerned with sociology, another in Santiago, Chile, in 1962, with economics. A third, held in 1963, was inter-disciplinary and resulted in a book of essays, *Continuity and Change in Latin America*, edited for the Joint Committee by John J. Johnson (Stanford University Press, 1964). The Committee has, in addition, joined in sponsoring and assisting in the financing of other conferences in the sphere of inter-American scholarly relations, most recently with the Hispanic Foundation and the *Latin American Research Review* in Washington, D.C., May 1966. This was the meeting that founded the Latin American Studies Association.

These and other sessions helped bring together academicians in the hemisphere and thus strengthen rather tenuous ties among Latin American scholars. The meetings also served to air some of the problems of training and research in the region and several discussions resulted in publications such as the article "Latin American Economists in the United States" by Aníbal Pinto and Osvaldo Sunkel. (A translation by Bryce Wood appeared in the

October 1966 issue of *Economic Development and Cultural Change*.)

By 1963 it had become apparent that it would be useful to take stock of social science research on Latin America. In furthering this aim, the Committee sponsored a Seminar on Latin American Studies held at the Center for Advanced Study in the Behavioral Sciences, Stanford, California, July 8 to August 23, 1963. The papers and proceedings of the Seminar were published in *Social Science Research on Latin America*, edited by Charles Wagley (Columbia University Press, 1964). This book represented primarily the interests of scholars in the United States concerned with research on Latin America.

As one means of developing intellectual contacts with social scientists in Latin American countries, the Committee then organized a conference focusing mainly, but not exclusively, on the volume edited by Wagley. Several Latin American scholars were invited to write comments on individual chapters of the book; others were asked to prepare critiques on the status of the social sciences in general as viewed by Latin Americans.

The present book contains their papers which were presented and discussed at the Conference on Latin American Studies, in Rio de Janeiro, March 29–31, 1965, under the sponsorship of the Joint Committee with the collaboration of the Latin American Center for Research in the Social Sciences. Part I contains the papers concerned with general evaluations of the social sciences, while the more specific disciplinary critiques are in Part II.

The two books have revealed certain research gaps and delineated areas in which distinguished scholars feel further investigation would be fruitful. Latin American social scientists, as this book indicates, have been particularly preoccupied with the development process of the region. While from an academic point of view scholarly inquiry cannot be dictated by policy considerations, the problem of development has been so overwhelming and has occupied such a preeminent place in the minds of the leaders of Latin America that some orientation in the direction of social science research has resulted.

Many studies on the problems of economic development in Latin America have already been undertaken. Much more work will be needed in this field. What is also recognized in this book, however, is that economic studies alone cannot shed sufficient light on the growth processes of nations. New and better research in the other social sciences is needed in order to gain further understanding of the nature of economic, social, and political development and to provide insights and useful information for public policy.

In the near future, the Joint Committee hopes to be able to sponsor conferences of a substantive nature which would not only extend and deepen the exchange with distinguished Latin American educators but would also help meet some research priorities. In these plans the Committee has sought the advice of Latin American social scientists; a small consultative meeting for this purpose was held at El Colegio de México in December 1966.

The Committee plans to give even more attention to cooperative undertakings over a longer span of time. An effort will be made to sponsor some conferences in collaboration with Latin American institutions. In addition to fostering such joint meetings, the Committee has recently initiated a new program of grants for collaborative research between Latin American and North American scholars. Cooperation of this kind gives promise of significant benefits.

The Joint Committee hopes that by these and other means it will be possible to reinforce the bonds among social scientists in this hemisphere, while at the same time continuing to advance social science research on Latin America. The kind of friendly and scholarly interchanges which have characterized the conferences underlying this book contribute greatly towards this end.

The Joint Committee is deeply grateful to Bryce Wood of the Social Science Research Council who carried the major burden of organizing the conference in Rio de Janeiro and who coedited this volume.

The Joint Committee appreciates the encouragement and financial assistance of the Ford Foundation which made this publication possible.

JOSEPH GRUNWALD, *Chairman*
Joint Committee on Latin American Studies
American Council of Learned Societies
Social Science Research Council

Washington, D.C.
December, 1966

Preface

On behalf of the Joint Committee on Latin American Studies, I wish to express deep appreciation to the authors of the papers in this book and to all conference participants for their contributions. In particular, the Committee wishes to thank Dr. Manuel Diégues Júnior, Director of the Latin American Center for Research in the Social Sciences, for his Introduction and for his editing of the following papers in a combined Portuguese and Spanish version,* and for the hospitality and efficiency with which the staff of the Center, under his direction, arranged facilities for the Conference at the Hotel Gloria, Rio de Janeiro.

In the preparation of the English language edition of the papers, the editors wish to thank their collaborators: Cecília Roxo Wagley, for bringing order into the several bibliographies and for checking citations; Margaret Cucci and Valentine Rosen, and Colin M. Campbell and Frederick Fuller who made the translations; Madora Harris, Joanna Mueller, Kay K. Ryland, and Jacqueline Quayle for technical and secretarial assistance.

It will be noted that some of the papers refer to and criticize features of chapters in *Social Science Research on Latin America*. This book does, in some measure, depend on its predecessor, but every effort has been made to render it an independent work, capable of being read as such. The authors of chapters in the previous book have not been asked, nor have they requested, to make replies to comments on their work by the authors represented here.

It has been the editors' view that the papers should be presented straightforwardly; no attempt has been made to synthesize or conciliate or thematize the contributions, and very few edi-

---

* *As ciênicias sociais na América Latina*, (São Paulo, Difusão Européia do Livro, 1967) edited by the Centro Latinoamericano de Pesquisas em Ciências Sociais.

torial changes have been suggested or made. The authors are members of different disciplines in a number of Latin American countries and they express their own, individual views about the roles of the several social sciences, both in the development of national societies, and as research enterprises worthy of consideration because of their intrinsic human and intellectual interest.

The translations have been read and revised by the authors and the preparation of the final text has been the pleasant task of the undersigned, to whom the authors have delegated the awesome responsibility for its accuracy. If slips 'twixt simple cup and nearby lip receive classical acknowledgment, honest endeavors at complex mutual understanding among distant authors, translators, editors, and printer may, we hope, receive universal indulgence.

Some of the papers have been revised by the authors since the submission of the texts for the Portuguese and Spanish versions, so that a literal comparison of the two would not in all cases be significant for critical purposes. The intent of the Committee has been to offer to a wide audience the current thinking of some Latin American social scientists on fundamental matters of mutual scholarly interest.

It is hoped that the acquaintance initiated in this meeting may be cultivated in various ways through a common concern for the furtherance of objective studies contributing to economic, political, and social development in all American countries.

BRYCE WOOD

New York City
December, 1966

Contents

Introduction

For three days—or more precisely, for one full day and two mornings—Latin American and United States specialists, representing different trends in the social science fields, met at Rio de Janeiro for an exchange of ideas. The main purpose was to evaluate studies, previously prepared by specialists, on research on the various social sciences in Latin America; these studies comprise the book edited by Charles Wagley (1964). This evaluation also served another purpose: that of ascertaining the present status of these studies, and more particularly of research, in the social sciences.

It was not a formal meeting: Various trends and opinions were outlined and, if no definite conclusions were reached during this exchange of impressions and ideas, at least some rather meaningful suggestions, observations, and information were assembled. This exchange was, in itself, a great step forward because Latin Americans and North Americans alike spoke to each other frankly and expressed their thoughts and opinions, in a genuinely scientific appreciation, based exclusively on the methodological and theoretical principles which they formulated, drawing on their experience of research and versed as they were in their respective disciplines.

It was therefore a symposium of ideas—of ideas on economics, sociology, anthropology, and political science, with an admixture of history and geography which are not always regarded as social sciences, even though they are included by some authors as human sciences or, at least, humanities. Since the distinction between the so-called "social" and the so-called "human" sciences is apparently very tenuous or virtually non-existent, the inclusion of geography and history made it possible to consider the others, which are recognized as social sciences, from equally interesting viewpoints: that of space, through the contribution of geography, and that of time, through the contribution of history.

The contribution of history brought out one aspect which attracted the attention of the participants: The fact that it is not always concerned exclusively with the past but is also concerned with the present and can serve, and here experience of the past comes into the picture, to interpret or translate current events. This contribution may be regarded as the most important one made to the Conference by the discussion of historical problems, although there were obviously other aspects which were not less significant. Generally speaking, it became very evident that none of the so-called "social" sciences, or sciences classified as such, precludes the collaboration of history. The time, or historical, factor is essential for a knowledge and interpretation of anthropological, sociological, and political phenomena.

It should be emphasized, and the geographer called upon to express his views stressed this point, that this was perhaps the first time in Brazil that geography was included in a symposium on the social sciences. While geography provides the physical or territorial basis for social studies, it has not acquired in this context the status of a social discipline; at the most it is an ancillary discipline and is never on the same footing of equality. But it was established that geography has developed to a meaningful extent and has advanced far along the road from the early conception of it as a "physical description of the earth," i.e. a cold, material, and inexpressive subject, because the important thing on earth is man's presence and activity and not the earth for the earth's sake. Today geography has a very valuable contribution to make to social studies, for, besides its purely territorial aspect, it also deals with social and human aspects, namely, man's presence in the world. And this world is precisely the modern field of geography: the earth inhabited by man, transformed by him, used by him, and changed by him; and not merely the bare and virgin earth as it was created.

This contribution, that of the territorial, or geographical aspect and that of the temporal, or historical aspect, placed the social sciences, considered in the traditional manner, in a context that led to an interesting and lively debate which was not confined to research devoted to these fields in Latin America; the debate went further and covered the relations existing between them, the common fields of interest, in short their possible integration and not merely possible interdisciplinary collaboration. The subject of interdisciplinary research was one which was fully discussed.

There are at present two problems which merit urgent consideration in Latin America: comparative research and interdisciplinary research. The first will enable Latin Americans to gain a better knowledge of our reality in its diversities and similarities. Culturally speaking, we do not constitute a unit, even though we have many more similarities than differences. Crossbreeding produces different results as can be seen if we consider, for example, the aspects of population structure; the extent to which the indigenous or African cultures participate differs according to the structure of each of our countries.

We Latin Americans are, however, less a cultural, homogeneous, and monolithic unit than a composite region; to paraphrase a concept of Holmes (Holmes 1944: 56): We are a combination of similar areas or subareas, adjacent to each other, with elements which can join together or combine to create a common concept of life. It is this common concept of life that brings us together, that brings us closer, that identifies us by means of converging ideas, in our efforts to develop. Thus, without prejudice to our cultural diversity and displaying a certain spirit of unity, we can be Latin America; this is brought out more clearly by detailed comparative research.

Interdisciplinary research, for its part, opens up a wide and fertile field leading to more efficient comparative research. We are not referring to the application of several separate or barely related disciplines; what we have in mind is a situation in which the approaches of the various disciplines are combined in a kind of intercommunication which makes it possible to work together and interpret the same fact in its various aspects. We do not mean the "invasion" of disciplines but a joint endeavor without discrimination, without this or that discipline predominating; we mean a perfect pooling of effort in which methodology is skillfully applied.

It is clearly important for a region such as Latin America to be the subject of an interdisciplinary, and not just a multidisciplinary, study in which specialists work in collaboration. Otherwise it will be impossible to have a complete picture of our cultural, ecological, social, and economic conditions or, broadly speaking, of man in all his fullness.

This prompted Duroselle to state that a regional study can be successful only if "systematic use is made of all the disciplines that can provide valuable explanations" (1952: 674) a point with which Simey (1952: 713) and Fenton agree; the latter is quoted by Herskovits (1952: 729) in his reference to the focusing of all the disciplines on one area of culture, whereby a composite picture can be obtained of the culture. In a nutshell, what we wish to establish is the idea that, when studying a region, the cooperation of various disciplines is necessary, especially or principally the social or human sciences; and a region can never be characterized or interpreted by only one of these disciplines, or from only one aspect.

It was mainly interdisciplinary research that attracted the attention of the Conference, and the discussion became more lively when the subject of economic research was broached. Stress was laid on the importance of economics which, perhaps because of its seniority in Latin America, especially in the form of political economy, has reached a fuller stage of development than the other sciences—sociology or anthropology, for example—which are much newer to us. Special emphasis was also laid on the mutual "invasion" of disciplines which is taking place: Economists are encroaching on other social disciplines, and other social scientists are using or abusing economics. This is what led to the idea of interdisciplinary action in the field of social research in Latin America.

While interdisciplinary research obviously does not mean encroaching on each other's fields, be it the economist encroaching on sociology or the anthropologist encroaching on economics, it is equally clear that, in carrying out interdisciplinary research, there should be a perfect integration of methods and working techniques. The primary objective of interdisciplinary effort should be the integration of research and not just of ideas, a point which was, moreover, stressed at the Conference. Hence it is necessary not to import models but, on the contrary, to find models that correspond to Latin America's national realities.

Another item which the Conference took up and which constitutes one of the main aspects of social research in Latin America,
particularly now that Latin America is undergoing a transformation which is adding increasingly to the value of such research,
was the applicability of European or United States models to an
essentially different milieu. Even if the models are valuable, it
would be misleading and perhaps harmful to apply them directly
to the Latin American environment. Nor would it be sufficient to
adapt them; given the transformation which the social sciences
are undergoing in Latin America, surely we can already find our
own models—models that are properly suited to our national
peculiarities.

There is no point in referring again to the interest of United
States scholars in Latin America. Wagley (1964:1–32) covers this
briefly in the introduction to his collection of essays. This interest has obviously grown of late, although historical and geographical studies, which are still preferred in some quarters, predominate. In making this observation I am not overlooking the
work which has also been done in other scientific fields; Wagley
himself points out that, so far as economics and sociology are
concerned, until the 1940s the contribution of the United States
or of United States specialists to the study of Latin America was
indeed a modest one.

It has been in the last few years, as Wagley remarks, that social
scientists have "discovered" the vast research laboratory of Latin
America. This discovery has developed a strong attraction for
United States specialists not only because of Latin America's
strategic importance for national (United States) policy but also
because it offers an excellent laboratory for studying a rapidly
changing social system (Wagley 1964: 13–14). This explains why
Latin American studies are being intensified in the United States.

It may be remembered that, at the beginning of this century,
there was a Brazilian who called upon United States scholars to
study Brazil in particular: In a speech of 1907, Joaquim Nabuco
told the Washington University Club that Brazil offered United
States scientists "a great opportunity to extend the horizon of
science" (Nabuco c. 1911:115) because America had the men and
the means for the purpose. Obviously Nabuco was referring
mainly to natural science which, of course, does not exclude the

possibility of other studies such as the study of man. It is precisely in this field that United States studies of Latin America have been intensified in the last ten or fifteen years.

Another Brazilian who tried to strengthen links between North Americans and Latin Americans was Oliveira Lima. The same may possibly have been true of Latin Americans from other countries. The result has been that in this relationship the United States and Latin America have tended to concentrate on the scientific fields, especially the human sciences, and that it has been possible to study Latin America's features drawing on experience in research if resources and adequate facilities have been available. Certainly the interest of this subject was not lost on the North Americans, who turned their attention to the Latin American human laboratory, including one specialist who became a virtual Brazilian, Charles Wagley, whose study of an Amazon community (1953) is one of the first works of its kind by an American not only in Brazil but, I believe, in any part of Latin America. This, moreover, may be one of the first contributions ever made to the study of a Brazilian community; another is the study of Cunha, by Emilio Willems (1947) antedating Wagley's study by a few years.

Community studies, which the North Americans have developed to such an extent, are widespread and have found an excellent field of application in Latin America. It should be stressed at the outset that it was United States anthropologists who began this type of research, the community study, in the first decades of this century and who created an entire methodological system and technical facilities which transformed the research into one of the specific fields of social inquiry. Subsequently it was Latin American communities which were used for the application of research outside the United States. The North Americans are also to be credited with studies of what we might call the major communities in dealing with the rural or nonrural features of Latin American countries. Examples of this are the books by Lowry Nelson (1950) on Cuba, George M. McBride (1936) on Chile, Nathan Whetten (1948) on Mexico, Carl C. Taylor (1946) on Argentina, Olen Leonard (1952) on Bolivia, and T. Lynn Smith (1963) on Brazil.

The United States has thus made its contribution to the development of social research in Latin America. Its contribution is more than the application of methods it has developed; it is also based on a knowledge of Latin American realities. And now that our region is passing through an acute transitional stage in the search for its own process of social change, or for a process of development compatible with its true nature, it is impossible to dispense with this continuing cooperation. This collaboration cannot, however, be regarded as a panacea; nor does it eliminate the need to improve the methods of study and research.

This is one aspect of the relationship between the social scientists of Latin America and those of the United States, and apparently of other parts of the world, which deserves close attention: We find United States specialists, full of the best intentions, masters of a very efficient technique or methodology, trying to apply their theoretical models to ourselves. This often explains the not infrequently dramatic clash which takes place; two totally different environments are involved, to the obvious disadvantage of the weaker, namely Latin America.

But this is not the only aspect of this relationship. There is another aspect no less important, which was emphasized in September 1964 at the International Conference on Comparative Social Research* at Buenos Aires. It is the following: United States specialists, sociologists, anthropologists, and economists, study problems or subjects in Latin America which are of particular interest to them, or are connected with their teaching activities or with the university courses which they give, or again because they have received a grant for this purpose from some university or foundation. But these problems or subjects are usually not those of most direct concern to Latin Americans themselves; they are not those which have the most direct bearing on the needs or aspirations of our peoples; nor are they problems or

* The International Conference on Comparative Social Research in the Developing Countries was initiated by the International Social Science Council and the Instituto Torcuato Di Tella, and sponsored by the Argentine National Committee for UNESCO, and was held September 7–16, 1964 at Buenos Aires. The text of some of the papers presented and a summary of all the papers were published in *America Latina* [8 (1): 3–100 and 175–83, Jan/March 1965].

subjects of importance for the regional development process. Hence there arises another clash, or clashes, because this comes up in more than one Latin American country.

For this very reason it is urgently necessary to establish a system of liaison between Latin American and United States specialists in order to harmonize their mutual interests, or, more correctly, so that the North Americans could use their experience, facilities, and resources to study problems of vital importance to Latin American development. There is another aspect of this relationship between specialists of different regions: First and foremost, United States scientists must understand and appreciate the effort which their Latin American colleagues are making in the field of social science, on the one hand to improve their methods, and on the other to expedite scientific progress as a basic contribution to the economic and social development of Latin America.

This situation should and must be understood, given the headway already made in scientific activities—and here we refer particularly to the social sciences—in Latin America. We are already moving away from improvisation and amateurism; we are no longer mere theoreticians describing nationality, creating those national sociologies which testified to the status of social studies in the region during the last century. Argentine sociology, Chilean sociology, Mexican sociology, and Peruvian sociology, for example, were attempts at national description which did not always have a sound scientific basis but were a kind of intellectual interpretation of the elements constituting nationality in the light of ethnic, social, and economic factors.

A radical change has taken place in the social sciences in Latin America in the last few decades. The sociological, or what we might term "intellectualized" tradition, has undergone a transformation; the tradition of economics, politics, and anthropology has also changed; and this transformation is precisely the outcome of the attempt to combine research with teaching, which is now taking place although not yet on an extensive scale. The experience gained has been mainly derived from courses by foreign, mostly European, professors in Latin American universities, or from the training of Latin American students abroad through fellowships. The "improvisers" of earlier times are thus being replaced by well-trained specialists. Scientific improvement has been supplemented by professional skill and we are now on the way toward full professionalization. This is particularly true of economics, and it is certainly beginning in sociology, anthropology, and political science.

The exchange of ideas among specialists in different fields is therefore acquiring importance not only because they learn about each other's field of work and because this will prevent the encroachments against which so many complaints were made at the Conference, but also because it leads to the formulation of more effective research programs, in which the exchange of scientific experience does not mean that a superior technique predominates over an incipient one but, on the contrary, in which the latter can show what it can do. In short, it is an exchange of ideas which enables methodological fields, technical experience, and theoretical problems to be defined, thus avoiding duplication and disputes.

In this connection the Rio de Janeiro Conference was significant because stress was also laid on Latin America's social research requirements in the light of our experience. Admittedly there was no fixing of priorities, nor was this the purpose of the meeting, but it was realized that, since Latin America is at present striving to develop social research, and interdisciplinary research in particular, it cannot dissociate itself from this effort or ignore its importance.

Development as such did not, of course, claim the exclusive attention of the specialists attending the Conference; aspects of the regional development process were also studied. Stress was laid on the importance of planning as a means of achieving development and the fact that the research to be undertaken must therefore conform to the requirements of planning, which will lead into appropriate paths of economic and social development.

The Conference thus emphasized not only the importance of creating an awareness of regional problems but also the need to focus research on development. From this it may also be deduced that another important point, implicit in the previous observation, was established: the need to understand social factors in order to achieve development. Development is not exclusively economic, nor should it be. Getting to know the problems of development and research in terms of these factors, therefore, constitutes the main challenge for the Latin American social scientist.

Obviously the university has a crucial role to play here. It should be the responsibility of the Latin American university, and we are referring to the university in general without specifying any exceptions that may exist, to ensure that this knowledge is acquired and also to train the specialists to investigate the problems relevant to regional development. The university has a role but it is not yet playing it. This was another point brought out in the debates at the Rio de Janeiro Conference: The Latin American university, generally speaking, requires an overhauling of its present structure to adapt it to the purposes of our development,* because it is not performing the functions which it should in this process of change which the Latin American peoples are undergoing.

It was stressed that the university in Latin America, as a cultural institution, retains archaic or rigid forms which prevent it from performing its basic task, that of promoting social research. The Latin American universities are focusing on teacher-training and have therefore not kept up with the pace of development in social science research. They are not what they should be, namely centers of incentive, of impetus, of the actual rebirth of the social sciences. The Latin American university is in need of a structural overhaul which will enable it to train, with the requisite flexibility, the researchers, transformers, and motive forces of regional development. This job it is failing to do at the present time.

There is also an awareness of the gap existing between the élite and the masses. The former almost invariably have a bookish or

---

* Rudolph P. Atcon in a report (1963) considers university reform to be the best, most direct, and shortest path to social reform. The report provides a not always very encouraging picture of the present situation of the university in Latin America, but offers suggestions for its reform, some of which are quite interesting. In addition to the report, *ECO, Revista de la Cultura del Occidente* publishes a study by Jaime Jaramillo Uribe (1963), of the National University of Colombia, containing comments on the document and a reply to various opinions expressed by Mr. Atcon. Both the report and the comments offer very useful information on the present position of the university in Latin America and on ways of reforming it.

doctrinaire university training and are often strangers to the true Latin American environment—the "national reality"—and the latter are forsaken and unaware of the social transformation process in the direction of which they do not participate. The university should be the instrument for integrating the elite and the masses: It should enable the former to have a training more in conformity with the interests of regional development, and it should facilitate the access of the latter to training which could adjust them to the pace of development. The elite's remoteness from reality almost always contributes to disequilibrium in power relationships. The lack of university training in leadership, genuine leadership for development, is becoming a decisive factor on the political scene, or more precisely, it is contributing to political turmoil which leads to disputes, internal dissension, military coups, and party strife.

There is no doubt that this situation, the estrangement of politics from reality, affects the development of the social sciences and especially the development of social research in Latin America. It is not uncommon for the social sciences to be presented as subversive. Nor is it unusual to find sociology confused with socialism and social sciences with socialist ideas, precisely because of the fact that, through them, the most direct route can be found to rational, peaceful, harmonious, and integrated regional development. The universities turn into centers of resistance, rigidly organized, yet assailed by the ideas of young people who see the future more clearly, whereas the ruling classes endeavor to hold the clock back. In Latin America and in the social sciences there is no time to hold the clock back. The changes are rapid and they lead to a future which is closer to and more in keeping with national realities, and Latin American reality as a whole. As a political mentor which should steer the course of Latin American countries, the university rarely plays a role; and yet it could contribute a great deal toward ensuring that the process of social change in Latin America is effective and peaceful. There are few political leaders with advanced university training. But there are trained specialists who, being aware of the social realities of their respective countries, could direct the national development process. However, such specialists are still

largely trained by foreign experts, whose models, although carefully prepared and highly refined, are rarely compatible with the
social reality of our own countries.

The Conference, therefore, thought that, as a matter of priority, the Latin American university should be reorganized. Instruction in social research is academic and limited at present,
but the university could be converted into a dynamic center for
transforming Latin America by adjusting its own structure and
activities to suit not only national requirements, but those of
Latin American reality as a whole. This would not entail any
vision of Latin America as a social or cultural monolith, but
rather as promising a unity that derives from balancing diversities which are complementary or which can be mutually
adjusted.

The structural crisis of the university is not, of course, peculiar
to Latin America; it is also a sign of the speed of social and
cultural change which is to be found in other areas such as
France, as was recently pointed out in an article by George
Gusdorf of Strasbourg (1965: 10). The periodical *Esprit* (1964)
recently devoted an entire issue to the university. That issue,
which bears the very expressive subtitle *"Dossier pour la réforme
de l'enseignement supérieur,"* contains many articles and findings on the need for a structural change of the university. The
introductory article points out that higher or university education has become one of the major problems of the developed
countries; and Paul Ricoeur observes, in his study, that the university is confronted with a twofold task, adding that this is true
throughout the entire world, namely "that of meeting the challenge of large numbers and becoming a mass institution, on the
one hand, and, on the other, of succeeding in the difficult internal selection operation of singling out a brain, training it in
research and retaining the initiative of innovation in all fields"
(Ricoeur 1964: 1,162).

The most urgent task facing social scientists in Latin America
may well be that of transforming the university and adjusting it
to the regional development process, making it an instrument of
social progress, and forging it into a link between the elite and
the masses so that they can be integrated and complement each
other in the process of transforming our countries. The task is

particularly that of successfully combining research and instruction without dissociating the latter from reality or national experience but rather giving it the necessary impetus. Social science teachers will thus be able to train the new protagonists of social change in Latin America consistent with the requirements of well-balanced and genuinely Latin American development in all sectors.

There is little doubt that research is vital not only for the training of specialists, including teachers, but also, especially, for regional development from which the social sciences cannot remain aloof; on the contrary, these sciences are necessarily destined to cooperate since man is the subject of this development. It must be admitted that research is a long-term task. First, in view of its importance, research will become an instrument for creating an awareness of Latin American problems, and, second, given this awareness, research will then play its leading role by providing knowledge of the problems, policy, guidelines, and obstacles in the field of development.

It is here that the social scientist can concentrate his efforts; he can embark on new activities, analyze the situation, point out the paths to be followed, and suggest the methods to be applied to each situation in the light of its historical background and future prospects; it will also be his role to indicate which research and analysis models are best suited for the region, having regard to the changes in the social structure required for development. The starting point for all this should be inter-disciplinary research. And that is what Latin America, at this historic juncture, is demanding of its social scientists: That they should become part of, and not just associate themselves with, an overall and effective interdisciplinary research process.

In this sense, the Rio de Janeiro Conference opened up avenues and prospects. These avenues can be entered upon and these prospects can be fulfilled, and that is certainly what the social scientists of Latin America desire.

MANUEL DIÉGUES JUNIOR

Rio de Janeiro
December, 1966

REFERENCES

America Latina.
Jan.–March 1965: 8(1); 3–100 and 175–83.
Atcon, Rudolph P.
1963 Clave para un enfoque conjunto del desarrollo coordinado social, económico y educativo en la América Latina. *In* ECO, Revista de la Cultura del Occidente, Bogotá, vol. VII (1–3), (May–July).
Duroselle, Jean B.
1952 Les "area studies"; problèmes de méthode. *In* Bulletin International des Sciences Sociales, IV(4).
Esprit
May/June 1964. Paris (5–6). Special issue.
Gusdorf, Georges.
1965 Les universités n'existent pas en France. *In* Le Monde, Paris, Jan. 23.
Herskovits, Melville J.
1952 Le rôle de l'anthropologie culturelle dans la poursuite des "area studies." *In* Bulletin International des Sciences Sociales, IV(4).
Holmes, J. Macdonald.
1944 The geographical basis of government: specially applied to New South Wales. Sydney, Angus & Robertson Ltd.
Jaramillo Uribe, Jaime.
1963 Comentarios a un estudio de la Universidad Latino Americana. *In* ECO, Revista de la Cultura del Occidente, Bogotá, vol. VII (1–3), (May–July) .
King, Herbert William Henry.
[1951] The pattern of human activities. (Modern regional studies.) Sydney, Wellington, London, Australasian Publishing Co., n.d., pp. 20–21.
Leonard, Olen.
1952 Bolivia: land, people and institutions. Washington, D.C.
MacBride, George M.
1936 Chile, land and society. New York, American Geographical Society.
Nabuco, Joaquim.
(1911) Discursos e conferências nos Estados Unidos, translated from Artur Bomilcar, New York, Benjamin Aguila.
Nelson, Lowry.
1950 Rural Cuba. Minneapolis.
Ricoeur, Paul.
1964 Faire l'université. *In* Esprit (5–6), special issue (May/June).
Simey, Thomas S.
1952 L'apport de la sociologie et de la psychologie aux "area studies." *In* Bulletín International des Sciences Sociales, IV(4).
Smith, T. Lynn.
1963 Brazil: people and institutions. Revised edition, Baton Rouge, Louisiana State University Press.
Taylor, Carl C.
1946 Argentine rural life. Baton Rouge, La.
Wagley, Charles.
1953 Amazon town: a study of man in the tropics. New York, Macmillan Co.

Wagley, Charles (Editor).
1964 Social science research on Latin America. New York, Columbia University Press, Introduction: 1–32.
Whetten, Nathan.
1948 Rural Mexico. Chicago.
Willems, Emilio.
1947 Cunha: tradição e transição em uma cultura rural do Brasil. São Paulo, Diretoria de Publicidade Agrícola, Secretaria da Agricultura do Estado de São Paulo.

General Papers

FLORESTAN FERNANDES

1

The Social Sciences
in Latin America

The results of the Inter-American Conference on Research and
Training in Sociology * and of the Seminar on Latin American
Studies † enable us to establish one important fact: The self-
styled "Americanists" or "Latin Americanists" tend to adopt a
national, and in a sense competitive, approach toward advances
made in the social science fields in Latin America. These scholars
lack both information and understanding about the Latin American scene, and they are excessively preoccupied with the academic status of Latin American studies in United States university circles, and vicissitudes in the stages of development of those
studies. Despite intensified effort, in both quantitative and qualitative terms, the Latin Americanists are purely and simply interested in accumulating knowledge about Latin America and its
human problems. Descriptive studies of problems or regions, and
the need for comparative and interdisciplinary studies therefore
loom large in their discussions. But the intellectual effort exerted
by Latin American countries to develop the teaching and application of the social sciences, as well as research in this field, is
usually not fully or thoroughly described, as if this effort were a
marginal activity of no great value or major importance. The
main impression one derives is that the Latin Americanists with
a few exceptions, are explaining, for a closed-circuit intellectual
audience, how they envisage their intellectual roles, like the

* Held at the Center for Advanced Study in the Behavioral Sciences,
Stanford, California, from August 25–27, 1961, under sponsorship of the Joint
Committee on Latin American Studies.

† Held at the Center for Advanced Study in the Behavioral Sciences, from
June 8–August 23, 1963 under the same sponsorship. See Wagley (Editor,
1964).

ethnologists of bygone days who displayed the same mentality in their explorations of exotic peoples. The margin between this and an active kind of "scientific colonialism" is a narrow one.

To the extent that this writer's competence allows, this paper is intended to suggest, frankly and sincerely, how Latin American social scientists could formulate special programs for cooperating with the colleagues just mentioned, whom they, quite rightly, would prefer not to call Americanists, or Latin Americanists.

It is essential to understand that the most important thing for us is to develop science and scientific technology in our countries. However, we regard this development not as an offshoot of colonialism but as a crucial aspect of the cultural legacy inherited by our countries in the course of their historical formation from the sixteenth century to the present day. We do not look upon our foreign colleagues as "civilizing heroes," and, in return, we would like them to understand objectively the significance and scope of the intellectual aims we are pursuing through the expansion of scientific research. Many of these aims, as now formulated, may appear elementary. But they are fundamental; they form a basis on which to erect and gradually extend the institutions which science and technology are weaving into the pattern of civilization that is taking shape in our countries.

From this point of view, the little headway we ourselves manage to make is of greater real importance for the success of these institutions than the welter of publications that European and United States travelers, settlers, scholars, and scientists have been amassing since the sixteenth century. This literature, which is important for reconstructing the past or for other intellectual purposes, is emerging and expanding for the most part independently of the rising tide of educational and research institutions in Latin America. It does not therefore interest us to the point where we feel that it would be worth while trying simply to add to what is available in foreign research centers. In order to interest us, it would have to evolve, at least in some essential aspects, in another way; it would have to contribute, at least indirectly, to the intensification of scientific research and the promotion of specialization in the Latin American institutions concerned with pure and applied science.

This is a prelude to the general approach of this study—the choice of the three topics to be discussed and the way in which cooperation with foreign social scientists is viewed. The three topics are as follows: the main purposes of the expansion of the social sciences as visualized in the Latin American environment by those responsible for such expansion,* the importance of the contribution made by foreign specialists, as seen by the Latin American social scientist, and the importance of sociology as a strategic discipline in the present context of the social sciences in Latin America.

The Expansion of the Social Sciences in Latin America

Latin American social scientists are obviously striving to intensify scientific research. But so far as the results of such research are concerned, the direct results, which contribute to theoretical advances in the social sciences, and the indirect ones, which further the progress of the relevant educational and research institutions, it is the indirect results which attract the greatest interest and attention. This means that owing to the conditions under which they work, these scientists must give exceptional weight to results transforming scientific research into a means for achieving other ends. Although these ends are essential for the expansion of science and scientific technology in Latin America, their importance entails choices that may seem strange to the social scientists of the more advanced centers which are mainly or exclusively concerned with theoretical advances.

This fact must be faced with complete frankness if the different positions and evaluations of the foreign Americanist, and of the Latin American social scientist are to be understood. In one way or another, the latter is a conscious agent of cultural change. His approach to social objectives and activities is that of an innovator in the field of cultural dynamics; he must be alert to whatever existing or potential opportunities, offered by the environment, favor the introduction, strengthening, and differentiation of the multifarious institutions required by the scientific

* Only the main objectives are recapitulated here. For a more thorough presentation of the author's ideas see Fernandes (1963: ch. 5, 2; 1958: ch. 5, 4, 1).

system. In some Latin American countries, any advance in this direction appears to be genuine "modernization."

The first sociocultural innovation to be undertaken in this connection is the actual merging of science into the culture and the social system. Before converting scientific and technological knowledge into permanent social and cultural influences, the social scientist must mold the inherited existing social institutions or help new ones to emerge, thereby laying the cultural foundations of science and scientific technology, and of education based on both. In some Latin American countries which are more advanced in the urban and industrial revolution, many of the principal conditions already exist for the normal operation and progressive specialization of the social institutions on which the growth of the scientific system depends. Nevertheless, even in these cases there are certain defects which impede the development of scientific research and of its educational and technological applications. The social scientist must carefully observe the effects of these factors and strive to find ways and means of overcoming them. In particular, he must recognize and make creative use of certain small advantages deriving from the collective desire for progress. He can, of course, devote systematic attention to the first type of objective, but only to a relatively limited extent, since the dynamism and pace of growth of the social institutions through which he operates continue to provide the main objectives of his working strategy.

It is necessary to delve into this sociocultural background in order to understand and evaluate properly the nature and importance of the course of intellectual development that has been carefully outlined by some Latin American social scientists. At a time when scientific knowledge, the teaching of the sciences, and the constructive application of scientific discoveries have reached such a level of refinement in western civilization, some Latin American social scientists are shunning the resulting intellectual roles (despite a completely up-to-date yardstick for evaluation), as if they had once again to pass through some of the *pioneering phases* of scientific training in the modern world. They need to produce a fund of knowledge commensurate not only with the intellectual requirements of the scientific method but also with its theoretical possibilities and present applications. But they have a further obligation: They themselves must create or improve the necessary working conditions. Generally speaking, they play two kinds of intellectual roles simultaneously and necessarily: first, roles similar to those played by social scientists during the pioneering stage of the expansion of the social sciences in Europe between the first quarter of the nineteenth and the early twentieth century, and in the United States in the first quarter of this century, and second, roles deriving from existing social science research techniques as applied by modern European and United States social scientists. An analysis of the condition and requirements of social science in Latin America is difficult because of the fact that most foreign scientists either are unaware of this combination of roles or tend to reflect on "what is being done" or "what should be done," and unilaterally apply a working strategy formulated for the second alternative, as if scientific research took place in a vacuum. They ignore both the lessons taught by the past history of the social sciences in their own countries and the fact that the limited resources of the "underdeveloped world" constitute an added burden. They also underestimate the intellectual achievements which would realistically and effectively meet the true requirements of the situation in the social and cultural environment concerned.

These observations do not mean that the Latin American social scientist is indifferent to the implications of his intellectual roles in the scientific community. On the contrary, he cannot afford to make the mistake of wasting the few opportunities he has by pursuing scientific aims of uncertain empirical or theoretical value. Such pursuits are relevant only to his personal career, and this is a secondary consideration from the overall point of view. First and foremost, he realizes the need for the institutionalization, specialization, and expansion of research—which implies that personal ambitions must take second place. However skilled a specialist may be and whatever his personal ambition, if he identifies himself with the collective aims of social and cultural change, he will give absolute priority to the teaching of students, to the continuity of a possible line of research, to progressive improvement of the training of researchers, to creating career opportunities that will attract young talent, and to understanding the value of science to the community. Hence, if he does not have the capacity to discern, in the intellectual cooperation of successive generations, a nobler motive than his own self-fulfillment, he runs the risk of being unpleasantly surprised and highly rewarding projects may have to be prematurely abandoned.

All this leads to something fundamental. Where the social sciences have already found an appropriate cultural niche in Latin America, scientific research is not regarded as an exclusive instrument for promoting certain theoretical advances in scientific knowledge. It forms part of a sociohistorical relationship which makes people highly conscious of the importance of social science projects for laying or gradually improving the ground for scientific production itself. This leads to a kind of virtually unavoidable strategic opportunism which, despite good intentions, perverts the individual applications of the scientific mind. On the other hand, it also leads to results which demonstrate how assiduous and unheralded effort may nevertheless further the expansion of science and better the lot of the human communities involved. Putting aside the first of these results which is of no interest to the present study and may be regarded as a passing phenomenon, it would be advisable to outline at least the main implications of the second aspect. To confine this matter to its essentials, there are four points which show the positive contribution made by the Latin American social scientists in the social and cultural context.

First, the determined concentration of creative effort which is designed to take advantage of the opportunities that the environment offers for the expansion of science and of its important applications is already producing fruitful results in two ways. On the one hand, the training of specialists in the social sciences is ceasing to be an adventure in improvisation. Some institutions, such as the University of São Paulo, can train specialists in all branches of the social sciences and in some cases its standards are as high as those prevailing in the best educational and research centers. On the other hand, the pursuit of an "intellectual career" in the social sciences is no longer an unusual activity. Not only are there a number of highly desirable and rewarding opportunities in higher education and pure research (in the university mentioned, with the advantages of full-time employment), but other alternative possibilities of using personnel with scientific skills in technical sectors, in public or private administra-

Library
I.U.P.
ndiana, Pa.

300.98
C,1
C76s

tion, and in establishments of applied science are also rapidly emerging. These two developments enable us to consider the training of social science specialists in new ways: in terms of number and quality, and in terms of the continuity of creative effort and of cooperation between successive generations. There is a steady increase in the number of opportunities open to young people who have an aptitude for a scientific career in the social sciences and, at the same time, the intellectual, institutionally organized activities which guide their careers are becoming steadily more varied. Problems of limitations on the number and quality of students are tending to disappear, thanks to resources which are widening the variety of specialized fields.

Second, these advances are clearly reflected in what might be termed the "cultural development pattern" of scientific research. As the training of specialists with national resources and the employment of these specialists in normal careers ceases to be a first priority problem, the main areas important to empirical or theoretical research expand. This constitutes substantial progress which can be objectively evaluated. There is a gradual transition from the historicosociological type of analysis, that has prevailed in the past, to larger-scale research projects mainly because teamwork becomes possible.* Again, the major effort must be concentrated on descriptive research, which is also of great scientific importance, because the region under study happens to be Latin America which is not well known, whatever the yardstick used to gauge its problems. But greater ambitions can now be encouraged because in addition to large-scale projects involving descriptive analysis, projects with limited theoretical objectives are also emerging. This process is extremely important because, at the same time, great strides have been made in differentiating among the various specialized areas of research and in achieving a

---

* Relevant data are to be found in Florestan Fernandes (1963: ch. 6, 8, and 9). Chapters 8 and 9 contain particulars of two research projects in progress on industry in São Paulo and the factors and effects of underdevelopment in Brazilian society. For an overall evaluation of the continuity and scope of either of these research projects, a group of publications should be consulted relating to a field which began to be explored in 1951 with a draft study by Roger Bastide and Florestan Fernandes (1951), and followed by: Bastide and Fernandes (1959); Cardoso and Ianni (1960); Cardoso (1962); Ianni (1962); Fernandes (1965). As independent contributions relating to the initial phase of the projects, see also Bicudo (1955: 227–310); Ginsberg (1955: 311–61); and Nogueira (1955: 362–554).

modicum of stability and equilibrium in the institutions concerned with education, research, and application in the social science fields.

Third, the creation of career opportunities in private enterprises, public bodies, and specialized institutions greatly encourages the extension of scientific research to social problems at the control stage. It is impossible, within the limits of the present study, to devote to this subject all the attention it deserves. However, it is a fact that the requirements of the situation have involved social scientists in two distinct organizational phases of social research. They find themselves obliged to take an interest in the "solution" of social problems out of simple self-involvement in the sociohistorical situation. The directions in which the scientist's intellectual responsibility lies in open societies and the social pressures exerted to transform emotional and moral involvement into *effective participation* are sufficient to explain scientific preferences for research projects of real national importance.* But this involvement also occurs impersonally at other times, with more or less complex implications. Although many experiments may be subjected to unavoidable sporadic or permanent distortions, often owing to the partly or totally uncontrollable pressure of powerful groups, this does not prevent the occasional or permanent employment of social scientists in projects of great practical scope. This employment arouses greater scientific interest in nationally important social problems and also substantially widens the social scientist's intellectual horizon; a specialist who, in other circumstances, would confine his activity to the exigencies of his academic career eventually gives a fair share of attention to the three aspects of scientific knowledge—the empirical, the theoretical, and the practical—and, in so doing, is aided by the fact that his intellectual activities are included in the normal operation of institutions and services concerned with the applied sciences.† The sources that

* The stages of this process may be illustrated empirically by another study of the same author covering the participation of Brazilian sociologists in education reorganization movements; see "A Comunicação entre os Sociólogos e o Grande Público" (Fernandes, 1963: ch. 4).

† A good analysis of the way in which the social scientist (especially the economist) plays constructive social roles in this transition is given by Octavio Ianni, *O estado e o desenvolvimento econômico no Brasil* (1964).

condition and guide the social scientist's intellectual activities exercise the same kind of influence. They force the specialist to pay greater attention to the practical implications of scientific knowledge and to adopt attitudes and patterns of behavior which break down the social scientist's traditional isolation. Despite all the risks and drawbacks that such a situation entails, especially in Latin America, it has greatly helped the development of the social sciences, particularly by facilitating a better understanding of the nature, problems, and functions of the applied social sciences.

Fourth, there is the old problem of the social scientist's relationship with the layman and of the function of the social sciences in the community. There are also choices which have to be made regarding the institutional environment in which scientific work is done. These choices go beyond the formal pursuit of scientific knowledge because social scientists identify themselves with the historical development of their countries. Like other human beings, they strive to find solutions which reflect the collective desire for social change and modern institutions. The layman can thus understand their demands that scientific research should be intensified, because these demands coincide with the common desire for a change in the historical pattern of inherited civilization. Furthermore, awareness of the historically important social problems of national communities broadens the range of communication between the layman and the social scientist. Hence, because of their intellectual production and sometimes also because of their activities in the social community, these scientists, as a group, ultimately play a creative role in the dissemination of ideas, aspirations, and even myths which are very important for communities at a transitional stage in the introduction of scientific technology. Although certain distortions and especially certain risks are not always avoidable, the fact remains that the influence these scientists exercise ultimately bears fruit. It helps to promote the emergence of social attitudes and ways of thinking which lead to three simultaneous results: first, greater understanding and tolerance of the nature, goals, and results of scientific research as it relates to social problems; second, the enhanced importance of rational factors in the layman's perception, awareness, and explanation of existing "social reality"; and third, a tendency to regard the social sciences as a necessary element of "modern civilization," therefore essential for man's rational control of social problems, and thus encouraging very poor countries to make sacrifices in order to intensify scientific research. If the Latin American social scientist were "indifferent" to the urgent need for the institutional development of science and "neutral" in the conventional sense, the indirect support he receives from the layman and the sympathy aroused by his "intellectual cause" would lose their impetus.

These considerations show how useful it is to approach the development of the social sciences in Latin America as a sociohistorical process. This makes it easier to understand more clearly how the social scientist is associated with something which emerges from his outlook and professional life as a struggle for honest and exciting intellectual roles, for educational institutions that have their own vitality and a certain measure of autonomy in their operation or growth, for understanding, tolerance, and social prestige for himself, for science, for the possible applications of the social sciences. In brief, the history of the social sciences is very much a part of socially organized and historically directed human activity. Nowhere does science spring forth as an intellectual miracle. It emerges and progresses everywhere as a creation of man's inventive genius and of his urge to achieve a new and authentic cultural pattern. If we consider the development of the social sciences in Latin America from this angle, the social scientist is no mere agent of cultural transplantation. At the same time that he explores the potentialities of inherited civilization, he helps constructively and creatively to promote aspects of this civilization for which the foundations necessary for their introduction and development are lacking in his environment. However inadequate this explanation may appear as seen from the outside, it is certain that seen from the inside these are the main elements on which the very future of the social sciences in Latin America depend.

We are now faced with a question of crucial importance: Can the foreign, so-called Americanist, social scientist afford to ignore these aspects of the situation? However advanced the research centers from which he operates, is there not an underlying problem of scientific ethics in all this complex historicocultural process which must compel him to take a stand when considering his own work, and to take into account, effectively and dynamically, the present situation and future prospects of social science research in Latin America? Again, would it be advantageous and constructive, from the purely scientific point of view, to perpetuate the present gap between the extensive external research into "Latin American problems" and the internal effort generated by the contribution of Latin American social scientists themselves? There is a more serious aspect: Given the likelihood of more intensive external research programs, would it not be advisable to avoid further sources of tension and distortion since the more advanced centers can easily bring about radical changes in prevailing trends and since it is uncertain whether such changes are indeed desirable and productive?

These and other questions are vital. The Latin American social scientist is not following the dictates of social imitation. He is trying to build the social sciences on bases conforming to the pattern of history which encourages science to be introduced and developed, so that Latin America can be integrated into modern civilization. Should the foreign social scientist, especially when he is considered to be or is an Americanist, change his course and consider this element of reality? In any event, such questions do not constitute the whole challenge that confronts our Americanist colleague, for there is now a Latin American yardstick for measuring the content and scope of his intellectual contribution. Unless this yardstick is applied, the foreign social scientist will never find the answers to such questions however great his indifference to (or his genuine love of) the people who are the subject of his research or the sympathy he may feel for his Latin American colleagues.

The Significance of "Americanist Studies" in Latin America

The Americanist is also involved in a historicocultural process. But his contributions are directly and immediately concerned with the "progress of science." Generally speaking, it is the "problems of Latin America" and not *the spread of science in Latin America* which remains uppermost in his thoughts. The publications which result from these thoughts often center around intellectual activities connected with academic, scientific, or technical careers, which are organized and promoted by institutions in his own country. Hence, the main centers which regulate, distinguish between, and encourage the intellectual activities of the Americanist are situated outside Latin America in all but a few exceptional cases. Regardless of whether he aspires to academic degrees, to enhancing his position on the staff of a university or institution concerned with scientific research, to competing for reasons of prestige, or simply to obtaining further material to add to the knowledge of this region and its problems, the links between the Americanist and a given historical and cultural situation involve him, emotionally and morally, in the fate of the institutions of the national communities themselves. It may even happen that "the problems of Latin America" may constitute, in this context, a mere alternative or expedient; an alternative, because the same extra-scientific, personal, and institutional objectives could be achieved by selecting other subjects for study, such as "the problems of Asia" or "the problems of Africa"; and an expedient because, in many cases, an assignment to study certain aspects of this region is seldom accepted for genuine, lasting, and deep-rooted intellectual reasons. The choice is made because it "facilitates" certain adjustments, depending on the circumstances, to the advantage of the person concerned, or for reasons which it would be preferable not to discuss in this paper.

Thus, a great number of research and scientific studies deal with Latin America and its problems as an area and a subject, but they fail to provide an intellectual appraisal of the situation, or of the possibilities or future for the social sciences in this region. Whatever the quality of such studies, they only serve to add to what the Americanists themselves call "knowledge of the area," and their practical value, so far as the level of scientific research in the "indigenous institutions" is concerned, is purely indirect. As I pointed out earlier, the example provided by these scientists, whose achievements are eventually used to furnish certain minimum data expected by those who are dealing scientifically in their own countries with similar research problems and techniques, may possibly bear fruit in any Latin American research centers that emerge (Fernandes 1965: ch. 5, 4, and 1). Obviously this in no way alters the intrinsic value of the contributions of the Americanists from the scientific point of view, but it clearly involves a difference of social and cultural aims and of historical outlook which must not be neglected, especially now that political factors are creating greater interest in the area and Latin American studies are acquiring a new academic status not only in the United States but also in Europe, Japan, and the Soviet Union.

The Americanists probably have to start with certain historical facts. First, the rate of social and economic growth in some Latin American countries is slow, uneven, and unstable, but there is no evidence to show that this growth will stop or steadily decrease. Second, the dynamic operation of institutions involves constant modernization and sporadic spurts in the overall research capacity of modern western civilization's inventive resources. Third, it may be assumed, as a result of this progress, that the spread of science and scientific technology in these countries constitutes a pressing current problem because it is becoming a social need, conceived of and tackled as such. The main external conditions which promote the emergence and success of the social sciences in Europe and the United States, and which transformed the development of these sciences in the modern world into a historicocultural process are therefore present, with a few variations, in Latin America. The question that arises is whether the Americanists should ignore or should make use of and encourage the apparently spontaneous tendency of this historicocultural process to repeat itself.

If we delve into this matter, we will find what the Americanists call "local interests," that is, social scientists in a given Latin American institute or university. Local interests are nowadays less concerned with the intensification per se of scientific research than with the establishment or strengthening of the institutions which enable this aim to be achieved. However scientifically brilliant and indispensable Latin American projects prepared abroad may be, for us they are unfortunately less important than the acquisition or improvement of skills which will enable any person to undertake research for his own purposes or needs. But this is not the only paradox of the prevailing situation. The

Americanist is interested, in varying degrees, in the different countries of Latin America less as a specialist in the narrow sense and more as a scientist in the wider sense. In other words, for many Latin American countries the possible scientific ability of the Americanist is less important than the sum of his specialized achievements, and these countries would actually like to take advantage of the latter. If we analyze such implications still further, it will be easy to find common ground. The association with local interests could be achieved through special joint projects linking research programs with other activities, whereby the Americanists would take up temporary employment in Latin American educational and research institutions and undertake whatever intellectual duties these institutions were in a position to make available.

From another viewpoint, this would mean introducing new forms of intellectual collaboration and cooperation. If this point of view were to be considered and accepted, the Americanists would have a heavier burden of responsibility to bear, but in many ways their approach would become less rigid and they could really concentrate on mutual points of interest in Latin America. An entirely new attitude would have to be adopted and developed, because the above-mentioned responsibilities would involve two main things: first, a search for ways and means of combining research projects initiated abroad with the operation (or, in some cases, the establishment) of certain institutions in the Latin American countries, and second, an additional effort directed towards the expansion of scientific research in the region. Examples exist to show that both things are feasible and they suggest that there is a kind of reciprocal enjoyment of the resultant advantages. It would, however, be necessary to direct the process along new lines in order to generalize and establish as a regular practice what was previously haphazard and incidental.

The fact that this alternative is also interesting and remunerative for the Americanists goes without saying. A longer stay in the areas under study must become part of the normal routine. Most of the "specialists" who come to us are, as a rule, completely ignorant of the language and of the economic, cultural, and social history of the areas selected and, what is really amazing, of the local, national, or regional bibliography relevant to the "problems" which form the subject of their research. In a short period of time, they manage with difficulty to compile unreliable data for highly superficial surveys of very dubious practical or theoretical value. The system involving a different and longer association would produce good results, because it would give a larger number of specialists a valuable opportunity to be both observers and participants. Thus the specialist would not only be reeducated to understand the area, the people, the institutions, and their history, but would also acquire a new outlook enabling him to redefine the theoretical or practical problems of his projects, which are often very difficult at the outset and hard to apply to the historical and social situation without a more thorough prior knowledge.

There is another more general compensation. The Americanists are always disappointed with the apparently cold reception which their studies receive. Despite the interest they may arouse, these studies are not digested and utilized in the same way as publications by Latin American social scientists. A deeper understanding of the pathos and logos of the communities under study would help the Americanists to plan their activities in a way which would reduce or eliminate the number of failures resulting from selecting projects of little scientific interest and of no dynamic importance for the processes of perception, awareness, and actual intervention in the sociohistorical field.

Difficulties would, however, still lie ahead. The quality of the intellectual processes of the Americanists (and prospective Americanists) derives from a sociocultural pattern. If far-reaching changes are to take place in the present situation, it will not be sufficient simply to obtain more liberal allocations from the sponsoring institutions with which to pay for research projects which will take longer to carry out and be more complicated because of the additional activities involved. It will also be necessary to create conditions that make the aforesaid processes possible both in the operation of the foreign academic institutions and in the mentality of the specialists (or prospective specialists) concerned. If we take the United States as our point of reference, it will not be very easy to link many research projects with local interests, because this would seriously jeopardize careers organized on a highly competitive basis and entail various drawbacks for working programs of institutions in the United States. Again, the first and foremost intellectual requirement for the success of such action, if it is feasible, would be to ensure intellectual collaboration in unusual conditions with foreign specialists (who currently are seldom regarded and treated as colleagues) in the pursuit of objectives which may not be first priority intellectual projects in the United States. It would therefore be necessary to launch a major revolution in the mind of the Americanist (or of his students) to enable him to face a new challenge and, especially, to make him redefine the main bases of his intellectual processes.

To speak quite frankly, a real obstacle arises here. The working atmosphere and evaluations prevailing among the Americanists are not conducive to any kind of systematic cooperation with Latin American social scientists. Both the scientific and extrascientific goals of the Americanists and the criteria they apply depend on the academic institutions, specialized circles, and the public of their own countries. Accordingly, their relationships with Latin American social scientists suffer from a fundamental flaw which excludes the latter, and often their scientific production too, from the standing rules for scientific communication. This is aggravated by a chronic tendency to regard the emergence and blooming of the social sciences as a limited historical phenomenon, as if they were the exclusive attributes of countries such as the United States, Great Britain, Germany, and France, and not as a dynamic, cultural potentiality, implicit in the varied patterns of civilization inherited from the western world by the Latin American nations. The tragic result is that the magnitude and significance of the spread of the social sciences in Latin America are ignored, and an even more disastrous tendency to base evaluations on preconceived ideas unworthy of social scientists becomes more firmly rooted. Unless there is a sweeping and far-reaching change in these underlying factors, it will be difficult to make any real headway toward the progressive establishment of new criteria for scientific communication, productive integration, and systematic cooperation among foreign and Latin American social scientists. Whereas the latter keep themselves reasonably well informed about the progress of the social sciences abroad, the former (including most of those who also consider themselves Americanists) do not yet have: first, an objective understanding of the nature and scale of the strides made in the past thirty years by the institutions concerned with teaching and research in the social science field in Latin America, second, respect for the Latin American social scientist as a colleague who deserves to be taken into account, or third, an undistorted picture of the scale of the scientific output resulting from the expansion of these institutions and of the Latin American scientists' intellectual work.

These conclusions indicate that anomalies persist which make it difficult to bring into harmony the expectations and evaluations which guide the intellectual processes of indigenous and foreign social scientists working in the common field of Latin American studies. Probably, these anomalies will tend to disappear in time, thanks to the indirect effects of the expansion of scientific research in Latin America or because of the gradual maturation of the Americanists.* But even now, when these anomalies are creating misunderstanding, wasting constructive effort, and causing intellectual isolation, much could be done to make the means of communication more efficient and to take advantage for mutual benefit of such opportunities for specialization as do exist. Basically, and in different ways, those who are engaged in important scientific projects contribute toward the same ultimate objective, namely, improving the techniques of observation and analysis used in Latin American studies. This common element is strong enough to enable the means of mutual understanding and intellectual cooperation to be progressively improved. What is important is the initial willingness to accept new forms of interaction, but these new forms cannot exist and develop until the social sciences emerge, take root, and prosper in Latin America. Provided the legitimate differences and similarities inherent in the sociocultural trend of the direct and indirect objectives of scientific research are clearly understood, funda-

---

* In this connection stress should be laid, by way of example, on the importance of the contribution made by Kalman H. Silvert, *La sociedad problema, reacción y revolución en América Latin* (Silvert 1962), translated into Spanish from the original *The Conflict Society* (Silvert 1961) and which covers aspects of political behavior and of the operation of the political institutions to which many of his predecessors were blind.

mental meetingpoints will gradually be reached and a new day will dawn when the creative activities of the specialists will merge and the differences which discourage and hinder intellectual activities will become less marked or disappear.

Sociology in the Expansion of the Social Sciences in Latin America

Sociology has been regarded, since the days of Comte and Mannheim, as the basic social science and the only one which provides a comprehensive understanding of the causes and effects inherent in the organization of human social life. Whether or not we share this point of view, one thing is obvious at the present stage of development of the social sciences in Latin America: In view of the widespread use of scientific explanation as a technique for arousing social awareness and because of deliberate efforts to influence the social situation, the macro type of approach is assuming greater importance. Thus, independently of any dogmatism on the sociologist's part, the sociological approach to interpretation is gaining ground in all the social sciences, and sociology is acquiring the status of a basic social science. Since the procedures used for isolating and integrating social phenomena do not fully meet the structural and dynamic requirements of the historically accepted models of civilization, any analysis, be it theoretical or practical, must concern itself with the influence of specifically social factors (or sociohistorical factors) in shaping psychological, economic, political, and cultural processes.* Hence, more than the great founders of the social sciences, who are noted for their clear views of sociology as a whole (to some extent because of their links with social philosophy), and even more than modern economists who are concerned with the current dynamics of development, Latin American social scientists † are obliged to resort extensively and intensively to sociological explanations. Wherever and whenever they fail to find ready-made explanations, and this often happens, they do not hesitate to assume the sociologist's intellectual

---

* The term "cultural process" is used in the strict sense to denote the dynamic aspects of cultural interaction and differentiation.

† Implying those who are not sociologists by training, specialization, or profession.

role, improving *ad hoc* descriptions and interpretations which are sociological in content or by nature. Moreover, the same phenomenon occurs among educated laymen, especially in circles toward which the essayists, educators, social reformers, "enlightened" or "advanced" politicians, and thinkers have gravitated. Sociology enjoys, in short, surprising scientific or extrascientific prestige, as if it were not only the "queen of the sciences" but also held the key to any social problem.

If we reflect on this peculiar situation, we shall easily recognize something that is both an element of greatness and, at the same time, a constant stumbling block to the expansion of sociology in this part of the modern world. Everyone is striving to decipher and solve the historical riddles which seriously frustrate Latin America's cherished desire for progress. Sociology is therefore acquiring great importance and the sociologist is enjoying unusual intellectual prestige both in Europe and in the United States. On the other hand, this vague and unrealistic approach may very easily turn into something disastrous and self-defeating. Educated laymen, and even social scientists specializing in other fields, are prone to propound their *own* views of sociological truth and to defend them rather crudely whenever the opportunity presents itself, even against the findings of rigorous sociological research. The situation becomes extremely complicated, because the opposing viewpoints center around values that have the backing of vested interests and national myths. More or less influential and powerful pressure groups finally take positions, and the contributions of sociology and the findings of systematic empirical research are exposed to ethnocentric or ideological criticism. Since some of these groups occupy strategic positions in the power structure, such reactions and their consequences necessarily lessen the opportunities available for education and research in sociology. In general, therefore, sociologists derive little real benefit from the intellectual over-valuation of "sociological explanations" and often find themselves in the strange position of having to defend scientific research in their sector. It is difficult to turn to good account the educated layman's favorable disposition without at the same time laying bare his ideology. Moreover, something similar happens in the relationship with other social science specialists who are generally loath to agree to any far-reaching changes in their *ad hoc* interpretations. At both levels, insurmountable difficulties arise which create not only bad feeling but also real obstacles to a better understanding, and to the expansion of sociological research.

Within this faintly outlined frame of reference, there is a contradiction between what one thinks of sociology and what one does with it and through it. The instinctive desire to know and grapple with historical riddles does not confer upon a man, whether or not he has a scientific background, the power to change his nature. An abstract understanding leads to an intellectual precocity which is not matched by similar advances either in the layman's capacity to tolerate or use sociological knowledge or in the prevailing predisposition of social scientists who are more or less opposed to replacing easy improvisation by teamwork. Hence, the appeal to sociology (or to substitutes taken from various techniques of historicosociographical or historicopragmatic analysis) is not made with a view to cultivating sociological research proper or to promoting the theoretical refinement of sociology, but rather to expanding the social outlook of the people concerned in order to: first, increase the layman's social awareness of the situation; and second, make social scientists more sensitive to the dynamic impact of social factors on extrasociological situations. In brief, sociology's main importance derives from practical or theoretical motives which ultimately limit the direction, scope, and value of its possible uses, whether the theoretical motives are legitimate or not. It is important in one way because of the need for objective and realistic analyses of the sociohistorical situation as they are developed by the different types of political thinkers.*

It is also important in another way, because it involves hypotheses which make the sociological approach an additional tool of analysis. Either way, sociology is acquiring a strategic importance which is intuitively absorbed, developed, and neutralized in the very act of perceiving reality.

This being so, there would seem to be little point in devoting close attention to the opportunities for interdisciplinary cooperation that are offered by some national and international institu-

* With reference to this need and the relevant analyses, see Karl Mannheim (1950: 101–77).

tions promoting teamwork in the social sciences. Despite the importance of the trends launched by these institutions, the nature of the research which they undertake extends beyond the above-mentioned common ground and therefore does not accurately interpret the implications in such a way that sociology can be understood and used on this common ground. The most productive course would be, purely and simply, for the Latin American social scientists to analyze the most important contributions made in whatever supplementary investigation is most essential and creative. In any event it would be impossible to avoid, by such analysis, the false impression that sociologists are hostile to this use of sociology. Only one course thus remains open, namely, to note (even if only superficially and unsystematically) the levels at which the different methods of extra-sociological analysis necessarily and logically converge with the sociological point of view.* For this purpose, we shall examine certain features of studies undertaken by specialists in other disciplines.

Sociology and Other Social Science Disciplines

Not infrequently the geographer is confronted with the problem of man's rational exploitation of natural resources. Where technology is sufficiently advanced to permit such exploitation, the rural system or urban concentration, with their direct and indirect effects on regional development, impose solutions which are in varying degrees irrational, inappropriate, and destructive and can only be explained sociologically. Thus, taming the natural forces of the environment is no longer a constant factor in the civilization pattern of human communities; it now includes various phenomena inherent in the process of adjustment of a cultural heritage transplanted to a tropical milieu. The transplanted institutions lose their original organizational structure and, at the same time, all or some of their ecological functions,

* This leaves aside the question as to why this happens. Several more or less well-known influences are contributory, such as the nature of the situations and phenomena investigated, consideration of processes in history according to interpretative "macro" models, and the combination of empirical, theoretical, and practical interests in the intellectual horizon of the researcher. However, a discussion of these aspects would exceed the limits of the present study.

and man becomes incapable either of maintaining the pace of life of the inherited civilization pattern or of defending and protecting himself against the incursions of nature in the areas in which he exists and survives and which should be made immune to disaster. There is an alternative possibility that presents two aspects which are often found together: first, the capacity acquired by the human environment to adapt the ecological functions of the transplanted institutions through changes in its internal composition, and subsequent combinations of interdependence between nature, culture, and society, and second, the emergence and development of external living conditions which, socially speaking, can more than satisfy the organizational requirements of these institutions. Both aspects are rooted in specifically social processes, although they testify to the fact that the outgrowths, new acquisitions, and metamorphoses of the inherited civilization largely arise from man's passive or active reactions to geographical influences.

Something similar happens to the historian who is concerned with the sequence and explanation of historical events. Even in a community which is in the middle of an economic and sociocultural revolution, he may discover a strange but constant contradiction. Historically important administrative and political decisions are taken in the light of social policies which do not meet the requirements of the situation and are even less compatible with the long-term course of history. This contradiction is a result of the values that make up the cultural horizon of the ruling classes and of the slowness with which the emerging pattern of civilization responds to the more or less rapid changes in the social structure. Hence, the man who participates as an historical agent in the creation or growth of the great city is, for one reason or another, rustic and anachronistic in varying degrees, and he either remains indifferent to the purely historical need to choose among inevitable alternatives, or rejects them as untraditional, revolutionary, or too advanced. To understand and interpret this historically very important contradiction it is necessary to resort to sociological classifications of reality. These classifications reveal that, in very full and varied senses, the actors and their settings are not completely historical. Since the resources of the inherited civilization have to be reconquered step by step, non-historical sociocultural factors which facilitate and guide this reconquest become more important. The influence of these factors not only impedes or prevents historical awareness, creatively focussed on the distant future, but also nullifies, detracts from, or obscures the importance of other historical factors, including the constructive channeling of group conflicts and of the resounding demands of the masses. A historic awareness full of dignity and human courage is probably evolving but it is out of step with the current pattern of civilization and the social environment from which it emerges, and it rejects the current pattern together with all its unsatisfactory and nonconformist components.

The social psychologist is also faced with a dilemma: He is confronted with attitudes, behavior, and actions in which the protagonists earnestly present themselves as *Christians, human beings, and democrats* while an objective appraisal reveals the existence of flagrant social discrimination, ethnocentrism, and authoritarianism. An analysis which concentrates exclusively on forms of social evolution and self-involvement would not be sufficient to explain such psychodynamic aspects of the situation. We must go further and seek out what is anachronistic in what seems to be synchronized. It will then be possible to understand two things which are otherwise paradoxical: Archaic and modern forms of social evolution, self-involvement, and reciprocal treatment occur simultaneously on the sociohistorical scene; and even intelligent social behavior reflects and molds, in various combinations, the dynamic products of these two forms. However, they are not moral weaknesses or a kind of irrepressible hypocrisy that lurk behind apparently spurious attitudes, behavior, and actions; they constitute a way of life which links man simultaneously to the changing requirements of the past and present. Only sociological techniques of observation and interpretation enable us to appreciate this fact; they show us how the tendency of the social system to crystallize, even in urban and economically developed communities, involves the merger of structures which are exclusive in different degrees—archaic, modern, and ultramodern.

The economist who claims to have a complete explanation for certain key phenomena, such as the recurrence of economic disequilibria, the continuous operation of factors which stifle economic growth, and the vicissitudes of an irregular pattern of economic development, must likewise resort to sociological techniques of analysis. On the one hand, there are the problems created by the stubborn persistence of a cultural outlook which is inconsistent with the material and moral requirements of economic activity (including initiative and the spirit of enterprise) in a capitalist economy. On the other, there are the problems connected with the social, regional, and racial concentration of income. All things considered, the crystallization of the social system, however swift, proves to be insufficient to absorb, guide, and regulate the economic processes which should evolve "normally" from the theoretical point of view. Conversely, the crystallizing social system produces, simultaneously with normal stimuli, lasting effects which give a purely social meaning to the distortions, bottlenecks, and mistakes of the capitalist type of production. For this reason, in Latin America the economist, more than any other social scientist, finds himself in a vicious circle consisting of economic processes too weak to destroy archaic social structures and social processes sufficiently strong to impede or distort modern economic structures.

The anthropologist too has occasion to use sociology, especially when dealing with the dynamics of culture at the national level or concentrating on the mechanics of cultural transition from a traditional society to an industrial society. Again a historical dilemma arises. As part of the traditional system of inherited power, the educated elite of the ruling classes considered themselves to be the exclusive historical agents of cultural innovation. Thus a virtual monopoly developed which in the course of time became the source and instrument of social control. So long as the pace and scale of a socioeconomic revolution did not affect the position of these social classes in the power structure, the elite showed themselves to be more or less sensitive to the requirements of the present, and tolerant toward subsequent cultural innovations. They encouraged such innovations and, in addition, derived advantages from their direct or indirect contributions toward increasing the social concentration of income, social prestige, and political power. Whenever the pace and scale of the social and economic revolution, owing to internal changes generally consisting of a combination of immigration, demographic concentration, urban growth, the spread of capitalism, and the more democratic use of power, affect the position of those social classes in the power structure and threaten their control of the situation, the classes turn a deaf ear to the demands of the present and are hostile to the required cultural innovations. They wield their social power intelligently to prevent modernization and oppose it in every possible way. The elite of the ruling social classes are sometimes called enlightened, progressive, and revolutionary and, at other times, traditionalist, reactionary, and obscurantist. Whether the trend is in one direction or the other depends, historically, on their purely social ability (which is, however, no longer to be relied upon in the Latin America of today) to absorb the benefits of progress. The important point is that these elites interpose themselves between the centers of external influence and those of potential internal cultural development, thus constituting a third force which regulates, from within, the changing pattern of civilization in their national communities. Moreover, thanks to the control which they exercise over their communities, they prevent them and, where necessary, debar them from making the free historical choices characteristic of modern western civilization. All this vast complex of factors, weakening and determining the effects of cultural dynamics, must be examined, described, and interpreted by the sociologist.

Similar problems confront the political scientist. He is faced with institutions which are imported but which, nevertheless, form part of the organization of political power under the influence of strong national interests and aspirations. However, in practice the physical and human environment does not allow the assimilated political institutions to function normally—i.e. as prescribed by the prevailing pattern of civilization. Like the social psychologist, the political scientist has to cope with the contradictions between what is apparent and what is real. Like the economist, he finds himself in a vicious circle which makes society destroy all or part of the political processes which should facilitate the balanced operation and development of the power structure. Like the anthropologist, he witnesses the destructive effects of a situation in which "modernization" is monopolized by social classes who, on the political scene, conceal their direct or indirect defense of social privilege or their undermining of the democratic way of life. However, the political scientist's frame of reference covers the link between the crystallization of the social system as a whole and the corresponding forms of national integration and democratization of political power.

The transition from a traditional society to an industrial society in Latin America involves the transition from a national state, organized on the basis of inherited power, to a state that is democratically organized. The extent of national integration and of democratic consolidation varies, and, even in the case of countries where both processes are advanced, it fluctuates in continuity and intensity. The social concentration of power and the persistent tendency to identify moral values with the traditional social system constantly undermine the constructive social influence of national pressure and democratic outlook, and serve to perpetuate, and sometimes also to strengthen, hardened political attitudes and behavior. Where constructive influences are weak, the same factors foster political corruption and demagoguery as preferable solutions. Unless he thinks like a sociologist and applies sociological techniques of analysis, the political scientist will be unable to understand this ambiguity. If he removes political behavior, institutions, and processes from their social context, he will never manage to understand that, basically, all this drama arises from a combination of forces which subordinates national solidarity and the prospective democratization of power to the tendencies, existing in societies as a whole, toward social stratification and maintenance of the status quo.

Last, the jurist will find himself in an impossibly perplexing situation unless he can separate the formal aspects of lawmaking from its practical usefulness as an instrument of social control over human relations. As a rule, what is legitimate and completely effective from the formal aspect of positive law appears totally or partly ineffective in the day-to-day operation of juridical institutions and in the individual enjoyment of fundamental human rights. Purely social influences, since they are identified sociologically in the motivation and organization of human action, enable the legal system to be considered as part of the machinery providing access to social roles which would be completely or partly closed to entire groups of individuals. Certain factors, such as the economic situation, the nature of prevailing social and political interests, and the intellectual level, exert influence in varying degrees upon the ways these groups of individuals approach or make use of the advantages offered by the law. Because of these social influences an entire system of institutions, of vital importance for the community as a whole and for the balance of the social system, suffers a kind of sociohistorical contraction and exhaustion, and some of the principal constructive functions of the law in modern civilization are entirely destroyed, distorted, or impaired. Again, in such psychosocial conditions, legal norms and institutions lose contact with the wishes of the community, the processes of social change, and the tendency of the social system to crystallize. Sometimes they move ahead of the average development of the society; at other times they lag far behind. In either case, legal norms and institutions become useless in the long run as instruments for helping man to exercise rational control over social forces and problems. In short, the jurist must also resort to the sociological method in order to establish in what sense and within what limits the juridical system: first, performs certain constructive social functions of the law (dynamically or otherwise), second, is a fiction devoid of historical content, or third, is virtually a prison in which upward mobility is rendered impossible by an obsolete social structure.

This general picture, presented in such brief outline, clearly suggests that a comprehensive and objective study of reality must include sociology. In this connection, three points must be made. First, the sociological improvisations of other specialists in the social sciences are due to the lack of specific contributions by sociologists toward explaining the different aspects of the transition from a traditional society to an industrial society in Latin America. In the absence of such contributions, each researcher does his best to obtain equivalent information which will enable him to understand and explain observed phenomena. This first point indicates that it will become essential to intensify sociological research in all the directions mentioned. Obviously it is important and useful for each scientist, independently of his own speciality, to be able to draw on the descriptive and interpretive resources of sociology. In the long run, this will certainly enable the other social scientists to evaluate sociology more realistically and efficiently, and this is not always done either in Europe or the United States. Really vital and sociologically meaningful relationships are not always noted and developed as they should be. Hence, the best solution would be to place sociology and the contribution it can make towards explaining reality in a new context in which the sociologists would concern themselves with their specific intellectual roles.

Second, a result of such an intensive and extensive use of sociological thinking and techniques of analysis is to downgrade sociology and make it a kind of general servant of the other social sciences. There is one important point about this development, however, and that is that it will make it easier to understand the significance of social factors in the organization and differentiation of human social behavior. Moreover, in analyzing many relationships in which other extrasocial factors become important, sociologists and sociology have only the discoveries of other social scientists to draw on. Nevertheless, these potential advantages will be lost unless a deliberate effort is made to reorganize the very bases on which sociological methods of observation and analysis are used. Actually when the Latin American social scientist unexpectedly uses sociological bases, he is pursuing a broader objective; he is trying to redefine the nature of theory in the social sciences. He is seeking a more comprehensive knowledge which will enable him to include elements in his research which were ignored when theoretical work distorted or detracted from the explanatory and practical objectives of the social sciences. Accordingly, if we go to the roots of this whole intellectual process, we will find that what is really important is the kind of theory to be encouraged in the social sciences. In Latin America there is deep dissatisfaction with what is being done in Europe and the United States, and the result has been a highly ambitious and creative effort which may result in a better combination of abstract, empirical, and practical objectives in the type of theory to be developed by social scientists. None of this will happen, however, unless the sociologists succeed in correcting the foreseeable shortcomings of *ad hoc* sociological knowledge and make a larger original contribution toward solving the logical and pragmatic problems inherent in the above-mentioned tentative outline, which make sociology, if not the basic social science, at least a fundamentally strategic discipline. Only then will it be possible, in a really scientific way, to further the underlying purposes of the attempt to discover more comprehensive explanations which, at the same time, enhance man's foresight and his power of control over the social environment.

Third, what is obviously lacking at present are cooperative research projects to facilitate the collaboration of different social scientists in the study of certain groups of phenomena. The expression "interdisciplinary approach" would sound false and pompous here, because all that is actually meant is the channeling of intellectual contributions along the same lines. A genuine interdisciplinary approach calls for well-defined empirical, theoretical, or practical objectives, and relatively advanced ones at that. What must be encouraged, and this appears to be generally agreed, is something less ambitious at the outset: separate research projects in which those social scientists participate whose talents may be necessary for conducting specific macroanalyses. Such projects occasionally are launched in certain institutions which include sociologists, economists, psychologists, geographers, political scientists, historians, and jurists on their research teams. Meanwhile, the practice must become more general and spread from the planning and applied research institutions to other sectors of social inquiry.

Independently of this frame of reference, mention should be made of another aspect of sociology which is important for Latin American social scientists. As scientists, they feel obliged to attack, clarify, and solve practical problems which rarely occur in the "advanced countries" of western civilization. As noted earlier, their social environment provides chronically inadequate physical, human, and moral conditions for the establishment and development of the institutions in which the scientist works. Radical and intolerable inconsistencies therefore emerge at all levels of the relationship between science and social organization. This is evident in three basic ways: first, in the chronic shortage of physical and human resources for the expansion of scientific research, second, in the insuperable obstacles to the normal operation and growth of the institutions engaged in pure or applied scientific research, which has predictable effects on the motivation of the researchers and on the continuity of their work programs, and third, in the layman's insufficient or warped understanding of the nature, functions, and meaning of science.

All this seriously detracts from the factors favoring the expansion of scientific research and simultaneously helps the factors operating in the other direction. Looking at the matter from this angle, the practical problems of Latin American social scientists therefore derive from the combination of the forms of organization of their intellectual activities and the moral obligations which they stubbornly accept. The choice is difficult: One must either accept these obligations and create conditions for the development of the social sciences, or ignore them and encourage society's hostility to this development. It is the duty of scientists to strive for conditions which favor, more or less, the expansion of science; it is the duty of social scientists to promote and even demand the creation of the best possible conditions for the expansion of the social sciences. In any event, it is virtually impossible to separate these objectives from something more general: the destiny of civilization which transforms science and scientific technology into cultural structures governing man's creative activity. Even the most recalcitrant spirits finally realize the nature of this truth and eventually make a simultaneous effort in both directions. If it were otherwise, the expansion of scientific research would be a sham achievement, devoid of historicocultural content and reality. This shows the complexity of the social, cultural, and moral background of the intellectual processes of Latin American social scientists. There is no way for them to understand the requirements of the situation and to find adequate solutions, as scientists, other than resorting to specifically sociological thinking and explanatory techniques. They need sociology, or logical equivalents thereof, not only in order to face the problems but also to tackle them and submit them to intellectual analysis. There is always a more efficient method which must be discovered and effectively applied.

In this moral context, any Latin American social scientist who is concerned with the expansion of the social sciences will ultimately adopt the sociological outlook as an intellectual technique in order to: first, acquire an objective picture of the growth of science both as a general historicocultural process and against the historical background of his own national community, second, identify, qualitatively and quantitatively, the creative social forces inherent in the constructive social functions of science and to consider the methods whereby these forces may be released in his own national community, thus converting them into factors of social change, and third, identify which psychosocial or sociocultural factors of the environment are conducive or are not conducive to science, scientific technology, and to the development of the relevant social sciences and social control techniques.

This picture is seriously complicated by the sociohistorical relationships which condition the Latin American social scientist's intellectual activities and the fulfillment of his corresponding moral obligations. These intellectual activities and moral obligations easily conflict with social claims and expectations nurtured by other social circles. There are social groups, which, with some ideological consistency, eventually take a stand on what the social scientist is doing or claims to be doing. His contributions inevitably contain certain implications connected with the "great historical choices," regardless of any intention in that direction. This leads to expressions of hostility and, in certain circumstances, deliberate social pressures which are clearly designed to ensure that the social scientists are subdued and controlled by the groups concerned. The only social group which can avail itself of this opportunity, in the present historical situation, is the elite of the ruling classes. In the traditionalist world, the elite has complete control over those phenomena of social change which could affect its position in the hierarchy and therefore its social interests and ideologies. Thanks to changes that are now visibly under way it is losing much of that control. As a result, each expression of intellectual independence and objectivity by the social scientist gives the impression that the stability of the social system is at stake. The social scientist sees the fruits of his intellectual efforts projected against a crude and potentially violent ideological background. He can escape from this conflict only if, by spontaneous loyalty or by extrascientific adjustments, he conforms to prevailing expectations. Furthermore, modernization in Latin America tends, in the long run, to make what might be called the "epicentric values" of social change more effective. In particular, certain psychosocial and sociocul-

tural stimuli, associated with national integration and the operation of democratic principles, combine to enhance the state's
autonomy or power of decision. As a result, the aforesaid elite
gradually loses some of its direct or indirect control over organized political power. The main result of this process, for social
scientists, is that new and creative intellectual activities emerge
to challenge them in the administrative or political field.* Since
they identify themselves through the development machinery of
the national, democratic state, and because of the nature of their
own scientific knowledge, which is dedicated to the interests of the
nation as a whole, social scientists are exposed to the antagonisms
of those who defend well-established economic, social, and political policies. They even run the risk of being branded as ex-
tremists and of being opposed as such. Both factors make it even
more necessary to make systematic use of sociological analysis;
otherwise the social scientist will find himself, unarmed and
defenseless, confronting opinions and pressures which have undesirable effects concerning the way in which scientific research
into historical and social phenomena is approached, used, and
developed.

Although these points do not cover the subject as fully as
might be desired, they indicate how and why sociology is of
strategic importance in forming the cultural horizon of the Latin
American social scientist. He requires it as a social technique,
necessary because of his intellectual pursuits. In order to play his
various intellectual roles, he must make decisive and constant use
of a kind of sociology of science and of the relationships between
the social scientist and society. The practical problems that arise
affect the type of intellectual work which has to be done and
involve something which does not allow of concessions. Even if
more productive opportunities are closed to it, sociology provides
a free knowledge of the adjustments that are possible and of their
foreseeable effects. This implies, in one way or another, an effective increase in the available ways and means of defending the
scientific criteria for ascertaining reality, propagating truth, and
changing society. All this goes to show that, besides its impor-

* With reference to the dynamic links between the intellectual roles of
social scientists and the demands of the historical and social situation, see
Florestan Fernandes (1963: 77–109).

tance as a more or less inevitable additional technique, sociology is a vital element in the social scientist's relationship with his own historic world.

Conclusion

So far as the objectives under discussion in this Conference are concerned, the subjects covered in this paper are provocative, although the general underlying spirit of them is constructive. The point is that a complete about-face must be executed. For one thing, the Americanists (especially when they are United States social scientists) must lose no time in revolutionizing their approach to observation and analysis. There is no excuse, particularly after the encouraging development of the social sciences in the main Latin American centers of research, education, and applied science, for the continued existence of old stereotyped opinions about the significance and scope of indigenous advances in social research at those centers. To say the least, if research is carried out under certain conditions, the wasteful duplication of effort will increase and the foreign specialist will continue to lose each day more and more of the small and doubtful advantages which he enjoys. These consist of material facilities that cannot outweigh the corresponding disadvantages, such as a degree of self-involvement and familiarity with various local or national situations, personal experience of the evolution of behavioral patterns, the molding of personality and social institutions, and direct and full participation in the processes of regional change. It also seems clear that the time for redefining the more comprehensive objectives of the Latin American social scientists' theoretical work is approaching. The latter need to free themselves even more from the immediate pressures of their scientific work, so that they can make greater use of their creative intellects for the main purposes of scientific explanation. Briefly, this means that they should participate in the campaign to expand educational and research institutions, but that the strategy they adopt should require an increasingly smaller sacrifice of their positive contributions to the current development of the social sciences.

From this angle, it seems obvious that there should be no difficulty in finding mutually advantageous forms of cooperation which will insure simultaneous fulfillment of the aims pursued by the Americanists and by their Latin American colleagues. With a few minor changes in the planning and execution of their research projects, the former will be able not only to take into account the development of the social sciences in Latin America but also to make a substantial contribution toward selecting and strengthening promising trends in research. If the relevant activities are scrupulously aimed at maintaining and promoting these trends the Latin American scientists would, in their turn, have further opportunities for research, with regard to the content, variety, organization, and scientific value of projects. Not only would it be easier to revitalize the existing educational and research institutions, but the continuity and progressive specialization of social research would also cease to be a troublesome problem.

For this twofold development to take place the main thing is to begin by defining mutually acceptable objectives, so that the incentive to expand the social sciences in Latin America does not frustrate the creative efforts of the Americanists and, conversely, so that the increase in foreign collaboration does not destroy or corrupt the productiveness and originality of the Latin American social scientists' intellectual work. Great caution and integrity of purpose must be shown, because a wrong step in either direction would irreparably jeopardize higher objectives connected with the flourishing of the social sciences. It would be an even greater risk, in the present historical and cultural situation, to encourage impractical or unimportant projects for developing social research and the social sciences in Latin America. What the Americanists seem to have in mind is not interdisciplinary research proper, but teamwork which would involve the cooperation of social scientists in macroanalyses. Since the latter is largely lacking in the Latin American centers of pure and applied social research, it may be possible to find a mutually satisfactory combination. Other examples lead to similar conclusions, which demonstrates the value of the discussion at this Conference, and show that various opportunities exist for fruitful and systematic collaboration.

What will presumably be more difficult is establishing the extrascientific scale of motivations and values that social scientists share. This evaluation of sociology depends both on intellectual needs for macroanalysis and on forms of self-involvement by researchers in sociohistorical processes. Even at this level opportunities still exist for understanding and adjustment. What will perplex the foreign scientist is the way in which the Latin American social scientist plays his intellectual roles, participating simultaneously, and, as we have seen, inevitably, in the general trends of sociohistorical development and in the specific trends of scientific development. But this source of diverging evaluations and interests is incidental and transitory. It is consistent with the more rigorous scientific spirit and it also ceases to be perplexing when viewed in the light of long-term objectives. No social scientist from any part of the world will fail to agree that it is essential to promote democracy, to combine economic development with social justice, to explore the resources of science for the benefit of human communities and social equity. However, the only important difference between the Americanists who are more or less indifferent to what is happening in Latin American communities and the social scientists living in these communities is the fact that the former can ignore, in their own countries, the means whereby these ends can be achieved within the context of our time and civilization. From this point of view, the strategic position of the Latin American social scientist can be understood and approved together with its peculiar intellectual implications. These implications bestow a special and unique importance upon sociology as a means of establishing a new pattern of theory, in which better empirical, theoretical, and practical objectives are combined, and of inventing and using scientific, rational, social control techniques on a growing scale.

REFERENCES

Bastide, Roger, and Florestan Fernandes.
  1951 O preconceito racial em São Paulo. Instituto de Administração. Universidade de São Paulo; publicação 118. São Paulo.
Bastide, Roger, and Florestan Fernandes.
  1959 Brancos e negros em São Paulo. 2nd edition São Paulo, Companhia Editora Nacional. 1st edition Editôra Anhembi 1955.
Bicudo, Virgínia Leone.
  1955 Atitudes dos alunos dos grupos escolares em relação com a côr de seus colegas. *In* Relações Raciais entre Negros e Brancos em São Paulo. São Paulo, Editôra Anhembi pp. 227–310.
Cardoso, Fernando Enrique.
  1962 Capitalismo e escravidão no Brasil meridional. São Paulo, Difusão Européia do Livro.

54 General Papers

Cardoso, Fernando Enrique, and Octavio Ianni.
1960 Côr e mobilidade social em Florianópolis. São Paulo, Companhia Editora Nacional.

Fernandes, Florestan.
1958 A etnologia e a sociologia no Brasil. São Paulo, Editôra Anhembi S.A.
1963 A sociologia numa era de revolução social. São Paulo, Companhia Editora Nacional.
1965 A integração do Negro à sociedade de classes. São Paulo, Faculdade de Filosofia, Ciências e Letras da Universidade de São Paulo.

Ginsberg, Aniela Meyer.
1955 Pesquisa sobre atitudes de um grupo de escolares de São Paulo em relação com as crianças de côr. *In* Relações Raciais entre Negros e Brancos em São Paulo. São Paulo, Editôra Anhembi, pp. 311–61.

Ianni, Octavio.
1962 As metamorfoses do escravo. São Paulo, Difusora Europeia do Livro.
1964 O estado e o desenvolvimento econômico no Brasil. São Paulo, Faculdade de Filosofia, Ciências e Letras. Universidade de São Paulo. Mimeographed edition. Later published as O estado e capitalismo. Rio de Janeiro Editôra Civilização Brasileira, 1965.

Mannheim, Karl.
1950 Panorama de uma política científica: a relação entre teoria e prática política. *In* Ideologia e Utopia translated by Emilio Willems. Pôrto Alegre, Editôra O Globo, pp. 101–77.

Nogueira, Oracy.
1955 Relações raciais no município de Itapetininga. *In* Relações Raciais entre Negros e Brancos em São Paulo. São Paulo, Editôra Anhembi, pp. 362–554.

Silvert, Kalman H.
1962 La sociedad problema reación y revolución en América Latina. Translated by Noemí Rosemblat. Buenos Aires, Editorial Pardos.
1961 The conflict society. First edition. New York, American Universities Field Staff. Revised edition 1966.

Wagley, Charles (Editor).
1964 Social science research on Latin America. New York, Columbia University Press.

LUIS ESCOBAR CERDA

2

An Economist's View of the Role of Social Sciences in Latin America

To begin with, I should like to thank the Social Science Research Council for inviting me to participate in the Conference. I believe that the effort being made by distinguished United States research workers and professors to stimulate the development of the social sciences in Latin America constitutes a valuable contribution to the economic and social development of our countries as well as a powerful stimulus to the work being done by their colleagues in Latin America. I should like to congratulate them on their effort and on the contents of the fine essays in the volume edited by Mr. Charles Wagley (1964), on whose useful suggestions the Social Science Research Council kindly invited us to express our opinions.

My comments will be based mainly on the book edited by Mr. Wagley, the reports on the project of setting up Latin American schools of economics and public administration (FLACSO 1961), and the report on the teaching of economics in Latin America (Pan American Union 1960) of which I am a coauthor; I have also reworked a few ideas which I have expressed on earlier occasions and which are to be found in my book *Organization for Economic Development* (Escobar Cerda 1961: ch. 1).

I should like to stress at the outset that, generally speaking, the economists have carried out their work in closer contact with the realities of life in the communities in which they operate than have the practitioners of the other social sciences. Economists have been taking an active part in defending and attacking public and private interests, whereas other social scientists have found themselves embroiled in such controversies only occasionally. Apart from the historical reasons for which economics has played a different role from the other social sciences in our countries, there are methodological reasons which have to do with the difference of intensity in the use of quantitative techniques. Although a good deal of ground remains to be covered, it is obvious that the science of economics in Latin America has reached a higher degree of development than the other social sciences.

However, the work accomplished by the economists has convinced them that a closer relationship between themselves and other social scientists has become an urgent necessity. They have begun to suspect that their science is much less impervious to outside influences than was thought by some classical economists. This means that the precepts of economic policy, which are derived from analysis, and economic analysis itself, are now being examined in the light of the particular historical circumstances in which the facts under consideration occur. We are thus in the process of making economic analysis more circumstantial and, at the same time, more objectively scientific, thereby increasing its capacity to ascertain and explain reality. The social sciences have taught us, for example, that the propensity to change is not so much a trait inherent in human nature as it is the result of social conditioning, shaped and influenced by a multitude of different factors. Many opinions can be quoted in support of this statement. Ellis, Furtado, and Hess (FLACSO 1961) state that "economists are becoming increasingly aware that economic development is conditioned by social and political environment. The problem of population pressure, for example, is a complex amalgam of these three elements and others as well." Gunnar Myrdal (1957) has said that:

Our traditional division of knowledge into separate and delineated social science disciplines has no correspondence in reality; concrete problems are never simply economical, sociological, psychological or political. A theory of under-development and development which works only with "economic" variables, is for logical reasons doomed to be unrealistic and thus irrelevant.

The staff of FLACSO has pointed out that "a scientific study of societies pursuing the goal of economic and social development in the framework of a democratic political structure of necessity requires a multi-disciplinary approach" (FLACSO 1961). Similarly, Rex Hopper, in his paper entitled "Research on Latin America in Sociology" (1964) and Joseph Grunwald in his article "Knowledge in Economics, Special and General Validity" (1964) make a number of remarks which are in line with what I have been saying.

The relative advance of economics over the other social sciences has made the economist aware of the limitation of his own working tools and those of the other sciences and of the shortage of professionals in these fields. Surely that is the reason why, in working out his models, he has ignored noneconomic variables or has simply included them as "constants," in other words, as neutral elements which come under the heading of *ceteris paribus.*

It may well be that the time has come for the economist to orient and stimulate the work of the other social sciences by expressly including noneconomic variables in his models, analyses, and discussions, and asking other social scientists to work on them. That, I think, would be the most practical and workable interdisciplinary approach: Each one would do his own work, with which he is familiar, but the object of the work would be the same.

Let us take the problems of agrarian reform as an example. Carlos Massad in his article (Massad 1964) says that no research has gone very far to date in the attempt to point out the most likely changes resulting from alternative policies with regard to agriculture in terms of out-put per unit of input and of total output and its composition, either in the short or in the long run. He adds that little has been done to describe the existing situation with respect to land tenure, agricultural policy, and possibility of introducing new techniques of cultivation, new products, existing marketing systems and their weak points, the degree of integration of the agricultural population with the market for manufactured products, the elasticity of demand of the agricultural population for manufactured products, or possibilities of profiting from economies of scale in industry through a redistribution of income in agriculture. For my part, I might add that the entire process of organization and modernization of society, which is closely linked with the agrarian problem, obviously requires much more thorough analysis than it has thus far received. Despite the lack of research on basic questions, such as those I have mentioned, Latin America has embarked on programs of agrarian reforms, many of which, for lack of complete information and a proper diagnosis of the situation, are proceeding much more slowly than the great mass of the people seem to expect.

What I am trying to bring out is that the "phenomenon of development" is a political, economic, and social complex in which all these variables are interdependent. I am sure that the overwhelming majority of social scientists would agree with this assertion. At the same time, I am aware that there are serious operational obstacles in the way of including this multitude of variables in the development models. I think that this difficulty could be overcome if we were to organize study and research with a view to formulating a diagnosis which I have defined as "a *national* interpretation of economic development." Economic policy in all countries and at various times has been based on some theoretical interpretation of the functioning of the communities concerned and of the laws which regulate the phenomena of social change. This obviously applies to Latin America today.

At the same time, one would seek in vain for a written formulation of government interpretations of the operation of society and of its change processes. To put it even more plainly, in my opinion the Latin American countries do not have a national theory of economic development. Rather, they base their policies on a diagnosis or interpretation which basically falls within the Keynesian model, although the powerful influence of classical theory still makes itself felt. But a statement making use of the classical and Keynesian models and indicating to the student of social science and to the politician a framework for the theory on which governments in fact base their decisions has not been elaborated. This lack of an explicitly formulated development theory in practice leads to many inconsistencies, so that measures are taken which are mutually contradictory or, at the least, not wholly compatible. This is one of the main causes of our weakness: The lack of a theory of economic development—by which I mean an adequate interpretation of the way in which our national economies function.

Why has no such theory been explicitly formulated? The reason is simple. We economists seem to have accustomed ourselves to dealing with universal laws applicable to everyone and to all circumstances. That is our great weakness. Every region has its own development problem, which should be interpreted in the light of the political, social, historical, cultural, and economic variables which give it its particular configuration. For that reason, too, the same country at different times has different development problems. To accept this principle means to recognize that no general development theory valid for all regions can be formulated; there have to be as many interpretations as there are situations; some of these situations may be similar, but others have very little in common.

It is certain that the higher the level of abstraction of economic analysis, the easier it is to generalize; this merely requires making use of a greater number of assumptions. Such generalizations may be presented as a general theory and on occasion they may indicate some basic relations applicable to nearly all situations and nearly all times. Thus, the example of Robinson Crusoe has been used to demonstrate certain basic economic characteristics and decisions. However, at the level of abstraction which can be used to interpret a particular case, the situation is different. As the assumptions are eliminated one by one, a specific situation emerges which requires a special diagnosis.

To be sure, the findings on the external characteristics of different degrees of development may in a sense be similar; for example, certain indices, such as rates of literacy, mortality, population increase, and industrialization, or the number of doctors and teachers per 100,000 inhabitants, are usually of the same degree of magnitude for the so-called underdeveloped countries. But this must not lead us to the conclusion that the internal characteristics of each one of these countries—which have resulted in these findings—are the same; we would be confusing definition with explanation. The task of the social scientist in each country is precisely to ascertain these characteristics which I have called internal, and which, in the last analysis, are national in order to be able to put forward a reasonable explanation of the operation of society and of the laws which govern its change processes.

The lack of a national interpretation of the development process has been made up for, to some extent, by the international economic theories which have originated and are being developed particularly in Europe and the United States, that is to say, in the highly industrialized countries. The influence of the classical and Keynesian models is of particular importance.

Charles Wagley, in his introduction to *Social Science Research On Latin America* (1964), expresses some interesting thoughts on this aspect of the problem. He says that:

The lack of interest in Latin America . . . on the part of economists, political scientists and sociologists is also a result of their own self-image as social scientists. In their fundamental preoccupation with methodology and theory, they tend to view themselves—more than historians, geographers or even anthropologists—as universalists. Their methods, theories and models, developed from studies made in Europe and the United States, have generally been regarded as universally applicable. These theories and models could be tested and refined by further research in those areas of the world where basic quantitative data were available, so they saw no reason to do research in regions where the paucity of data kept them from developing their scientific theory. A Ph.D. candidate could contribute to economic, social or political theory more easily by a study of New Haven, Connecticut, than by a laborious study of Mendoza, Argentina. This way of thinking has been especially true of economists, but in a limited way it has also applied to sociologists and political scientists.

Wagley offers an explanation of this phenomenon when he discusses the historical and social characteristics of the area and remarks that, despite all its Indian and African traditions, Latin America is fundamentally an extension of Europe and that the Latin American nations have adopted governmental forms, constitutions, and ideologies borrowed from Europe or the United States. Nevertheless, he adds that while Latin American economic systems are formally patterned after Western capitalism, in reality there are important structural differences and dual economic systems which bedevil economic theorists and that "the Europeanness of Latin America can be deceptive."

If we agree that the principal responsibility of the social scientists in Latin America is to formulate what I have called a national interpretation of economic development, the question of how this task should be approached at once arises. That brings us directly to the next question, which is, what kind of research should be done in our countries? I wonder to what extent the role of the social scientist in Latin America should be that of a pure scientist or whether, on the contrary, he should be a committed scientist. Those two approaches mark the profound difference between pure and applied research. I think, however, that if the social scientist is called upon to do applied research, he should not renounce the strict application of scientific method in his work; the purpose is simply to direct his attention to those tasks which have the highest priority for the solution of specific problems confronting Latin America. Moreover, the social scientist would gain greater influence in Latin American societies and would be able to command greater support, sympathy, and understanding in the pursuit of his task. The fact is that we really know little of the societies we are attempting to construct in Latin America through the process of more or less rapid change in our different countries. (Please note that I say "our different countries," because I do not think it correct to speak of Latin America as a homogeneous whole. Since its components have functioned as independent nations, they have developed marked differences in their cultural, social, political, and economic structures, so that they now represent social groupings to which the same treatment cannot be applied.)

The interesting essays on which we are commenting at the present meeting contain a number of ideas which coincide with mine. Thus, for example, Charles Wagley (1964: 28) says that:

At the same time, Latin America suffers from poverty, illiteracy, political instability, inflation, food shortages, lack of educational facilities, and a multitude of other serious social and economic problems. These concerns are reflected in the research and theory of Latin American social scientists, which focus upon practical immediate political and policy problems. Latin American social scientists are interested almost exclusively in social and economic change.

Naturally, I am aware that it is extremely difficult to make any significant progress in applied research unless we can rely on the findings of adequate basic research. This point has been discussed in the report on the teaching of economics in Latin America which I wrote in collaboration with Messrs. Ellis and Cornejo, and Carlos Massad also refers to it in his interesting paper. Nevertheless, any existing gaps in basic information can be filled more readily and with greater enthusiasm when the information is needed for the conduct of applied research.

I believe that social scientists in Latin America should not fear the possible political implications of the results of their research. If we seek to avoid such implications, our work will have little value where the urgent needs of our countries are concerned. The important thing is to form teams which have a scientific approach, that is to say, which do not start out with a priori notions which they seek to bolster up with such data as they may collect. Rex Hopper (1964: 245) says in his essay that "it is the social responsibility of sociologists to contribute to a body of scientific knowledge which will illuminate social situations, could inform social action and might even influence political decisions." He then quotes Adams (1963: 5) and remarks: "I would like him to speak for both of us":

> It is clearly evident from the direction of the work that the Latins themselves do that the attention to real contemporary problems is the important thing. This is, somehow, separated from the improved techniques that have developed in the U.S. and Europe. The logical thing, it would seem, would be to encourage the development of methodology and theory of problems of importance. If it is possible to make detailed analyses of personal pronouns and firewood, why cannot such attention be given to economic choices and political bents?
>
> In summary, the history of anthropological development in Latin American studies indicates that both theoretical and applied work should be encouraged, but that also some special attempt should be made to focus the interest of competent theory and methods on problems of greater importance.

And Miguel S. Wionczek (1964) has said: "This is one of the many examples of wishful thinking so much in vogue among Latin American politicians and economists: if you don't speak about the real problems, they will somehow disappear."

If Latin America is embarked on a process of change, and no one seems to deny that now, we must have a clear understanding of its actualities; in other words, we must be able to formulate an intelligent diagnosis of the manner in which societies really work and use it as a starting point to evolve a national interpretation of the development process. I sometimes think that we are endeavoring to change a society without really knowing how it operates, and that this lack of knowledge could endanger the process of change or lead it in an undesirable direction. Nevertheless, we are caught up in an irreversible process. Our lack of adequate knowledge of the society's operation will not delay the process of change, nor will it serve to excuse any such delay or to defend the status quo. Political events in Latin America will follow their course, for they cannot wait for the social scientists to declare themselves satisfied with their work. It is therefore our duty to organize ourselves properly in order to make up for existing deficiencies, provided that we agree that they do, in fact, exist.

The task ahead of us is very great in relation to the available resources. The state of relative underdevelopment of the social sciences in Latin America is due, as has often been noted, to the fact that they began to be seriously taught only late in the thirties and were poorly organized: without research, without full-time professors, with poorly selected students, most of whom also were part-time, without a college which would offer courses in the humanities at a university level, and without schools renowned for the teaching of economics, sociology, anthropology, and political science.

Although much has been done in recent years, there is still an obvious shortage of social scientists in Latin America, so that the door is open to an effective collaboration on the part of United States and European scholars. However, it seems to me essential that this collaboration, if it is to be highly productive, be oriented in the direction I have indicated—toward the formulation of national interpretations of the phenomenon of development. This approach may not be easy to accept for those who fear that the conclusions of their studies may be put to political use. Nevertheless, this is a factor which must be ascertained with the utmost accuracy since, as pointed out by Orlando Fals Borda (1961), whom Rex Hopper cites in his interesting paper:

We have the grave responsibility of studying the sweeping changes which envelop us. This we must do in order to provide the scientific data necessary to the alleviation of the conflicts inherent in the transition period and to the reduction of institutional disfunctioning.

Nothing less will justify our science and our profession. Anything less will reduce our professional "caucuses" and congresses to irrelevant academic disquisitions held in ivory towers. And we'd do well not to forget that the social processes operating in the real world are not only undermining the traditional social structure; they are also destroying the foundations of the ivory towers (Hopper 1964: 259).

This also explains why, when FLACSO asked a group of experts to draw up a report on the establishment of a Latin American school of economics, the experts said that:

The true function of this school will to be to promote, in a systematic manner, basic research relating to Latin American realities and supplement university teaching at the highest level. The ultimate objective will be to create an institution which will play in Latin America the part that in Europe and the United States is carried out by the great universities, that of acting as centers for the advancement of economic science in accordance with the real social needs (FLACSO 1961: 14–15).

I conclude my comments on the topic assigned to me, "An Economist's View of the Role of Social Sciences in Latin America," in the hope that I have made sufficiently clear not merely the possibility, but the urgent necessity of collaboration among all social scientists in formulating national interpretations of the development process which will enable us to see clearly the type of societies we are trying to build in the next few decades. In order to emphasize the importance I attach to such collaboration, I can do no better than to quote a felicitous passage from Rostow (1965):

Economists have an important part to play in economic development. But I would say about economists and development what Clemenceau said about generals and war, that war is too serious a matter for the generals. In the same way, economic development is too serious a matter for the economists, or at any rate for the economists alone.

REFERENCES

Adams, Richard.
   1963 Some supplementary notes on the work of anthropology in Latin America. Unpublished paper presented to the Seminar on Latin

American Studies of the American Council of Learned Societies and the Social Science Research Council. Center for Advanced Study in the Behavioral Sciences. Stanford, California.

Escobar Cerda, Luis.
1961 Organization for economic development. Santiago, Chile, University Publications.

Fals Borda, Orlando.
1961 La transformación de la América Latina y sus implicaciones sociales y económicas. Revista la Nueva Economia 1: no. 2.

FLACSO (Facultad Latinoamericana de Ciencias Sociales).
1961 Publication of the University.

Grunwald, Joseph.
1964 Knowledge in economics, special and general validity. *In* Economía, published by the Facultad de Ciencias Económicas, University of Chile, Nos. 83 and 84.

Hopper, Rex.
1964 Research on Latin America in sociology. *In* Social Science Research on Latin America, edited by Charles Wagley. New York, Columbia University Press, pp. 242–89.

Massad, Carlos.
1964 Economic research in Latin America. *In* Social Science Research on Latin America, edited by Charles Wagley. New York, Columbia University Press, pp. 214–42.

Myrdal, Gunnar.
1957 Economic theory and underdeveloped regions. London, G. Duckworthy.

Pan American Union.
1960 Studies and monographs, III. Washington, D.C.

Rostow, W. W.
1965 The chapter that Keynes never wrote. (Talk given to a group of students in Buenos Aires, Argentina, in February.)

Wagley, Charles (Editor).
1964 Social science research on Latin America. New York, Columbia University Press.

Wionczek, Miguel S. (Editor.)
1964 Integración de la América Latina; experiencias y perspectivas. Mexico City, Fondo de Cultura Económica, Introduction.

JOSÉ NUN

3

Notes on Political Science
and Latin America

Merle Kling has produced an excellent report on the development of Latin American political research in the United States
(Kling 1964: 168–213). However he has centered it on a dangerous
image: the passage from the traditional to the modern.

Thus, he confronts us with the well-known problem of "the
only revolution": the one which is supposed to link up a historical past with a suprahistorical present, the *modern* present of the
developed countries, which is the embodiment of progress and,
therefore, the goal of the countries that are beginning to become
"modernized" (Walzer 1964: 432–33). In this way, Kling tempts
us to gauge ourselves intellectually by that standard, to see how
modern we Latin Americans are in our work. This prospect is
rather alarming, because for some time we have been hearing—
and saying—that political science does not exist in Latin America.

However, sometimes two doubts can provide one measure of
reassurance. Because as it happens, the scientific status of this
branch of learning is not only dubious in our part of the world
but it is also questioned in the countries in which the study of
the social sciences is most advanced. After all, the question posed
by Mannheim* more than thirty-five years ago has still not been
fully answered, unless, of course, we adopt a bureaucratic criterion and consider that the specialty exists where there is an
establishment that purports to teach it.

* "There is scarcely a sphere of life about which we do not have some
scientific knowledge as well as recognized methods of communicating this
knowledge. Is it conceivable then, that the sphere of human activity on the
mastery of which our fate rests is so unyielding that scientific research cannot
force it to give up its secrets?" (Mannheim 1936: 110).

This makes it even more interesting to study the case of Latin America. First, because there is no doubt that ever since the days of Independence, politics has increasingly become a matter of prime concern to our intellectuals. It is also a fact that books and articles on the subject exist in great abundance. On the other hand, evidence of academic interest in the subject is to be found in the nineteenth century, as witnessed, for instance, by the competition sponsored in 1886 by the *Consejo de Instrucción Pública* of Chile on the topic: "The State of Political Science in Chile and Means of Promoting its Advancement".*

Are these facts at variance with that skepticism? Should the scientific validity of such efforts be questioned? What are the criteria of relevance and significance to be applied? What is being done at present and what prospects can be discerned? Is it possible to generalize about trends of thought in Latin America or are there differences? What is the source of our very legitimate dissatisfaction with the present status of the discipline?

A great many questions for a single report. I shall nevertheless try to approximate an answer. But first of all, a paragraph on the famous idea of *scientific progress,* that constitutes a basic assumption of the continuum "traditional—modern."

Conceptual Revolutions

In their efforts to be didactic, textbooks have conditioned us to conceive of the process of learning as one great stream, periodically swelled by the contributions of the man of genius.

However, the difficulties implicit in this position have become increasingly apparent even in the field of the formal sciences, whose historians tend more and more to reject the idea of mere cumulative progress and to think in terms of conceptual revolutions—resulting in each case in a redefinition of the corresponding discipline after a more or less prolonged crisis (Kuhn 1962).

* The contest—and its by no means negligible prize of six hundred escudos—was won by Valentín Letelier, the brilliant disciple of Lastarria. For an analysis of his essay, see Luis Galdames (1937: 259–72). To continue with the Chilean example, the statute of the University of Chile—drafted by Andrés Bello and promulgated on November 19, 1842— established the Faculty of Law and Political Science (art. 3).

What occurs is spiral development in which all significant progress is a new beginning, at a higher level, of a process that has already been completed. While the process is at work, the scientific community shares certain models to which it adjusts its work; mere cumulation is then possible. However, when those models prove unsatisfactory, some specialists begin to depart from the prevailing standards and to restructure their object of analysis so as to be able to normalize important phenomena which would otherwise have to be considered anomalous. And then it is no longer a technique that changes; it is no longer a question of adjustments in the limited sphere of a particular specialty; a parallel dialectization of the frame of applied reference occurs.* With varying degrees of rapidity new models take the place of previous ones.

The conflict implicit in these transformations is almost inevitable. The construction of a model presupposes the acquisition of a body of closely interrelated theoretical, methodological, and technical knowledge. A change of model therefore means questioning not only the solutions previously put forward, but also the actual terms in which the problems were stated. The fewer the possibilities there are of compromise in the transitional stage the more acute the confrontation will obviously be, and in the transitional stage there are no intrinsic evaluation criteria to resolve the differences; as a result there is a real crisis of scientific legitimacy.†

For reasons that will be discussed, this is the condition which prevails in the field of political science. If the majority of political scientists begin their work by asking themselves what the object of their discipline is they are motivated far less in doing so by any real interest in the definition—there are dozens of them—than by a fundamental concern about the specific possibilities for the development of their particular field. Each investigation is an adventure because there are no shared models to guide it. And this, although it is becoming less true in the United States, as

* For the idea of the "dialectization of the frame of reference," see Gilles Granger (1961: 21–38).

† Max Planck wrote, pessimistically, that "a new scientific truth does not triumph by convincing its opponents and making them see the light, but rather because its opponents eventually die, and a new generation grows up that is familiar with it" (Planck 1949: 33–34 or Kuhn 1962: 150).

Kling's article suggests, is very much the case in Latin America, where political studies are still in search of science.

As Eckstein says, "When consensus breaks down . . . when a field is marked by dissent or is in transition from one framework of inquiry to another—the fundamentals always come to the forefront; *the silent major premises cease to be silent."* (Italics supplied.) (Eckstein 1963: 5–6.)

Conflicting Models

As noted before, the danger of the "modernization" metaphor is that it tends to limit the range of possibilities: *volens nolens* it leads one to embark on a unidirectional process, with a predetermined point of arrival. Instead, in order to show the different opportunities open to Latin American political scientists, and adhering to the rule that every observer is his own taxonomist, I am going to set forth a very simple typology which, by classifying some general models, will allow a discussion of the contributions made by each category.

The two dimensions which I shall apply have to do with the approach of the observer: first, as regards the political phenomenon proper and second, as regards his conception of man.

Both have a lengthy tradition in the realm of political ideas. However, to prepare the ground I need only point out a key moment in the period of the secularization of state sovereignty. While the social order was cemented by "metasocial warrantors" (*garants métasociaux*) (Touraine 1964: 1–24), the ethicoreligious tie encompassed the political, and it was impossible to discern a general will other than the divine. When the people took up arms it was only to ensure compliance with God's law, not to defend their own threatened rule.

The weakening of these metasocial warrantors does not, however, imply the immediate transition from a principle of transcendent legitimacy to a strictly human principle. As Cerroni (1963b: 21) rightly observed, it is not enough for authority to cease to be exercised "by the will of the nation." The state is no longer based on a recourse to the absolute, but it is still not based on popular representation: At that moment of transition it can only find justification in itself, i.e. in its *success.* It is an admirable device and Machiavelli took it upon himself to provide instructions for its use.

But the seventeenth century, fascinated by the prospect of evolving a moral or political ethic, goes further, and begins to inquire about society. Politics had been a religious matter; it was a technical problem; it was becoming a social question. Note how radical these changes of model are; either one must deny the entire tradition of political science, on which, however, its critics base their skepticism, or one must admit that it is characterized by genuine conceptual revolutions. This is the meaning of the natural law argument as opposed to the feudal ideology: "To say that human society arises out of a contract is, in effect, to declare that the origins of all social institutions are *human and artificial*" (Althusser 1959: 17).*

Natural law is precisely the original source of the two perspectives which will permit a dichotomization of the first dimension I am proposing, the conception of politics, and which I shall term liberal democracy and socialist democracy. The other dimension, the conception of man, will, in its turn, be divided according to the observer's reference to an abstract man or to a situated man.

Before proceeding to consider the models that emerge from combining these criteria, it seems advisable to discuss briefly the concepts mentioned, the use of which no doubt evokes a variety of often contradictory meanings.

The Conception of Politics

I do not think the significance of the cleavage between the liberal and the socialist views can be questioned. To establish a common language however, it is as well to summarily emphasize the distinction.

Liberal democracy: The terms of all classifications must be diluted in the interest of clarity. If I relate this statement to only

* Further on this author adds: "*Then* it is generally a fairly sure sign of differentiation between trends to consider that the doctrine of natural sociability or sociability as an instinct is a theory of feudal inspiration and the doctrine of the social contract is a theory of 'bourgeois' inspiration, even when it serves the interests of absolute monarchy" (e.g. in Hobbes) (Althusser 1959: 17).

two ideas which I regard as fundamental, this does not imply that I am unaware of the complexity of the subject; I am merely trying to reduce it to proportions that are suitable for the comparative purposes I have in mind. These fundamental notions are first, equality as a function of liberty, and subordinate to it; and second, the irreducible dualism: society and state. The former derives from Locke and the latter is clearly formulated by Hegel. It will be sufficient for my purposes to review rapidly their respective positions.

The contractualist thesis of Locke, who is rightly regarded as the "philosopher of the American society" (Goldwin 1963: 467; see also Hartz 1955), actually involves two contracts: a permanent *pactum unionis* establishing civil society, and a *pactum subjectionis* founding the political order and whose existence depends on the consent of the governed. However, it is taken for granted that anyone who enjoys the right of ownership is tacitly agreeing to it. Furthermore, there will be no breach of the agreement so long as the government fulfills its function of upholding private natural rights—to life, liberty, and especially, property. A rising middle class thus seeks ideologically to consolidate Cromwell's victory and to assert its right to rule a state tailor-made to its aims. Locke's liberalism provides it with philosophical support with which to withstand not only the traditional elites but also the premature attempts by the Levellers or Winstanley's agrarian communists to introduce radical democracy. The argument that "the supreme power cannot take from any man part of his property without his own consent" (Locke 1947: 191)* is monotonously repeated. The political order can no longer be considered an invention, in the manner of Hobbes, but only as a "rediscovery of the natural" (Wolin 1960: 306) whose preservation is its function. At that natural and prepolitical stage property appeared as the maximum expression of liberty, so that now any political measure that adversely affects the former immediately jeopardizes the latter. In other words, the contem-

* As the author adds, on the same page: "For the preservation of property being the end of government and that for which men enter into society, it necessarily supposes and requires that the people should have property, without which they must be supposed to lose that, by entering into society, which was the end for which they entered into it—too gross an absurdity for any man to own" (Locke 1947: 191).

porary world is naturally divided into owners and nonowners of property and, consequently, equality is a function of an original and metahistorical liberty. This is not the equality existing between one man and another but the equality among men before the state, a purely formal and juridical equality. "Having made inequality an implicit article of its faith [liberalism], then invites to freedom those who are denied the means of reaching it" (Laski 1936: 156).*

In a way, Hegel brings these principles to their logical conclusion. By his time, of course, a century and a half have elapsed spanning the first stages of the Industrial Revolution and the French Revolution. Hegel's youthful writings reveal his first concern: how to overcome the dualism of bourgeois private man, enclosed in the particular, and the citizen, an element of the universality of a common will. But he observes the failure of the 1789 revolution which was unable to reconcile the two aspects and to convert the individual will into an *immediate* general will (Hyppolite 1955: 124). He then notes that there is nothing in the nature of the individual will that makes it possible to overcome "this mutual exclusion of 'mine' and 'thine' and unify the two in some common third" (Marcuse 1960: 187). The hypothesis of the social contract is of no use because the contract between individuals does not transcend the field of private law (Hegel 1942: 155–59). As Marcuse observes, the "Philosophy of Right" is the philosophy of a middle class society which becomes completely aware of itself. The state thus appears as the necessary instrument to protect that society. Bourgeois man may continue to enjoy the benefits of the market provided he submits as a citizen to an objective whole which is the unity and *raison d'être* of the concrete life of individuals. Hegel thus retrieves a universal principle from the various particulars and differentiates between two societies: the society of necessities, or civil society, and the political society, or state—or more simply, between material life and spiritual life. The former, although apparently autonomous, is governed by a law that it does not control and which leads it to its self-realization, that is, the reabsorption in the absolute idea.

---

* Marx extensively analyzed "the myth of original accumulation" on which Locke's liberalism is based. See Karl Marx (1919: ch. XXVI: paragraph 2).

Socialist Democracy: Assuming the relative advantage of smymetrical arguments, we can now define Socialist Democracy by briefly contrasting Rousseau and Marx with Locke and Hegel. Rousseau paved the way for a radically different concept of equality; Marx placed the separation between society and state in historical perspective and introduced the possibility of a complete unification.

First of all let us remember the famous paragraph with which Rousseau opens the second part of his *Discourse On Inequality:*

> The first man who, after enclosing a parcel of land, thought of saying "This is mine" and who found people simple enough to believe him was the true founder of civil society. How many crimes, wars, deaths, miseries and horrors the human race would have been spared by the man who pulled down the stakes, filled up the ditch and shouted to his fellow men: "Don't listen to that impostor; you are lost if you forget that the fruits of the earth are for all and the land belongs to no one" (Rousseau 1963: 88–89).*

It is not just a matter of defending a primary liberty and of subordinating equality to it but of distinguishing between two kinds of inequality. One is the natural or physical inequality established by nature "and which consists of the difference of age, health, physical strength and intellectual or spiritual qualities" (Rousseau 1963: 47). The other is moral or political inequality which depends on the consensus and "consists of the different privileges which some enjoy to the detriment of others" (Rousseau 1963: 47). Rousseau's conceptualization of this difference leads to the remarkable paragraph with which he concludes the *Discourse:*

> It follows . . . that moral inequality, which is authorized only by positive law, is contrary to natural law, provided it does not coincide in the same proportion with physical inequality, a distinction which is sufficient to determine what one should think in this connection of the kind of inequality existing among all civilized peoples, because it is quite obvious that it is contrary to natural law, however defined,

---

* Rousseau states further on: "Such was or must have been the origin of society and laws which placed further restrictions on the weak and further strengthened the rich; they destroyed natural freedom beyond all hope of recovery; they laid down for ever the law of property and inequality; they made irrevocable law out of crooked usurpation and, for the benefit of a few ambitious men, they subjected the entire human race for all time to come to labor, servitude and misery" (Rousseau 1963: 107).

for a child to give orders to an old man, for an imbecile to act as a guide to a wise man, and for a group of people to live in superabundance while the hungry multitude lacks the necessities of life (Rousseau 1963: 128–29).

Della Volpe is therefore right when he points out that the idea of a nonleveling egalitarian society is the part of Rousseau's argument which, because it was never fulfilled, outlives the French Revolution (della Volpe 1963: 35). Egalitarian insofar as it implies the elimination of every privilege which is not based on individual-empirical differences in strength, talent, etc.; nonlevelling, inasmuch as the social values are ultimately distributed in accordance with individual merits.

This position is consistent with that adopted by Rousseau vis-à-vis the society-state dualism. In contradiction to Hobbes's statement that the people do not exist until the stage has established itself, Rousseau advances the theory of preexisting popular sovereignty, that is summed up in his dictum: "The Sovereign, by merely existing, is always what it should be" (Rousseau 1960: 183). Hence the idea of direct democracy, of the ruler as the mere instrument of the general will, of *"un gouvernement sans gouvernement";* and hence also Rousseau's rejection of the theory of representation which threatens to set up a dangerous intermediary between the majority decision—which is potential law—and its execution, which is actual law.

It would be tempting to contrast Rousseau to Locke and Hegel. Rousseau's whole construction is still based on a natural law metaphysics, for, ultimately, Rousseau "unifies the people politically and morally without remedying the real or social dissociation, and superimposes a political democracy over an inorganic society which is substantially incapable of supporting it" (Cerroni 1963a: 49). This view is divested of its natural law content and fully exploited by Marx, who starts out with a structural analysis of the dissociated *being* of the people in order to uncover the irrationality of the social fabric. This is the key function of his theory of social classes, which does away with Rousseau's utopia of a pure ethico-political unification of the people and heralds the solution to Hegel's problem.

The unyielding individualism of civil society proves to be the individualism of the class society:

The *State* and the *structure of society* are not, from the standpoint of *politics, two* different things. The State is the structure of society (Marx 1964a: 216). The positive abolition of *private property,* as the appropriation of human life, is *thus the positive* abolition of all alienation, and thus the return of man from religion, the family, the State, etc., to his *human,* i.e. *social,* life (Marx 1964a: 244).

In short, the dualism is inevitable so long as classes exist because the state is an instrument of class. The separation between political life and social life will end with the socialization of the modern atomistic society, and then the life of the individual will accord immediately with the general will, thus achieving the direct democracy conceived by Rousseau:

> Human emancipation will only be complete when the real, individual man has absorbed into himself the abstract citizen; when as an individual man, in his everyday life, in his work, and in his relationships, he has become a *species-being;* and when he has recognized and organized his own powers *(forces propres)* as social powers so that he no longer separates this social power from himself as political power (Marx 1964b: 31).

The Conception of Man

This dimension can be identified quite simply by taking Burdeau's clear statement as our starting point:

> The emergence of the real people has introduced a completely new person to the political scene: the concrete man, defined not by his essence or by his belonging to an abstract type, but by the peculiarities he derives from the specific situation in which he finds himself. . . . To describe this new being, who does not fit perfectly into either the category of citizen or of subject *(sujet)*, I can think of no better term than "situated" man *(homme situé)* (Burdeau 1956: 26–27).

The entire natural law thesis is based precisely on the idea of abstract man as a prehistoric and presocial person. As I have already mentioned, it is this pure or metahistorical rationality which Marx attacks in Rousseau, positing instead a material or historical rationality—the rationality of the real man.*

What I wish to emphasize at this point is that the consideration of this "situated" man is not an automatic correlative, in the

* The first chapter of Della Volpe's (1963) excellent study is aptly entitled: *Criticism of Rousseau's Abstract Man.* I refer the interested reader to it.

political field, of the emergence of democratic theories. We shall see how the abstract man continued to predominate—on an equal footing with his fellows because of being outside time and space—in this ideal community of citizens which, as an entrance requirement, divested its members of all individuality.

It is convenient to bear in mind that what is meant by *abstraction* in this context is not the necessary, logical way of defining an object of analysis, but is the kind of reflection that poses nonempirical entities as its starting point. Therefore, I am not referring to an abstract conceptual construct with empirical referents, in this sense, a proletarian would be also an abstract man, but to a conception that is metaphysical by its very nature; in this sense, the designata of human essence would always be nonempirical.

Basic Typology

By crossing the two dimensions analyzed, the following chart may be drawn up. Admittedly it is only of instrumental value, and that to a limited extent. For example, the various fascist conceptions being neither liberal nor socialist do not fit into the table, but their absence does not affect the purpose of this article since they are of virtually no importance so far as Latin American political science is concerned.

The Four Common Parts of the Conception of Politics [a]
and the Conception of Man [b]

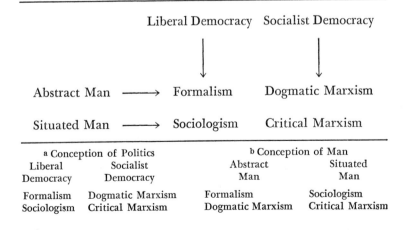

	Liberal Democracy	Socialist Democracy
Abstract Man ⟶	Formalism	Dogmatic Marxism
Situated Man ⟶	Sociologism	Critical Marxism

[a] Conception of Politics		[b] Conception of Man	
Liberal Democracy	Socialist Democracy	Abstract Man	Situated Man
Formalism	Dogmatic Marxism	Formalism	Sociologism
Sociologism	Critical Marxism	Dogmatic Marxism	Critical Marxism

This will provide a tentative framework for conceptualizing the four basic models orienting the work of contemporary political scientists. I shall go on to analyze each of the different categories, with particular reference to Latin America. (Obviously the label applied to each part is intended solely to facilitate its manipulation. Where I write "formalism," I could just as well have written "institutionalism," and where I write "sociologism," "behavioralism" would have done as well. I should add that in this case the "isms" do not have a pejorative connotation.)

Formalism

This category comprises the legal-formal and institutionalist trends and, partly, the decision-making approach.

The juridicization of the political phenomenon constitutes the culmination of the conceptual separation of society and state. In the realm of ideas, it is interesting to note that the same process which fostered the development of juridicization simultaneously promoted the growth of disciplines such as sociology and psychology, which were ultimately to produce the sternest critics of this process.

The common process to which I refer stems largely from positivism. The reaction against historicism, the disrepute into which the speculations on human nature of a Bentham or a Spencer had fallen, led students of politics to avoid—as Wallas complained (Wallas 1920: 37)—"the analysis of man." The positivists considered it essential to work with concrete, irrefutable facts: What better, then, than to concentrate on the study of laws, statutes, and documents? Furthermore, the nineteenth century was the century of constitutionalism, so there was a vast wealth of material to satisfy the demand. There were other reasons to account for the rise of formalism such as the determination to ensure that the discipline enjoyed unquestionable autonomy, and the emphasis in the new states (especially Germany) on rapid political socialization of the citizenry (Eckstein 1963: 10–11).

However, this genetic explanation of the phenomenon is not sufficient to explain why, when positivism can no longer be taken as an explanatory variable, formalism continues to be the dominant trend in Latin America. Equally unsatisfactory as an explanation is the connection between political science and the law schools, which we shall discuss later on, since it ends in a tautology.

What should be noted is the relationship between this model and the evolution of the representative state. The foundations of liberalism were consolidated in the age of limited suffrage, and the whole rational basis for this lies in the possibility of finding, each time, the transcendent truth of the political order. By this I mean: limited suffrage does not yet aim to determine the will of the people, but to discover the *rational principles* to which the government must adapt. In this way the abstract sovereignty of the people is logically reconciled with the concrete activity of a narrow elite, because it is this elite who, by its education and its independence of judgment, constitutes the enlightened minority which is best equipped to find the rationality sought (Cerroni 1963b: 22–23).*

However, with the gradual extension of the vote, it is no longer a question of investing an elite but of appointing representatives of the general consensus. Social differences cease to be politically relevant and all individuals become equal *as citizens*.

Two observations may be made: First, the attainment of universal suffrage *as a fact* is a very recent phenomenon in Latin America and the process of achieving it is not yet complete in many countries of the region; second, even where the extension of the vote has been completed, formalism allows a theoretical solution of the contradiction with which liberal thought is confronted.

For the logical development of political equality should lead to direct democracy, to the more or less immediate passage from the representative mandate to the *mandat impératif;* in other words: to abolition of the separation between society and state. The sovereign general will ought to be sovereign at all times,

* As Cerroni rightly points out, few thinkers have stated the problem with the clarity of Benjamin Constant, who concluded his analysis by affirming: "Property alone makes men capable of exercising political rights." It is appropriate to ponder these questions at a time when several Latin American countries still restrict the right to vote, maintaining the distinction between *hommes éclairés and populace*—obviously a *populace* which these *hommes éclairés* have not taken the trouble to enlighten and for whose plight they are mainly responsible.

since it is the dictum of the will that is involved. This poses a threat which Hauriou lays bare when he notes that "public power . . . is the only form of political protection which is compatible with individual property" (Hauriou 1938: 13).*

The current solution of formalism is to convert the people into an element of the state.† In this way popular sovereignty is reduced to the technical process of designating those who are to implement the law as organs of the juridical system and not as agents of the popular will. To quote from a recent North American study on electoral behavior: "The explicit task of the public is not to decide what the Government will do, but rather *who will decide* what the Government will do" (Campbell *et al.* 1964: 281). The people are a purely juridical creation: On election day the law assembles as voters a number of scattered individuals, to endow itself with the human instruments necessary for its execution, and when they have accomplished that task it disbands them. If one considers that the condition for the exis-

---

* Edward Shils. (1960: 79) shares the same concern but expresses it more elegantly thus: "Liberty and privacy live on islands in a consensual sea. When the tide rises they may be engulfed."

† This transition from *popular* sovereignty to *state* sovereignty is clearly formulated by Hegel (1942: para. 279, 182–83): "So opposed to the sovereignty of the monarch, the sovereignty of the people is one of the confused notions based on the wild idea of the 'people.' Taken without its monarch and the articulation of the whole which is indispensable and direct concomitant of monarchy, the people is a formless mass and no longer a State . . . (S)overeignty is there as the personality of the whole and this personality is there, in the real existence adequate to its concept, as the person of the monarch." This is the organicist conception which is nowadays extended into the liberal theory of the state. Thus Kelsen explicitly considers the people to be an element of the state which it presupposes: "The people of the States are the individuals whose behavior is regulated by the national legal order; that is, *the personal sphere of validity of this order*" (1946: 233, my italics). "Only a normative order can be 'sovereign', that is to say, a supreme authority, the ultimate reason for the validity of norms which one individual is authorized to issue as 'commands' and other individuals are obliged to obey" (p. 383). "In the infinite chain of causes and effects, that is to say, within natural reality, there cannot be a first cause, and, therefore, no sovereignty" (p. 384). This does not prevent Kelsen from making an admirable analysis of the ideological character of the modern theory of representative democracy: "The function of this ideology is to conceal the real situation, to maintain the illusion that the legislator is the people, in spite of the fact that, in reality, the function of the people—or, more correctly formulated, of the electorate—is limited to the creation of the legislative organ" (Kelsen 1946: 291).

tence of the people is the same condition that denies the people existence, there is nothing strange in the fact that the chief actor in this charade is nothing but a shadow, an abstract man without profession and without history.

With political theory transformed into a branch of legal theory, the natural tendency of the political scientist is to reify the juridical norm, which comes to be considered as a natural, suprahistorical, and metasocial phenomenon—not recognizing that, as Van Dyke ironically remarks, the law is ultimately nothing more than a temporary "score-board" in the political game (Van Dyke 1960: 140).

In the institutionalist school formalist emphases are so conspicuous, that at present it is hard to distinguish it from the legalist school.

One of the contemporary representatives of institutionalism who has had great influence in Latin America is Maurice Duverger (1961), whose assumptions are often used acritically in studies of the political parties of our countries. The author explicitly states his criterion: *"Present-day parties are characterized far less by their programs or by their type of adherent than by the nature of their organization:* a party is a community with a particular structure." (Italics mine.) (Duverger 1961: IX-X.)

It seems appropriate to quote the vigorous retort of Lavau: "Political parties do not constitute, in the abstract, communities defined primarily by their structure: in the first place, they are groups of a given national society and, within it, particular groups formed on the basis of more or less differentiated and distinctive interests, affinities or forms of sociability." And further: "Arguments about the electoral system and the number and nature of the parties distract attention from the only things which are real and which count in transforming the world: bread, housing, education, social inequalities and the spiritual life of mankind" (Lavau 1953: 8 and 165).

I have emphasized formalism because it dominates the field of Latin American political science at the present time.* My inten-

* I refer the reader to the reports by S. V. Linares Quintana (Argentina), Djacir Menezes (Brazil), L. Mendieta y Núñez (Mexico), and Isaac Ganón (Uruguay) included in the composite volume: *Contemporary Political Science—A survey of methods, research and teaching* (UNESCO 1950). See also Bullejos (1960: 141:68).

tion has been less to repeat the well-known criticisms, with which I agree, than to reveal some of the ideological reasons for its prolonged existence. Formalism is the political theory of a liberal elite which manages to pay tribute to Rousseau while legalizing "patriotic fraud" and laws "in defense of democracy." But formalism *is* a political theory and, unless we opt for an unjustifiably narrow definition of the term, its proponents are political scientists.

If I am right in saying this it will also be obvious why political science continues to be closely linked to juridical science in Latin America. The question is more than just the bureaucratic problem of allocating subject matter: Latin American political science is not predominantly formalistic *because* it is taught in law schools but, rather, these schools teach it because it is predominantly formalistic. Many directly bureaucratic interests have clearly become crystallized over the years and this structure is thus preserved, but it should be borne in mind that the main problem is one of ideology and is linked to a general conception of society and politics.

Of course I have no objection to this type of study being regarded by Kling as representative of traditionalism in political science. But we must decide what "modernization process" means. I must add that the category of formalism should also include the attempts, as yet relatively few (Shubik 1964), to analyze processes of "decision-making" by means of game theory, insofar as it requires working with abstract agents who are perfectly rational and aware of the criteria for appraisal of all the competitors involved. I do not know of any study on those lines that has been made by Latin American political scientists.

Sociologism

In this category I include the contributions of political sociology and the various trends which, at times without any specific denomination, are covered by the generic term "behavioralism": *

---

* I use (1962: 2–3), *"behavioralism"* and not "behaviorism," on the recommendation of Easton who fears that the movement may be confused with the psychological school of Watson. That that fear is not unfounded may be seen by reading, for example, Carlos A. Tagle: *"Una sugestión respecto de la doctrina del comportamiento político"* (1961).

theories among others of interest groups, decision-making, communication, and influence.

Strictly speaking, the work of the North American behavioralists is practically unknown in Latin America. That fact does not prevent a vogue for studies on pressure groups, which is due to European contacts, and, in particular, to the work of Jean Meynaud.

The contributions of sociology are a different matter. For the impact of sociology marks a new stage in the study of political science. It is worth our consideration because Latin American sociologists are actually paving the way for a renovation of our political studies.

As noted before, while positivism stimulated the juridical-formalist approach on the one hand, it also gave impetus to the development of psychology and sociology which, in turn, were to react upon it.

In Europe, the labor movement finally gained recognition through trade unions; socialist groups gave shape to the first modern political parties; the right to vote was extended. For the "independent" property owner any progress in the public sphere constituted a threat to his private interests; then emerges the "dependent" worker, who sees associationism as "an instrument of individual emancipation in public form" (Cerroni 1963b: 32). That man, defined by the realities of his condition, makes his appearance on the political scene and suddenly his entire situation becomes relevant for the political scientist.

The reaction has been taking shape since the beginning of the century. Graham Wallas, for example, makes a passionate psychologistic plea against the artificial separation established by formalism between "the study of the thing done and the study of the being who does it" (Wallas 1962: 38–39). As we know, Harold D. Lasswell headed the American movement attempting to assimilate the contributions of psychology and which has, admittedly, met with scant response in Latin America.*

As I pointed out before, what happened in the case of sociology is different. It must be admitted that even "behavioralism,"

* As is obvious, I am making necessarily general appreciations. See, for example, as an interesting exception, Cílio Garcia (1962: 51–66).

if it wishes to be something more than the introduction of greater methodological rigor into political studies, is increasingly obliged to resort to sociological theory in order to find an adequate conceptual framework.*

The central figure in this development is Max Weber, whose work represents a noteworthy attempt to establish an acceptable compromise between German legal theory and cultural history, on the one hand, and sociological and psychological reductionisms, on the other (Bendix 1960: 486 *et seq.* Also 494). A discussion of Weber's contribution would not, of course, be appropriate here; it is sufficient for my purpose to point out how his theories of domination and bureaucracy restore concrete man to the political sphere from the point of view of liberal democracy.†

There is no need to emphasize the importance of Weber's influence on United States sociology in which, paradoxically enough, it has become "the means of justifying a Parsons' conservatism, a Merton's liberalism and a Mills' radicalism" (Horowitz 1964: 354). However, since it is mainly through structural functionalism that this influence has made itself felt and since the allegiance of the leading Latin American sociologists to this school is well known, some comments are called for, especially in connection with the subject of sociopolitical development.‡

I drew attention earlier to the importance of Marx's critique of the limitations of Hegelian historicism, the flow of which comes to a standstill in a kind of crystallization of the social process (state-civil society dualism) and makes this crystallization seemingly irreducible as a juncture in history. One century later,

* Of course, the other alternative for *"behavioralism"* is to confine itself to miscroscopic analyses, replacing theoretic construction by common sense propositions. But that obliges it to work within the cultural frontiers of a common sense shared by the observer and the observed. It is what in fact is happening, which explains the strictly national character of most studies in this trend. For a strong defense of opening up political studies to the other social sciences, see Heinz Eulau (1963: 19–24).

† Although Weber's liberalism has been seriously questioned, it seems clear that there was a liberal starting point for his reflections. See Roth (1965: 213–223) and Cerny (1964: 57–9).

‡ The following is not intended to be a general critique of structural functionalism. I have merely selected some points relevant to the purpose of this study. For fuller analyses, I would refer *inter alia* to Lockwood (1956); Dahrendorf (1958: 115–27); Wrong (1961: 183–92); Geertz (1957: 32–54); Hempel (1959: 271–307); Moore (1958: 89–110) and Black (ed.) (1961).

exhausted by the effort to fathom concrete man, structural functionalism triumphantly rediscovers Hegel: The journey has ended; the Western model has materialized; society has finally coincided with reason.* The cycle of ideologies has been closed and, in the best Machiavellian tradition, politics becomes a purely technical problem again.

Thus, the purpose of studying the underdeveloped countries is less to discover the actual rationality of their individual adventures than to show them rationality in operation from outside: The objectives which they unconsciously pursue are already a fact in some countries, and the whole problem of the peripheral areas, and, indeed, of the Soviet Union and China, is how to catch up with the major Western countries. This is a conservative theory of progress, insofar as it means progress already achieved, which explains why a United States intellectual who is conservative in his own country may sound progressive when he gives advice to the backward nations.

The danger of ahistoricity was implicit in the criticism of evolutionism which is the starting point of functionalist thought. Whereas, at a time of radical change, Comte or Spencer earnestly tried to discover the clue to the process and thought they had found it in the postulation of a series of stages through which the potentialities of the social organism would develop, Radcliffe-Brown and Malinowski established a more reasonable order of priority: Before studying *how* society is going to evolve, we must know *what* society is. In other words, synchronic examination is visualized as a necessary preparation for diachronic analysis, to which the social scientists must return at a second stage. The strongly integrated primitive society described in social anthropology seemed to be the right reference model, and some sociologists deliberately turned their backs on the future in order to take a long introspective look at the operation of modern society.

From the methodological point of view, that procedure may nowadays be criticized as incomplete or inadequate. Regarding the criticism of incompleteness, structural functionalism is ac-

---

* "A basic premise of this book is that democracy is not only or even primarily a means through which different groups can attain their ends or seek the good society; it is the good society itself in operation" (Lipset 1960: 403).

cused of having forgot that initial program and for claiming to exhaust sociological analysis. In this sense it would now be guilty of the same mistake to which it previously took objection: "Whereas evolutionists can explain *persistence* only by reference to historical events not comprehensible in terms of their theory, functionalists can explain initiating *change* only in terms of historical events extraneous to their theory" (Bock 1963: 233). Thus structural functionalism would seem to be one of the stages, and as such a necessary stage of sociological research but in no sense the only one; Dahrendorf (1958: 127) and Touraine (1964: 71–94) maintain this, although in different ways. Criticism, on the other hand, becomes more radical from a logicodialectical point of view: If social reality is history in operation, a constant "becoming"—the permanent totalization that Sartre speaks of—any analysis which tries to freeze it at a given stage of the process will be not only incomplete but also conceptually inadequate until it is integrated in a totality that supersedes it as partial and static knowledge. In other words, there is, in the social fabric, a constant interpenetration of synchronic and diachronic factors which, by giving meaning to each other, make any attempt to disentangle them an arbitrary operation. Social anthropology provides mounting evidence to support this thesis, as is illustrated, for example, by the successive changes introduced by Margaret Mead in her interpretations of the society of the Manus (Mead 1956).* Strongly integrated traditional society is showing itself to be a delusion of the social sciences rather than a paradise that has actually been lost by modern man. Of course, the existence of a prevailing system of values, without which it would be impossible to speak of a society, is not open to question:

> But beyond the prevailing theme, there are always different sets of values to which some social groups cling to a certain extent, and which are a kind of counterpoint to the main melody. . . . Hence, a description of the social structure in purely synchronic terms seems to be basically inadequate, since the conflicting systems of values cannot be understood unless a diachronic approach is adopted (Wertheim 1960: 37 and 44).

* Among social anthropologists, Boas was particularly aware of the difficulties involved in separating the synchronic and the diachronic perspectives (Boas 1936: 137–41). See also Lévi-Strauss (1958: 12 *et seq.*).

In any event, both critiques of the structural-functionalist *theory* agree on the need to question its lack of historical perspective. (I italicize the word "theory" to avoid any misunderstanding. Nobody, to my knowledge, doubts the ability of the sociologists of this school to describe historical processes, as is evident from the abundant literature on the subject. What is disputed are the theories for explaining historical processes systematically.*

This attitude has, of course, far-reaching effects on the study of political phenomena and I am therefore interested in briefly reviewing the ideological content of the two structural-functionalist critiques.

Structural functionalism's predilection for the status quo has been denounced *ad nauseam* and there is no point in dwelling thereon. But, while every period of history produces a number of different rationalizations, only those which are best suited to their purpose really prevail. Previously, I tried to emphasize the functionality of formalism as an ideology of liberal capitalism. What has not been properly analyzed is the remarkable coherence of structural functionalism as an idealization of the particular conditions in which monopolistic capitalism operates. One of the reasons for structural functionalism's great importance is that, through it, the United States no longer limits itself to "masticating old European culture," to use Gramsci's expression, but is trying for the first time to express its own conception of the world.

This must not be oversimplified, as if sociologism were part of a mighty conspiracy engineered by Wall Street. Marx rightly noted that there are no absolute boundaries between science and other ideologies. It is true that the essence of ideological knowledge is to universalize particular situations, but in contemporary society, dominated by the dialectic of alienation the "taking root in the particular, the establishment of a closed world system, should not be regarded simply as a mistake or escape from reality, because this is how the attempt is made to grasp the univer-

---

* "The difference between description and theoretical explanation is precisely that between the isolation of particular propositions and their integration with each other in such ways that logical inference is possible" (Parsons 1961: 32).

sal" (Léfort 1955: 53). But, at the same time, in anxiously trying to avoid a relapse into mechanistic determinism, it would be naïve not to heed the context in which a line of theory, conditioned by and conditioning the reification process, is developing.

It was precisely concrete historical circumstances which heralded the paralysis of liberal thinking. The manager replaced the captain of industry; the old independent middle class was ousted by the white-collar worker and bureaucrat; the outer-directed man supplanted the inner-directed man; and eventually the Keynesian state took the place of the "good guardian" of Smith and Ricardo; manipulation of the masses destroyed the hopes of a sovereign and independent public opinion. And, in the meanwhile, liberalism continued to cling with sullen stubbornness to the dogma of laissez faire and the laws of the market. Its supreme hero, the individualistic and creative entrepreneur whose slogan is the most cutthroat free competition, had gone out of fashion at the beginning of the century; some decades later he was a real anachronism (Mills 1963: 263–73).

To avoid stagnation it was imperative to carefully demolish the myth of the rational and competitive *homo oeconomicus,* always ready to seek the maximum benefits for himself. Parsons deals with this subject in his critique of Spencerian utilitarianism.

> It is not difficult to see that the initial concepts of the "theory of social action" constitute a simple antithesis to the views defended by the ideologists of free competition. Parsons sees the stimulating motives of individual activity where the adherents of utilitarianism saw its major limitations (Novikov 1964: 40).

The secret of success is no longer independent economic initiative but rather the abandonment of that initiative, and perception of the phenomenon displaces the center of intellectual thinking, from conflict to consensus, from the production to the consumption of values. Dahrendorf is right in denouncing the Utopian nature of structural functionalism; what needs to be added is that this is the Utopia of a society dominated by large monopolies and rigorously controlled by the State which protects itself from the anarchy of free competition. The individualism of *homo oeconomicus,* controlled by the "invisible hand," has been supplanted by the conformism of *homo sociologicus,* governed by the organization.

This means that the virtual suprahistoricism of the European functionalists—I am referring both to the British anthropologists and to Durkheim—finds, in the United States, historical conditions that are extremely favorable to its consolidation. It should be remembered that the entire first period of United States sociology is dominated by the study of conflict and social disorganization. The change of direction takes place in the thirties. During the twenties, the large corporations established their empire once and for all, after thirty years of instability and social and political conflicts. Previously, the principle justifying capitalism had been private ownership; but "with the dominance of the corporation property recedes into the background and 'public consensus . . . indefinite, completely unorganized, without traceable form . . . becomes the final arbiter of legitimacy' " (Powell 1965: 351–52 from Berle 1959: 98). As Powell himself points out, Americanism is the essence of this consensus and means "above all else a belief in the sanctity of the prevailing order of society" (Powell 1965: 352). In this context in which the consensus is sanctified, a theoretical approach which stopped history analytically had to become the doctrine par excellence for those who believed, and still believe, that history had actually stopped.

The typology from which we started nevertheless reveals the contradiction inherent in this model: The basic historicity of the model's conception of man stands in contrast to the suprahistorical character of its conception of politics; the problem then consists of including one open and moving system within another system which is closed and static. To avoid this contradiction of terms, two main and mutually compatible methods have been devised.

In essence, the first method dehistoricizes situated man, universalizing that particular experience which is the starting point of analysis. This can be illustrated by various passages in Lipset's *Political Man.* Although the author begins by announcing that "from the standpoint of sociology, the debate between the 'supporters' of the state and those of society is closed" (Lipset 1960: 23), his solution leaves the problem intact. In the final analysis, it consists in freezing the historical process, statistically correlating political behaviors and social or economic phenomena, and classifying the results in relation to the model of liberal democracy, explicitly postulated as the objective. It will be seen that there is thus a tendency to accept the necessity of the datum without analyzing it, i.e. without including it in the historical dimension which gives it meaning. This is, of course, Lipset's own explicit choice. But if, to use his own terms, democratic stability is also a function of the effectiveness of the political system and if "in the modern world, such effectiveness means primarily constant economic development" (Lipset 1960: 82),* the reasons for his choice are not evident. In addition, man situated in the structure of the Western developed countries is taken out of his context and placed, without theoretical justification, in others where he necessarily becomes abstract. By thus attributing the same ontological status to different phenomena i.e. comparisons between indexes of wealth of industrialization regardless of the type of relations of production existing in each case, or of the form of income distribution), the necessary interdependence between variable and system is overlooked, and what is finally found is what was originally contributed.

The second method has become a feature of sociologism: I mean the psychologistic reduction of situated man. As Homans states in his critique of the functionalists, "They keep psychological explanations under the table and bring them out furtively like a bottle of whisky, for use when they really need help" (Homans 1964: 818).†

* Both in this work and in a previous one (Lipset 1959: 69–105) Lipset does not include in his correlations any rate of variation in time, so that, for example, the differences between stagnating and expanding economies cease to be relevant. James S. Coleman (1960: 352–576) does the same thing. It is interesting to note that, when the latter makes a breakdown by countries of the regional averages of Lipset, there are substantial discrepancies (Coleman 1960: 543–44). A recent study on Latin America shows that there is *no* meaningful correlation between the "democratic" level (the definition of which is basically not far removed from that of Lipset) and growth of the gross product, and a low correlation if the growth of per capita income is used. See Wolf (1965: 13–14). See also the comments of Morris Janowitz (1964: 18–23).

† Note the significance of the title of Homans' article: *"Bringing Men Back In"*; I support the critique but not the conclusions of Homans.

This is the corollary of the sanctification of Americanism, "If you have not found your share of happiness here [in America] something is wrong. Our history proves that there is nothing wrong with our institutions, so the individual must be wrong." *
Reification of the established order leads one to interpret normality and statistical averages in the best Durkheimian tradition: The pathological is defined as a departure from the average cultural pattern, which may be referred to only with negative expressions such as "deviation," "marginality," "lack of integration," disregarding the positive and real aspects of that same culture (Foucault 1961), and its ultimate potentialities for renewal. By diverting the tensions and conflicts which upset the consensus to the field of psychology, sociologism finally recommends individual remedies for those problems which thus cease to be collective. Since sociologism has refused beforehand to change society, the only reasonable solution is to try to change the individual.

The examples are all too plentiful. The tendency to particularize in defense of the system is well illustrated by a recent study on political alienation. The authors state that "the average voter believes that he is not part of the political structure and that he has no influence upon it" (Levin *et al.* 1960: 61), and they therefore arrive at the following diagnosis:

> *In effect, democratic theory is one of the sources of political alienation.* Feelings of political alienation will arise when the political role that an individual expects to play and believes is rightfully his cannot be realized.
>
> . . .
>
> We suggest that a *more realistic* theory must start from the fact that *the masses do not and cannot play the active role, and that elections seldom reveal the "will" of the majority* (Levin *et al.* 1960: 73–75).

* From the speech by a spokesman on Americanism to an audience of immigrants at Buffalo. *Buffalo Express,* Jan. 30, 1920, quoted by Powell (1965: 352). Almost a half-century later an observer of American society made the following critical remark: "The reason for the failure, for the unsuccessful pursuit of happiness, always lies with the individual, his inadaptability, his lack of a sense of togetherness. Equality of opportunity, the metaphysical essence of the whole United States tradition, cannot be disputed" (Giammanco, 1964: 11).

In other words, to preserve representative democracy the voters should cease to imagine that it really can be attained. Instead of fighting the distortions of the political process, it would seem a better course to attack the awareness of them that the individual acquires.

Similar emphasis is to be found in Shils:

> An extremist group is an alienated group. This means that it is fundamentally hostile to the political order. It cannot share that sense of affinity to persons or the attachment to institutions which confine political conflicts to peaceful solutions. Its hostility is incompatible with that freedom from intense emotion which pluralistic politics needs for its prosperity (Shils 1956: 231; Lane 1962: 161–86).

Alienation is limited to being a particular disorder, and what was a rejection of present society finally becomes self-rejection.

The epistemological inconsistency of this reductionism is all the more striking when we remember that the social sciences do not differ from each other in their empirical referents—all deal with human behavior—but in the way they structure their respective objects of analysis. This phenomenon becomes meaningful and is explained at different levels of emergence which systematically organize cognitive activity. Without a more general theory justifying it, the change in levels only creates confusion and makes discourse incoherent by injecting variables into it that are arbitrarily taken out of their original theoretical contexts (Lipset 1959: 77–111; Germani 1963: 127–43).

I said that the two methods are mutually compatible. It could even be maintained that actually any distinction between them is purely analytical. Perhaps one of the best illustrations is provided by the much discussed hypothesis of the authoritarianism of the working class (Sigal and Verón 1964). As I understand it, this hypothesis combines both elements: first, reifications of pluralist democracy as the *only* nonauthoritarian means of political expression, which certainly does not reveal a very pluralistic attitude on the observer's part, and, second, an extrapolation of psychological variables, the appropriateness of which has been criticized by the psychologists (Miller and Riessman 1961: 263–75).

If my brief observations on structural functionalism are correct, one of the causes of the ethnocentric tendency for which United States sociologists are so often criticized will be revealed. I am referring not just to the "scientific exporting" of the Western political model but also to the uncritical generalization of unique historical experiences, naturally their own; the difficulty of dealing with theories in problems of historical development tends to be "solved" by a transposition of the empirical phenomenon, which is mediated only in appearance. The normal movement of scientific knowledge from the undifferentiated empirical to the determinate abstract is replaced by a movement from the determinate empirical to the undifferentiated abstract.

I think this accounts for the ambivalence often apparent in the work of Gino Germani who is, perhaps, the best exponent of structural functionalism in Latin America. Leaving aside his valuable sociographical contributions, when Germani deals with historical materials he frequently manages to avoid that ethnocentric pitfall but at the cost of his own theoretical premises; this is the separation revealed by "the two halves" of his *Política y sociedad en una época de transición.* His conceptual model, the only part that interests me at present, shows the above-mentioned limitations. Even with the acceptance, at a high level of abstraction, of the analysis of the traditional and modern poles which Germani presents, the reader is left without a systematic guide for understanding the process of transition. When the author is later confronted with the problem, he tries to solve it by resorting to historical description (Germani 1963: 147–62).* But here the risks finally increase; the point of arrival being the ex post facto translation of modernization processes that have already happened—as if the future of the developing countries were fated to be the deferred present of the developed countries.

The merit and limitations of this approach are to be seen in his key concepts of mobilization and national and popular movement. The former, defined as excessive participation in relation to the preexisting patterns, takes the traditional pole as its point of reference; the latter, taken to mean a form of total participation distinct from representative democracy, takes, as its point of reference, the modern pole of the "Western" model. In both cases,

---

* This does not imply that the descriptive value of the periodization proposed by the author is being called into question.

Germani, as a good functionalist, reveals deviations from certain standards, either because of excessive participation or because the participation overflows the institutionalized channels. In other words, synchronic analysis alerts us to important disequilibria that will have an impact on the development process. But this still does not enable us to understand the meaning of such deviations, nor their effect on the production of new values, nor the actual essence of the conflict in progress. For that, a conceptual plan that normalizes such anomalies would be necessary. At its present stage of formation, the idea of mobilization tells us more about traditional society than about developing society, just as the concept of national and popular movement reveals a short-coming of parliamentary democracy rather than the actual nature of that social process.

While these brief observations on Germani's studies refer largely to his theoretical position, the main emphasis of my criticism of the already substantial work of the University of Minas Gerais group, is on the absence of a definite line of theory. The empiricism in most of the work of this group * prompts me to restate Hegel's comment: "To judge from their words, they observe and say what they see, but this is not true, because unconsciously they transform what they see into a concept" (Hegel in Lefebvre 1955: 56). The observer "unconsciously" finds himself ultimately operating with common-sense meanings and prejudices about evidence which he does not control, and it is very possible that this tendency to succumb to the demands of the experienced fact is strengthened in the Brazilian case by the prevalence of electoral studies which, moreover, refer to recent elections.† In this connection their efforts are certainly praiseworthy. Nevertheless one specific caveat must be entered, because the great "empirical" wealth of election data paradoxically con-

* Since 1956 the University of Minas Gerais has been publishing the *Revista Brasileira de Estudos Políticos*, under the direction of Orlando M. Carvalho. The most representative of Dr. Carvalho's works is his *Ensaio de sociologia eleitoral* (1958). See also Nelson de Sousa Sampaio: *O diálogo democrático na Bahia* (1960). Of course, my general remarks leave room for exceptions. Among them, for instance, are articles by Oliveiros S. Ferreira (1960), and Tocary Assis Bastos (1964).

† See issues of the *Revista Brasileira de Estudos Políticos* dealing with the 1958 elections (VIII, April 1960) and 1962 elections (XVI, January 1964). Also on the 1962 elections see Cavalcanti and Dubnic (1964).

tains some theoretical problems very resistant to analysis. For example, it is possible to determine how a region votes, or to correlate occupational structure and political participation, or to recognize that a wife usually supports her husband's party (Germani 1955: 247–63; Briones 1963: 376–404; Soares 1961). These data, which are valuable in themselves to the sociologist *must* still be linked by the political scientist to the political process proper. In other words, a high correlation between the women's vote and support of Christian democracy gives us certain clues about women's conduct or enables us to evaluate better the electoral campaign of one or more parties and even the political role of the Church, but it does not provide information on the actual impact of that behavior on the overall political system, the specific attitude of the government, or lawmaking (Key 1960-63 54–61). Obviously a researcher may, in practice, always furtively introduce his opinions about these relationships, while the reader is distracted by a pile of statistics.

Among the recent contributions to Latin American political sociology mention should be made of *Los que mandan,* by José Luis de Imaz (1964)*, and *La democracia en México,* by Pablo Gonzáles Casanova (1965a). Both have the merit of contributing valuable statistical material. Imaz's book is the main source of information for studying the power-elite of Argentina, and González Casanova's book accurately reveals the disequilibria in Mexico's development. But in both there is a noticeable absence of a defined theoretical approach: Imaz tries to solve the problem by constant references to his neutral and objective approach to facts, which is all too often contradicted by numerous value judgments; González Casanova, on the other hand, prefers an apparent eclecticism and concludes his book with a "Marxist" analysis and a "sociological" analysis, which, while they contribute little from the scientific point of view, are perhaps useful from the political aspect, provided that the reader manages to conceive that Mao Tse-tung and Seymour Martin Lipset would agree in their diagnosis of the Mexican situation.

A great deal of research is now being carried out. In Brazil, Nelson de Sousa Sampaio is working on an analysis of political behavior, while the University of Minas Gerais group has been

* For a detailed commentary, see Canton (1965: 129–34).

engaged for eight years on a similar study in two communities of that State—Cachoeira do Campo and Barroso.* In Venezuela, José A. Silva Michelena, in collaboration with Frank Bonilla is supervising an advanced project on the composition and policies of the elite (Ahumada 1964: 192–202). In Argentina, Torcuato Di Tella is organizing a data bank in terms of a formal model of sociopolitical change in Latin America.†

Dogmatic Marxism

Historically speaking, one of the best illustrations of dogmatic Marxism is the Rousseauian conception of direct democracy based on an abstract idea of man. However, I am calling it dogmatic Marxism in order to emphasize the deformation that Marxism has undergone as a result of Stalinism and because of the far-reaching impact it has had on Latin American leftist thinking.

It may be worth while to point out that interest in political science generally springs from an interest in politics per se. The "organic" intellectual ‡ of the rising Latin American classes, who used to advocate the economic development of his country in terms of egalitarian democracy, obviously tended to reject the legal formalism prevailing in the world of the academic political scientists and to distrust, and quite rightly so, the sociologizing offers that were extended to him from the United States. His obvious alternative was the anti-status quo ideology proposed to him by the left. But that ideology left little room for the growth of political science.

While the formalism of liberal democracy refused to admit the circumstances of concrete man, the dogmatism of socialist democ-

* I wish to thank Orlando M. Carvalho for this information.

† See the preliminary report "Political effects of intra-country discontinuity," presented at the International Conference on Comparative Social Research in Developing Countries (Buenos Aires, September 7–16, 1964) and the version published in the *Revista Latinoamericana de Sociología*, I, 1, 1965. The research I have cited by way of example does not, with the exception of the case of Brazil, strictly belong to the field of political science, although its findings will obviously be of great value for developing that science.

‡ Antonio Gramsci (1959: 429–38) makes the distinction between *organic* intellectuals—identified with the emerging social groups—and *traditional* intellectuals, who were formerly organic and now strengthen the traditions and the *esprit de corps* of the *intelligentsia*.

racy simply did away with them: "The heuristic principle 'to seek the whole through the parts' became the terrorist practice 'to eliminate the particular' " (Sartre 1963: 34).

Let me explain that I am not indulging in a moral condemnation of Stalinism, but stressing its obscurantism as a pseudoscientific interpretation of reality. When della Volpe regards it as a form of neo-Platonism, or Lukács as voluntarist idealism, or Sartre as leftist idealism, they are all aiming in the same direction—that absolute conceptualization which destroys the unity of theory and practice and seeks to establish practice a priori.

Thus, instead of studying situated man, dogmatic Marxism merely situates abstract man and, in pretending to be truth revealed, actually closes the door on the acquisition of further knowledge. Knowledge is replaced by entities and by a theological cogitation in which the concept deduces from itself the singular features of specific historical processes. If Croce-style idealism paralyzed the development of the social sciences because human behavior was not predictable, Stalin-type materialism brought it to a halt because that behavior was already predicted.

Obviously, political studies are among the main victims of that attitude, since the entire truth of superstructural phenomena was presumed to lie in the laws governing the dynamic of the forces and relationships of production: "The Marxist intellectual believed for years that he was serving his party by violating experience, disdaining troublesome details, grossly simplifying data and, especially, conceptualizing facts before he studied them" (Sartre 1963: 30).*

In Latin America, dogmatic Marxism has dominated a considerable mass of political literature, from which only a small number of books can be salvaged. One of the most important of them is perhaps the study by the Peruvian Mariátegui (1928),† whose talent raises him above abstract schematicism and enables him to rediscover men of flesh and blood in his analysis.

A discussion of the possible historical reasons for dogmatic

---

* The critique of Stalinism will become clearer in the section that follows. For a remarkable analysis of mechanistic determinism see Gramsci (1958).

† José Carlos Mariátegui: *Siete ensayos de interpretación de la realidad peruana* (1928). It is worth noting that, in 1929, the Communist Conference at Montevideo rejected Mariátegui's thesis as "Trotskyite" (Niedergang 1962: 279).

Marxism as an ideology is beyond the scope of the present article. I think the most cogent such reason was stated by Gramsci and its applicability to the case of Latin America seems persuasive to me: "When the initiative in the struggle is lost and when the struggle itself finally becomes identified with a series of defeats, mechanical determinism becomes a formidable source of moral strength, solidarity, and patient and stubborn perseverance" (Gramsci 1958: 33). But as Gramsci remarked, political propaganda is obviously one thing and scientific research another, and the greatest danger lies in confusing the two. This danger increases when circumstances prevent a formal division of labor between men of action and thinkers, and politics becomes an inescapable obligation of the intellectual.

Critical Marxism

Generally speaking, it may be said that in Latin America formalism and dogmatic Marxism are oriented in terms of their membership groups, the academic world in one case, and the Party in the other, whereas sociologism selects, as its reference group, either the schools of thought prevailing in Europe, or, today to an overwhelming extent, those prevailing in the United States.

What I call critical Marxism * can, for the time being, be defined only in terms of a "reference project." Apart from my personal interest in this approach, I wish to dwell on it because it can potentially enrich the discipline and because the model seems to be taking shape among recently trained sociologists and political scientists, especially in Argentina, Brazil, Mexico, Chile, and Uruguay.

In order to integrate situated man in the context of socialist democracy, it was necessary to overcome the abstractness of eco-

* While aware of the danger of fundamentalism which the use of *"Marxism"* as an epithet has come to represent, its positive connotations are too important for it to be replaced, for the time being, by a more neutral designation. I add the word *"critical"* (which would otherwise be redundant) in order to distinguish this model from any form of prophetic or essentialist Marxism. As Ossowski so aptly put it: "One would wish the fertile ideas of Karl Marx not merely to be kept under a glass case like the jewels of socialist tradition, one would like them to awaken creative unrest, one would like them to revive the pioneering spirit among socialists in the field of science as well" (Ossowski 1964: 16–27).

nomic reductionism, because it so happens that dogmatic Marxism is in fact, as the well-known and unfortunate metaphor puts it, *inverted* Hegel: Civil society becomes the *truth* of the state, whereas previously it was its pure phenomenon (see Althusser 1962: 3–22; della Volpe 1956; Rossi 1960-63: 295–423). Marx would seem to have taken over the Hegelian method, transforming the system in the process.

But, in Hegel the simplicity of the contradiction is precisely a result of the internal principle of the system which claims to be the essence of every period in history, i.e. not its material, complex, and specific reality but its most abstract ideology, the linear development of an idea that always discovers itself as the inevitable presence of the universal in every particular, so much so that it is not even correct to speak of a fundamental level—the state, philosophy, religion—since its reality is also absorbed by the self-development of the idea (Poulantzas 1964: 280). Method and system thus appear inextricably linked, and it is hard to understand how Marx could proceed merely to "extract the former without assuming the burden of the latter." (The best proof of this is the idealism into which mechanical determinists slip when they try to do so.)

Of course there is no point in repeating the essentialist contention that "the true Marx is the Marx that is true." In this connection, the subject is tackled directly in one of the books of his youth, his critique of the Hegelian philosophy of right (Marx and Engels 1927: 403–533), written about 1843. This book takes issue with a purely speculative dialectic that is interested exclusively in finding the abstract determinations corresponding to singular concrete determinations so that the latter become the predicate instead of the subject and are thus not known in their objective and material reality, i.e. as particular structures existing outside the cognizant subject and distinct from the universality of the idea. By this shortcut the mediating role of scientific knowledge is frustrated and replaced by the mystical "transubstantiation" of existence into essence. The result is foreseeable: The unmediated universalization of the particular degrades the universal, converted into a simple vehicle of a gross empiricism which that "transubstantiation" has preserved as such. Acritically accepted as a mere aspect of the idea, "vulgar reality"—the phenomenon—becomes the substance of the idea, its essential truth. Marx therefore writes: "Hegel slips consistently from his political spiritualism into the crassest *materialism*. . . . The State in its highest functions assumes an *animal* reality. Nature takes vengeance on Hegel for disdaining it" (Cerroni 1965: 101). A philosophical certificate has been awarded to the empirical datum and the opportunity of knowing it in its specific determinability has been lost.

It will be seen that this criticism is leveled not only against the system but also against the method, rightly conceived as a variable of the system, as a purely logicoabstract and a priori dialectic. The problem cannot therefore be solved by a formal change which puts matter in the place of the idea and civil society in the place of the state, changing the sign and maintaining the *same* relationship between the *same* terms. Obviously the result will be the *same* mistake but the other way round: Or, to turn Marx's comment around, "There will be a consistent slipping from political materialism into the crassest *spiritualism*," as happened with dogmatic Marxism, in whose metaphysical deviation may be found the vengeance of a superstructure reduced to a pure unmediated phenomenon.

Instead of confining himself to extracting, Marx radically transforms the fundamental structures of Hegelian dialectic. For one thing, "Every social datum is not materiality but *real;* however, *within this global real* . . . [Marx] discovers the primacy . . . of the *real-material* (base) *over the real-ideal* (superstructure). . . ." (Poulantzas 1964: 280). But it should be noted that both are recognized to have an identical status of realness. Hence, there can be no question of a simple contradiction between the economic and the political, guided linearly and inexorably by the economic, by an infrastructure which exhausts the truth that the system contains. Clearly, if there were no needs, there would be no project to overcome them, but it is equally clear that needs become genuinely human, i.e. conscious, only when they are integrated in a project which expresses and transcends them.

Not only the relationship but also the Hegelian terms change, as we saw when we discussed the problem of the separation between state and civil society. The contradiction does not impose itself upon history from outside; it is inherent in history's various processes and at the various levels at which history occurs. This is why Althusser proposed to differentiate between the former *"simple* contradiction" and this *"over-determined* contradiction": "The overdetermination becomes inevitable and conceivable as soon as we recognize the real, largely specific, and autonomous existence, which is irreducible to a pure *phenomenon,* of the forms of the superstructure and of the national and international situation" (Althusser 1962: 20). Thus any claim to absolute determinism collapses: The specific contradictions can accumulate and merge in a revolutionary unit, but they can also amalgamate in such a way as to inhibit the development postulated as rational by the observer. Egalitarian democracy appears as an alternative necessity: After all, Marx himself forsaw socialism *or* barbarianism. Revolution ceases to be a duty of history and becomes an obligation of men: It is the price that must be paid if history is to become entirely human.

Strictly speaking, it must be admitted that the temptations of reductionism are much more difficult to resist when we study the phenomenon of the state than when we study any other field of the superstructure (Poulantzas 1964: 278). Since it is the state which legitimizes and defends the system of ownership of the means of production on the basis of which the social classes are defined, there is a natural tendency to establish an immediate link between the base and the superstructure, the state being conceived of as a pure machine for coercing the oppressed classes.

Actually Stalinism is a logical consequence of this premise. If the analysis of the state is reduced to the class dictatorship aspect, it follows that the struggle for socialism can, in its turn, be limited to a struggle for control of that coercive machine and also that the most effective instrument is a strongly centralized party, transformed not into a vanguard but into a general staff of the masses whom it must subordinate and regiment for the fight. Furthermore, once the bourgeois state is overthrown, the bureaucracy, which becomes a paternalistic and oppressive machine, will be strengthened in the period of transition: "So conceived, the state is not a state of direct democracy which gradually reintegrates society but the ubiquitous guardian of the classes it represents" (Vincent 1964: 575). It will be seen that the separation between the state and civil society finally becomes more

marked, and that the latter is reduced to total impotence, mitigated only by the promise of a happy future in which it will be
allowed to become all-powerful. (When it is recalled that, in
September 1917, Lenin wrote that the transitional phase "must
be carried out not by a State of bureaucrats but by the State of
the workers in arms," (Lenin 1958) the political and personal
tragedy of his latter years will be more readily understandable.)

It is hardly surprising that anti-Marxist critique has centered
"scientifically" on the striking weakness of this interpretation: In
what developed Western country can it be claimed that coercion
is an immediate element of political life? How can the thesis of
the state-dictatorship be reconciled with universal suffrage and
the freedom to act of large workers' parties in the capitalist nations? Where is the empirical proof of the existence of a united
power-elite?

Since it failed to recognize the specific efficiency and relative
autonomy of the superstructure, reductionism observed the dictatorship element but was not able to apprehend the state as
integral society, as the structuring of a system of values and
norms through which a hegemonic group obtains the consensus:

> The spiritualization of domination is the real duty of the modern
> bourgeois State and should be carried out with the help of the spir-
> itualization of violence which is never really discarded. The purpose
> is democracy "freely desired" by all, actually achieved through this
> spiritualization in the form of rule by a minority (Koffler in Vincent
> 1964: 570).

In other words, the state is the dialectical unity of a force component and a consensus component, a unit that is clearly illustrated by its two medieval arms: the *church,* responsible for
moral indoctrination, and the *army,* established as the permanent keeper of order.

This is the subject foreshadowed by the Hegelian dialectic of
the Master and the Slave (Hegel 1949: 228–67), which Marx
takes up in the Manuscripts of 1844, when he examines the
alienation process piece by piece. Years later in that letter to
Bebel which made such an impression on Lenin (Lenin 1938:
47–66). Engels draws a clear distinction between the state as a
tool of repression, destined as such to disappear, and the state as

an organized society, and proposes to distinguish the latter by the "word *Gemeinwesen* (community), a good old German term which can be used very well to render the French word *commune*" (Marx 1938: 31). But, although both Marx and Engels maintain this distinction in many passages of their works, for obvious political reasons most of the emphasis in their analysis falls on the domination aspect. It was Lenin who later developed the concept of hegemony which is also dealt with from another angle by Lukács (1960: 109–256; 293–308). But it is Gramsci who has delved the furthest into this subject.

Gramsci's work is certainly a central reference point for the development of critical Marxism. Regarding the problem I am concerned with, his position is repeatedly made clear, "The supremacy of a social group is expressed in two ways: as domination and as intellectual and moral direction. A social group rules its adversaries whom it tends to liquidate or to subject, even by armed force, and it is the leader of the sympathizing and allied groups" (Gramsci 1949: 70).* Hence Gramsci's conception of the state as "the whole complex of practical and theoretical activities with which the ruling class not only justifies and maintains its rule but also manages to obtain the active consensus of the ruled" (Gramsci 1962: 107–8). His conclusion is thus completely logical: "If political science means science of the State . . . all the essential questions of sociology are clearly nothing more than questions of political science" (Gramsci 1962: 107–8).

It is necessary to discover and locate historically the specificity of the superstructural processes which combine to create the hegemony of a fundamental social group over a series of subordinate groups. Thus, that "true historical mysticism," which Gramsci criticizes in Trotsky and Rosa Luxemburg, must be set aside; because it is based on the assumption of an economic crisis that will spontaneously dislocate the prevailing system of domination without heeding the fact that "at least as far as the more advanced States are concerned, . . . 'civil society' has become a very complex structure resisting the calamities of the immediate

---

* For a good introduction to the Gramscian political theory, see Grisafulli (1951: 583–609); Spinella (1957: 819–40). Also, Instituto Antonio Gramsci, *Studi Gramsciani* (1958) and articles by Cambareri, Alberto Caracciolo, Umberto Cerroni, C. Tamburrano and Palmiro Togliatti.

economic situation (crises, depressions, etc.); the superstructures of civil society are like the trench system in modern warfare" (Gramsci 1962: 94). The electoral system, political parties, religious groups, trade unions, "intellectual public services," and bureaucracy, form part of that system and must be studied from this aspect in the same way as the concrete historical values which form a structural link between the base and the normative pattern. The problem of the power-elite is therefore more complicated than C. Wright Mills' presentation or Robert A. Dahl's critique of Mills' presentation would have us believe: The fact that there is no unified and homogeneous elite empirically observable as such does not mean that there is no unified power system, a hegemonic consciousness that rationalizes and preserves the internal disunity of bourgeois society (see Lavau 1961: 80–87; Hacker 1964: 134–36; and Bachrach and Baratz 1962: 947–52).

We can now complete the critique of Stalinism: Because, by maintaining the separation between the state and civil society, Stalinism renounces the basic objective of socialist democracy, i.e. a program of collective reconstruction which reintegrates from *within,* and not from outside and by force, the isolation and fragmentation which the system of capitalist production imposes on that civil society. It is therefore logical that the de-Stalinization process should concentrate on transferring control to society to an increasing extent: decentralization, self-management, and respect for the consumer's decisions.

Paradoxically, this brief outline has brought us from a model of dogmatic Marxism in which there was no room for the discipline of political science to a model of critical Marxism in which top priority was assigned to the discipline, regarded as "a complex and arduous scrutiny of the entire fabric of social life and not just its skeleton or 'anatomy' " (Spinella 1957: 837).

A Provisional Balance Sheet

Of the four conceptual models examined, only two obviously offer sufficient possibilities for the future development of political studies: sociologism and critical Marxism. Despite all its illustrious predecessors, the latter is the younger of the two. It should be remembered that Gramsci's complete works were published for the first time only as recently as 1947, and that Lukác's main work only became available to the public in its French translation in 1960. Thus, although rather arbitrarily, it seems possible to place the first phase in the present formation of this model in the fifties, a phase which might be regarded as ending with the appearance of Sartre's *Critique* (Desan 1965; Lévi-Strauss 1964: 355–90). In other words, it is presumably only recently that we have entered the phase in which that concept, not always either coherent or systematic, will bear fruit.

An oblique reading of our typology suggests a trend toward imbalance that seems to be borne out by the previous observations: While a historicist conception of politics would lead to an abstract conception of man (who actually changes the nature of politics) as in the case of dogmatic Marxism; an analysis of situated man would, on the other hand, encourage a dehistoricization of the situation (in practice destroying the concrete determinability of the analysis) as in the case of sociologism.

I think that critical Marxism contains possibilities of overcoming the difficulty, to the extent that its theoretical principles make it possible to sum up in historical perspective the partial knowledge that synchronic examination has gleaned concerning situated man. This requires critical Marxism to maintain a continuing dialogue with sociologism, not only in order to evaluate the structural-functionalist contribution but also to make use of the substantial contribution of hyperempiricism that nowadays characterizes the rest of sociological literature. To fail to do so once again entails a very real risk of abstract thinking and, ultimately, dogmatism. Again, this dialogue does not imply postponing the main themes of discussion between both models, facticity versus historicity, formal knowledge versus dialectial knowledge, a purely reflexive relationship between isolated parts versus a permanent demand for totalization, but rather placing oneself in a better position to set the course best suited for the advance of scientific knowledge.

Of course to totalize does not mean, as many advocates of sociologism seem to think, to constitute a priori totalities or eventually to accept the notions of interaction or reciprocal causation without further methodological foundation, and reverting, in the final analysis, to the unhelpful tautology "everything is in everything" of which the least that can be said is that it is not particularly stimulating for research.

The phenomenon is always a mystified form of objectivity insofar as it is an apparent manifestation, although necessary and specific, i.e. irreducible, of a reality that must be discovered. And the latter can only be found by destructuring the object perceived and restructuring it in the light of its function within the unity of the historical process, i.e. of reality as social becoming.* To do this, one basic proposition should serve as a guide: Humanity proposes to undertake only those tasks which it can accomplish, i.e. for the accomplishment of which the material conditions already exist (or are coming into existence). On the basis of this proposition, the study of concrete situations must determine the fundamental social groups whose tensions and conflicts make it possible to understand the historical trend, provided that it probes into them, as I think I have stressed sufficiently, at their various levels of emergence: "Actually only the struggle can be 'scientifically' predicted, but not the concrete aspects of this struggle; these can only be the result of conflicting and constantly moving force that can never be reduced to fixed quantities, because in them quantity is continuously becoming quality" (Gramsci 1959: 142). As may be seen, the structuring of a significant set of social groups always confronts us with the Marxian gnosiological universe: the historical nature of every social fact whose meaning can be grasped only within a current totalization intelligible as a dialectical relationship between man and nature, man and other men, and man and himself.

To return to a previous example, the process of alienation will not induce a psychological reductionism, as in the case of sociologism, nor will it lead to the metaphysical construction of an essence of man, as in the case of the different kinds of fashionable Marxian humanism (Fromm 1956: 104–36; Goldmann 1959: 280–302; and Althusser 1964: 69–88).

"Alienation exists only when society actually lives in the mode

---

* The wording is that of Georg Lukacs (1960: 32). The *"totality"* category is a central theme in Lukác's book, although Lefebvre rightly criticizes his tendency to give it a "class subjectivism" bias (Lefebvre 1955: 70).

of alienation, i.e. of self-contradiction: when the most real is also, and simultaneously, the least real" (Léfort 1955: 51). With the transition from manufacture to industry, which implies not just the organization of the forces of production into new units but the radical transformation of its technical apparatus, the conditions for a basically contradictory capitalist system are created. An internal analysis of the social fabric itself shows the continous intercrossing of warp and woof, revealing a process of self-unification and a process of self-fragmentation. It is in this sense that the alienating structure of the system becomes irreducible, unless it is radically altered, because the reality of capitalist society is its lack of cohesion. With industrial production the subjective principle of the division of labor disappears, because all individual activities are subordinated to a collective project of creation which unites them and gives them meaning, but, at the same time, their capitalistic form degrades this socializing tendency, tries to "reproduce the old division of labor with its petrified individualities" (Marx 1919: 174) and closets the worker in a fragmentary occupation which has no intrinsic purpose and hence no meaning: "The contradiction is not between universalization and particularization but resides in the fact that the experience of the particular is self-criticizing because it appears as a deprivation of the universal, and the experience of the universal degenerates into particularization" (Léfort 1955: 51).

An examination of this basic disunity enables us to place the concept of alienation at the level of social relationships. Thus understood, the concept becomes peculiar to a given social system and it is *not* incorporated in a continuum of progressive struggles of a human essence against its alienations, as humanistic metaphysics would have us believe.* It must also be recognized immediately that, since all social activities are to be found in the mode of alienation, this also includes critical Marxism as an aspect of the process. Far from falling into irrationality, to admit this does not detract from the claim of critical Marxism to

* In this sense—and unless the observer introduces normative criteria from without—it is impossible to speak, for example, of the alienation of the medieval craftsman in his work: His work was full of meaning to him and there was no gap in the twofold activity of creating and controlling the product (Mills 1951: 220; Pappenheim 1959: 113–15).

present the problem correctly by revealing the contradictory structure that creates it and which indicates the direction in which the solution may be found.*

The aforesaid contradiction in the realm of material production has its correlate in the political sector. As the very adjective implies, "universal" suffrage aims at bringing all citizens together in a general consensus. The particular clearly shows its concern with universality: By my vote I bring about a collective entity which, in its turn, contributes to my fulfillment, establishing the dialectic between me and the others which is the essence of my participation.

However, here the process also goes awry; two separate themes interlink, and once again a collective creative project is broken into fragments to which only the unity which denies them can restore any meaning. On the one hand, such decisive sectors of the political machine as the armed forces and the bureaucracy, which cover their private interests with a cloak of generality, remain beyond my reach. On the other hand, the system limits its universalist offer and maintains the crystallized particularity of the privilege which denaturalizes it. Above all it prevents me from having effective means of control over what it invites me to create. My vote thus becomes a parody of the universal, a ritualism that is devoid of any real meaning.

Hence, although it is more usual to compare the vote with consumption phenomena I think a valid analogy may be made between the vote and capitalist industrial production. The operation performed by a workman adjusting a screw in the assembly line has no meaning for him because only the collective creation that results from his and all the other fragmentary operations subordinated to the overall production process can give it meaning; and that is where private appropriation comes in, preventing the socializing potential of industrial labor from being consumed. Similarly, the act of voting has no meaning in itself

* I cannot at present take up this basic question. Obviously, socialization of the means of production is a necessary but not sufficient condition for a disalienated society. Not only do other relatively autonomous forms of alienation remain to be eliminated, but it is also questionable whether any disalienation process will be complete so long as man does not overcome the problem of scarcity. The express admission of this point in recent Soviet literature is noteworthy. See, for example, Oiserman (1964: 43–7).

and can acquire a meaning only through effective control of the result which the voting has thus helped to produce; this again is a proposition of radical socialization to which a separate and nonsocializing subject is linked, that of privateness, which interrupts the twofold movement of creation and control and breaks social reality into two different registers that render it structurally contradictory (Fromm 1956: 156–62; Schumpeter 1947: 250 *et seq.*). As Fromm puts it so well: "There is a *mysterious* link between the act of voting and the great political decisions. It cannot be said that there is absolutely none, nor that the final decision is the result of the voter's will. That is exactly the situation of an alienated expression of the voter's will" (italics mine) (Fromm 1956: 161). Again we thus find instances of a gap between the real and unreal that are typical of the alienation process, because since both strands merge into one, the particular will appear as universal (thus, the liberal democratic state) and the universal will be reduced to the particular (thus, human rights).

Conclusion

In a recent book on United States political science (Somit and Tanenhaus 1964: 2–6), the following are mentioned as attributes of a consolidated discipline as such: first, a certain mental attitude on the part of its members, expressed in a consensus on methods and objectives and in the satisfaction derived from identifying themselves therewith; second, a formal organization (in education, professional associations and publications); and third, a shared gallery of great men.

To return for a moment to our typology, the standards would enable us to establish a continuum between the two boxes in the table corresponding to the liberal democracy columns. At one extreme (formalism) the Argentine Political Science Association, for example, would be clearly situated, and at the other extreme (sociologism), the *Revista Brasileira de Estudos Políticos* team of the University of Minas Gerais. Between these two extremes, although definitely closer to sociologism, would be the School of Political and Social Sciences of the University of Mexico. (If I hesitate about where to place this school, it is because the School has so far been mainly concerned with the training of civil servants and diplomats.*) On the other hand, if the concept of formal organization is not limited to the strictly academic field, dogmatic Marxism would, in its turn, come close to meeting the aforesaid requirements of a discipline, at least in countries like Argentina, Chile, and Brazil.

These observations prevent us from generalizing about a "Latin American political science," since the few groups engaged in studying political science here are far from sharing common models. But there is another aspect which these observations leave out: social recognition of the task which is being carried out, or, more specifically, recognition of that work by the rest of the national and international scientific community. In other words, it is doubtful whether all the validation criteria can be referred to the in-group, whereby the autonomy of a discipline might ultimately become a purely bureaucratic matter, dependent on the position of relative power, and divorced from scientific considerations, held by its representatives.

In thus amplifying the validation criteria, it may be said that the work of Latin American political scientists has not yet won full recognition in some cases or lost it in others. The first statement is true of the pioneering effort of the Minas Gerais group, and the second of the authors identified with the formalist school that is being gradually abandoned throughout the world.

It must be admitted that this lack of recognition is generally justified. So far there are very few specific replies which the specialist can offer to a continent vitally concerned with the political problem; and there is practically none which has not already been presented more brilliantly in essays or political commentaries.

Hence we should go back to the question raised at the outset: How is this situation to be explained in a Latin America where even a place at a café table may be regarded as a chair of political science?

First and foremost I must stress the subject around which I have organized these notes: the crucial importance of the con-

* This is borne out by the report published in *Ciencias Políticas y Sociales* [IX (34) 1963: 645: 56], which is confirmed in statements by the Director of the School, Pablo Gonzáles Casanova (1965b).

ceptual models used. This, of course, obliges me to relativize to a considerable extent my previous statement concerning the difficulties encountered by the political scientist in finding useful answers. Actually any change depends on the frame of reference —because the validity or relevance of the question formulated may be denied. Thus, there is no apparent reason why a formalist should become too engrossed in the subject of social mobility or a dogmatic Marxist too engrossed in analyzing the political system as a possible generator of class situations.*

With this proviso, the question becomes less all-embracing and is actually limited to sociologism and critical Marxism. To explain slow progress, attention should be drawn immediately to the conditions which have created the solid institutionalization of formalism and of dogmatic Marxism, respectively: formalism blocking the academic road to investigation, and dogmatic Marxism nipping many careers in the bud.

Moreover, the outside stimuli that might help to change this situation have been relatively few, because it should be borne in mind that the conceptual crisis of the discipline is not limited to our continent alone: There is no consensus among political scientists either inside or outside Latin America. There have been no substantial contributions to political theory since Weber, on the liberal side, or since Lenin, on the socialist side. If this is true in places where the environment and resources are conducive to the progress of new trends, and to analyze the reasons would provide material for another article, the situation can be well understood in countries where these conditions do not yet exist, and where McCarthy-type pressures and budgetary limitations combine to delay their appearance.

The "official" prevalence of formalism creates an apparently paradoxical situation in which there are dozens of schools which teach political science and only one or two that engage in re-

---

* I say this especially because of the confusion often caused by the failure to discriminate between critiques relating to particular stages of the development of political science and to the science as a whole. To change a conceptual pattern must be rewarding in the sense that it should make it possible to solve problems that were previously insoluble, without thereby renouncing what has been attained by using the discarded model. Hence the risk implicit in rejecting political science is that of not utilizing the contributions of a rich intellectual tradition.

search.* So it is not surprising that the former is a backward-directed teaching, concerned with past researches, with little or no connection with the present.

It is therefore a good idea to avoid facile criticisms of Latin American *ensayismo* which, after all, has been a heterodox instrument for encouraging thought, especially since the Latin American political essay is not a descendant of tedious sixteenth century Spanish doctrinalism but of Montaigne and the British essayists. Thus instead of being a stuffy scholastic dissertation, such essays are usually incisive interpretations of current affairs. As the illustrious author of the *Essais* says: "I do not describe the essence, but the passage." † It is, of course, rather aggressive prose, tinged with militancy, that necessitates a rigorous reformulation of its contributions, and care must be taken to avoid being misled by that particular kind of metaphor which is so shining that it appears to be a concept. But with these provisos in mind, *ensayismo* provides valid elements for writing the first chapters of Latin American political science.

It is said that the study of development problems is entering the political stage after first passing through an economic and then a sociological stage (Lacoste n.d. 7–10). The fact is that the urgency of the new problems confronting our discipline coincides with a time when "the silent major premises [have ceased] to be silent." Paying attention to them would seem to be the first step to be taken to get out of the mess. In times of transition it is advisable to place more emphasis on consensus as the acceptance of conflicting points of view, than on legitimacy as exclusive conformity to a model. It may even be reasonable to refrain, over the short run, from aiming at a Euclidian political science.

Hence, while the recommendations with which Merle Kling concludes his report are valuable suggestions for the context of

* This is based on a rapid survey I carried out from January to March 1965 in Latin American schools of political science, from which I requested information on current or completed research.

† Montaigne (1964: vol. III, ch. 2). I refer especially to Arturo Torres-Rioseco (1963: 36–42). In Spain, the essay as it is known in Latin America only started to flourish in the nineteenth century and reached its peak with the generation of 1898 which has had such an influence on our intellectuals. For a good general introduction to the subject, see Zum Felde (1954).

discovery, my intention has been rather to discuss the context of verification designed to establish the most fruitful directions toward which the political scientist should guide his work in a continent which has no time or energy to lose.

REFERENCES

Ahumada, Jorge.
  1964 Hypothesis for the diagnosis of a situation of social change: The case of Venezuela. International Social Science Journal, XVI (2): 192–202.
Almond, Gabriel A. and James S. Coleman (Editors).
  1960 The politics of the developing areas. Princeton, N.J., Princeton University Press.
Althusser, Louis.
  1959 Montesquieu—la politique et l'histoire. Paris, P.U.F.
  1962 Contradiction et surdétermination. La Pensée, 106: 3–22.
  1964 Marxismo o humanismo. *In* Crítica Marxista II(2) (March–April): 69–88.
Arciniegas, Germán.
  1963 Nuestra América es un ensayo. *In* Cuadernos, 73 (June): 9–16.
Bachrach, Peter, and Morton G. Baratz.
  1962 Two faces of power. American Political Science Review, 56: 946–52.
Bastos, Tocary Assis.
  1964 Análise das eleições em 1962 em Minas Gerais. Revista Brasileira de Estudos Políticos, 16 (Jan.): 306–91.
Bendix, Reinhard.
  1960 Max Weber: An intellectual portrait. New York.
Berle, Adolph A.
  1959 Power without property. New York, Harcourt, Brace & World.
Black, Max (Editor).
  1961 The social theories of Talcott Parsons. Englewood Cliffs, New Jersey, Prentice-Hall.
Boas, Franz.
  1936 History and science in anthropology—a reply. American Anthropologist, n.d. 38: 137–41.
Bock, Kenneth E.
  1963 Evolution, function and change. American Sociological Review, XXVIII(2).
Briones, Guillermo.
  1963 La estructura social y la participación política—un estudio de sociología electoral en Santiago de Chile. Revista Interamericana de Ciencias Sociales, II(3): 376–404.
Buffalo Express.
  1920 January 30. Buffalo, New York.
Bullejos, L.
  1960 Fuentes para el estudio político de América Latina. *In* Ciencias Políticas y Sociales, 6(19) (Jan.–March): 141–68.

Burdeau, Georges.
  1956   Traité de science politique. VI. Paris, Librairie Générale de Droit et Jurisprudence.
Campbell, Angus, *et al.*
  1964   The American voter. New York, Wiley.
Canton, Darío.
  1965   Review. Revista Latinoamericana de Sociologia, I(1): 129–34.
Carvalho, Orlando M.
  1958   Ensaios de sociologia eleitoral. Belo Horizonte, Revista Brasileira de Estudos Politícos.
Cavalcanti, Themistocles, and Vladimir Reisky de Dubnic (Editors).
  1964   Comportamento eleitoral no Brasil. Rio de Janeiro.
Ciencias Políticas y Sociales.
  1963   IX(34) (October–December): 645–56.
Cerny, Carl.
  1964   Storm over Max Weber. *In* Encounter, XXIII(2) (August): 57–59.
Cerroni, Umberto.
  1963a Aspetti teorici del rapporto democrazia-socialismo. *In* Critica Marxista, I(1) (Jan.–Feb.): 45–74.
  1963b Per una teoria del partito politico. *In* Critica Marxista, I (5/6) (Sept.–Dec.): 15–60.
  1965   Marx y el derecho moderno. Translated by Córdoba. Buenos Aires.
Charlesworth, James C. (Editor).
  1962   The limits of behavioralism in political science. Philadelphia, The American Academy of Political and Social Science.
Coleman, James S.
  1960   Conclusion. *In* The Politics of the Developing Areas, edited by Gabriel A. Almond and James S. Coleman. Princeton, New Jersey, Princeton University Press, pp. 532–76.
Dahl, Robert A.
  1961a Who governs? Democracy and power in an American city. New Haven, Yale University Press.
  1961b The behavioral approach in political science: Epitaph for a monument to a successful protest. American Political Science Review, 55(4): 763–72.
Dahrendorf, Ralf.
  1958   Out of utopia: Toward a reorientation of sociological analysis, American Journal of Sociology, LXIV (Sept.): 115–27.
della Volpe, Galvano.
  1956   Logica como scienza positiva. Florence.
  1963   Rousseau y Marx y otros ensayos de critica materialista. Translated by R. Raschella. Buenos Aires.
Desan, Wilfred.
  1965   The marxism of Jean-Paul Sartre. New York, Doubleday.
Duverger, Maurice.
  1961   Les partis politiques. Paris, Armand Colin.
Easton, David.
  1962   The current meaning of "behavioralism" in political science. *In* The Limits of Behavioralism in Political and Social Science, edited by James C. Charlesworth. Philadelphia, American Academy of Political and Social Science, pp. 1–25.
Eckstein, Harry.
  1963   A perspective on comparative politics, past, and present. *In* Com-

parative Politics, edited by Harry Eckstein and David E. Apter. New York, The Free Press of Glencoe, pp. 3–32.
Eckstein, Harry, and E. Apter (Editors).
1963 Comparative politics. New York, The Free Press of Glencoe.
Engels, Friedrich.
1938 "Letters" from F. Engels to A. Bebel. 18–28/III/1875. *In* Critique of the Gotha Programme. New York, Dutt, pp. 47–66.
Eulau, Heinz.
1963 The behavioral persuasion in politics. New York, Random House.
Ferreira, Oliveiros S.
1960 Comportamento eleitoral em São Paulo. Revista Brasileira de Estudos Políticos, 8 (April) : 162–228.
Foucault, Michel.
1961 Enfermedad mental y personalidad. Translated by Kestelbeim. Buenos Aires.
Fromm, Erich.
1956 Psicoanálisis de la sociedad contemporánea. Translated by Torner. Mexico City.
Galdames, Luis.
1937 Valentin Letelier y su obra. Santiago, Chile, Imprenta Universitaria.
Garcia, Célio.
1962 O problema das comunicações em política. Revista Brasileira de Estudos Políticos, 14 (July): 51–66.
Geertz, Clifford.
1957 Ritual and social change. American Anthropologist, 59 (February): 32–54.
Germani, Gino.
1955 Estructura social de la Argentina. Buenos Aires.
1963 Política y sociedad en una época de transición. Buenos Aires.
Giammanco, Roberto.
1964 Dialogo sulla società americana. Turin, Einaudi.
Goldmann, Lucien.
1959 Recherches dialectiques. Paris.
Goldwin, Robert A.
1963 John Locke. *In* History of Political Philosophy, edited by Leo Strauss and Joseph Cropsey. Chicago, Rand McNally, pp. 433–68.
Gonzáles Casanova, Pablo.
1965a La democracia en México. Mexico City, Era.
1965b [statement] *In* El Universal, Mexico City, February 19.
Gramsci, Antonio.
1949 Il Risorgimento. Turin.
1958 El materialismo histórico y la filosofía de Benedetto Croce. Buenos Aires.
1959 Oeuvres choisies, translated by Morget-Monjo. Paris.
1962 Notas sobre Maquiavelo, sobre política y sobre el estado moderno. Translated by Aricó. Buenos Aires. (Italian edition 1952.)
Granger, Gilles.
1961 Le progrès en tant qu'outil conceptuel. *In* Cahiers de l' I.S.E.A., no. 110 (February): 21–38.
Grisafulli, Vegio.
1951 Stato e società nel pensiero di Gramsci. *In* Società, VII(4): 583–609.
Hacker, Andrew.
1964 Power to do what? *In* The New Sociology: Essays in Social Science

and Social Theory in Honor of C. Wright Mills, edited by I. L. Horowitz. New York, Oxford University Press, pp. 134–46.

Hartz, Louis.
1955 The liberal tradition in America. New York, Harcourt, Brace.

Hauriou, Maurice.
1938 Précis élémentaire de droit constitutionnel. Paris, Sirey.

Hegel, Georg Wilhelm Friedrich.
1942 Hegel's philosophy of right. Translated by T. M. Knox. London, Oxford University Press. (First edition 1821.)
1949 The phenomenology of mind. Translated by Baillie. London.
1955 Leçons sur l'histoire de la philosophie, traduit de l'allemand par J. Gibelin. Paris, Gallimard, vol. I, p. 352.

Hempel, C. G.
1959 The logic of functional analysis. *In* Symposium on Sociological Theory, edited by L. Gross. New York, Row, Peterson, pp. 271–307.

Homans, George C.
1964 Bringing men back in. American Sociological Review, XXIX(6) (Dec.): 809–18.

Horowitz, Irving L.
1964 Max Weber and the spirit of American sociology. The Sociological Quarterly, V(4) (Autumn): 344–54.

Horowitz, Irving L. (Editor).
1963 Power, politics and people. New York, Oxford University Press.
1964 The new sociology; essays in social science and social theory, in honor of C. Wright Mills. New York, Oxford University Press.

Hyppolite, Jean.
1955 Études sur Marx et Hegel. Paris, Marcel Hivière.

Imaz, José Luiz.
1964 Los que mandan. EUDEBA, Buenos Aires.

Instituto Antonio Gramsci.
1958 Studi Gramsciani. Roma, Editori Riuniti.

International Conference on Comparative Social Research in Developing Countries.
1964 Preliminary report. Political effects of intra-country discontinuity presented at the International Conference. . . . Buenos Aires, September 7–16.

Janowitz, Morris.
1964 The military in the political development of new nations. Chicago, University of Chicago Press.

Kelsen, Hans.
1946 General theory of law and state. Cambridge, Mass., Harvard University Press.

Key, V. O. Jr.
1960 The politically relevant in surveys. The Public Opinion Quarterly, XXIV(1): 54–61.

Kling, Merle.
1964 The state of research on Latin America: political science. *In* Social Science Research on Latin America, edited by Charles Wagley. New York, Columbia University Press, pp. 168–213.

Koffler, Leo.
1960 Staat gesellschaft. Ulm, p. 34.

Kuhn, Thomas S.
    1962   The structure of scientific revolutions. Chicago, The University of
            Chicago Press.
Lacoste, Yves.
    n.d.   Introducción bibliográfica al desarrollo económico y social. Trans-
            lated by N. Minello. Montevideo, Taller Universitario, pp. 7–10.
Lane, Robert E.
    1962   Political ideology. Glencoe, Ill. The Free Press.
Laski, Harold J.
    1936   The rise of European liberalism. London, George Allen and Unwin.
Lavau, Georges.
    1953   Partis politiques et réalités sociales—contributions à une étude réaliste
            des partis politiques. Paris, Armand Colin.
    1961   Les élites politiques. Bari, pp. 80–87.
Lefebvre, Henri.
    1955   La notion de la totalité dans les sciences sociales. Cahiers Inter-
            nationaux de Sociologie, XVIII (Jan.–June): 55–77.
Léfort, Claude.
    1955   L'aliénation comme concept sociologique. Cahiers Internationaux de
            Sociologie, XVIII: 35–54.
Lenin, V. I.
    1938   Marxism on the state. *In* Critique of the Gotha Programme by Karl
            Marx. New York, Dutt, pp. 47–66.
    1958   El estado y la revolución In Obras Completas. Buenos Aires, Vol. XXV,
            Chap. V, Sect. 4.
Levin, Murray B., *et al.*
    1960   The alienated voter—politics in Boston. New York, Holt, Rinehart
            & Winston.
Lévi-Strauss, Claude.
    1958   Anthropologie structurale. Paris, Plon.
    1964   El pensamiento salvaje, translated by Gonzáles Aramburo. Mexico
            City, pp. 355–90.
Lipset, Seymour Martin.
    1959   Some social requisites of democracy. American Political Science Re-
            view, LIII (March): 69–105.
    1960   Political man: The social bases of politics. Garden City, New York,
            Doubleday & Co.
Locke, John.
    1947   Two treatises of government, edited by Thomas I. Cook. New York,
            Hofner Publishing Co.
Lockwood, David.
    1956   Some remarks on "The Social System." *In* British Journal of Soci-
            ology, VII(2).
Lukács, Georg.
    1960   Histoire et conscience de classe. Translated by Axelos-Bois. Paris, pp.
            109–256; 293–308.
Mannheim, Karl.
    1936   Ideology and utopia. Translated by Louis Wirth and Edward Shils.
            New York, Harvest. (1st ed. 1929.)
Marcuse, Herbert.
    1960   Reason and revolution—Hegel and the rise of social theory. Boston,
            Beacon Press.

118 *General Papers*

Marx, Karl.
  n.d. Le Capital. III. Translated by Costes.
  1919 Capital. A critique of political economy. Translated by Moore and Aveling. Chicago, Kerr and Co. Vol. I, Chapter XXVI, paragraph 2.
  1938 Critique of the Gotha programme. New York, Dutt, pp. 47–66.
  1964a Selected writings in sociology and social philosophy. Translated by T. B. Bottomore. New York, McGraw-Hill.
  1964b Early writings. Translated and edited by T. B. Bottomore. New York, McGraw-Hill.
Marx, Karl, and Friedrich Engels.
  1927 Historisch—gesamtausgabe. Berlin, I, pp. 405–533.
Mead, Margaret.
  1956 New lives for old. London, Victor Gollancz.
Mead, Robert.
  1956 Breve historia del ensayo hispanoamericano. Mexico City, Estudios.
Miller, S. M., and Frank Riessman.
  1961 Working-class authoritarianism: a critique of Lipset. British Journal of Sociology, XII(3) (Sept.): 263–75.
Mills, C. Wright.
  1951 White collar. New York, Oxford University Press.
  1963 The competitive personality. In Power, Politics and People, edited by Irving L. Horowitz. New York, Oxford University Press, pp. 263–73.
Montaigne, Michel Eyquem.
  1964 Selections from his writings. New York, McGraw-Hill. Vol. III, chapter 2.
Moore, Barrington, Jr.
  1958 Political power and social theory. Cambridge, Mass., Harvard University Press.
Niedergang, Marcel.
  1962 Les vingt Amérique Latine. Paris.
Novikov, N. V.
  1964 Modern American capitalism and Parson's theory of social action. The Soviet Review, V(1) (Spring): 39–49.
Oiserman, T. I.
  1964 Man and his alienation. The Soviet Review, V(2) (Summer): 43–47.
Ossowski, Stanislaw.
  1964 Excerpts from the works of Stanislaw Ossowski. The Polish Sociological Bulletin, I: 16–27.
Pappenheim, Fritz.
  1959 The alienation of modern man. New York, Monthly Review Press.
Parsons, Talcott.
  1961 An outline of the social system. In Theories of Society, edited by Talcott Parsons and others. Glencoe, Ill., Free Press, pp. 30–70.
Planck, Max.
  1949 Scientific autobiography and other papers. Translated by F. Gaynor. New York, Philosophical Library.
Poulantzas, Nicos.
  1964 L'examen marxiste de l'état et du droit actuel et la question de l'alternative. Les Temps Modernes, (219–20): 274–302.

Powell, N. V.
1965   Reform, revolution and reaction: a case of organized conflict. *In* The
        New Sociology, edited by Irving L. Horowitz. New York, Oxford
        University Press, pp. 331–56.
Ray, Donald P. (Editor).
1960   Trends in social science. New York, Philosophical Library.
Revista Brasileira de Estudos Políticos.
1960   VIII–April.
1964   XVI–January.
Revista Latinoamericana de Sociología.
1965   Vol. I(1).
Rossi, Mario.
1960–63   Marx e la dialettica hegeliana. Rome, Editori Riuniti, II, pp.
           295–423.
Roth, Gunther.
1965   Political critique of Max Weber. American Sociological Review,
        XXX (April): 213–23.
Rousseau, Jean Jacques.
1960   The social contract. *In* Social Contract, edited by Sir Ernest Barker.
        New York, London, Oxford University Press.
1963   Discurso sobre el orígen de la desigualdad entre los hombres. Trans-
        lated by T. López y López. Buenos Aires, Aguilar.
Sampaio, Nelson de Sousa.
1960   O diálogo democrático na Bahia. Belo Horizonte, Revista Brasileira
Sartre, Jean-Paul.
1963   Cuestiones de método. *In* Crítica de la razón dialéctica. Translated
        by de Estudos Políticos. Lamana. Buenos Aires, I, pp. 15–156.
Schumpeter, Joseph A.
1947   Capitalism, socialism and democracy. New York, Harper & Brothers.
Shils, Edward A.
1956   The torment of secrecy. Glencoe, Ill., The Free Press.
1960   The macrosociological problem: Consensus and dissensus in the larger
        society. *In* Trends in Social Science, edited by Donald P. Ray. New
        York, Philosophical Library, pp. 60–83.
Shubik, Martin (Editor).
1964   Game theory and related approaches to social behavior. New York,
        Wiley.
Sigal, Silvia, and Eliseo Verón.
1964   Relaciones entre psicología y sociología: un análisis sistemático.
        Buenos Aires.
Soares, Glaucio Ary Dillon.
1961   Classes sociais, strata sociais e as eleições de 1960. *In* Sociologia,
        (Sept.)
Somit, Albert, and Joseph Tanenhaus.
1964   American political science: a profile of a discipline. New York, Ather-
        ton Press.
Spinella, Mario.
1957   Gramsci, la revoluzione d'Ottobre, la scienza marxista de la politica.
        In Società, XIII(5): 819–40.

Strauss, Leo, and Joseph Cropsey (Editors).
1963 History of political philosophy. Chicago, Rand McNally.
Tagle, Carlos A.
1961 Una sugestión respecto de la doctrina del comportamiento político. Revista Argentina de Ciencia Política, II(3) (Jan.–June): 73–8.
Torre, Guillermo de.
1961 Ensayo y algunos ensayistas americanos. *In* Cuadernos 53 (Oct.): 166–70.
Torres-Rioseco, Arturo.
1963 El ensayo en la América colonial. *In* Cuadernos (April 17): 36–42.
Touraine, Alain.
1964 Pour une sociologie actionnaliste. European Journal of Sociology, V (1–24).
UNESCO.
1950 Contemporary political science. A survey of methods, research and teaching. Paris.
Van Dyke, Vernon.
1960 Political science—a philosophical analysis. Stanford, Stanford University Press.
Vincent, Jean-Marie.
1964 Vers une théorie marxiste du droit moderne. Les Temps Modernes, (219–20): 552–76.
Wagley, Charles (Editor).
1964 Social science research on Latin America. New York, Columbia University Press.
Wallas, Graham.
1920 Human nature in politics. London, Constable. 3rd edition reprinted in 1962.
Walzer, Michael.
1964 The only revolution: note on the theory of modernization. *In* Dissent, XI(4) (Autumn): 432–43.
Wertheim, W. F.
1960 La société et les conflits entre systèmes de valeurs. Cahiers Internationaux de Sociologie, 28: 33–46.
Wolf, Charles, Jr.
1965 The political effects of economic programs: some indications from Latin America. *In* Economic Development and Cultural Change, XIV(1) (Oct.): 1–20.
Wolin, Sheldon S.
1960 Politics and vision: continuity and innovation in western political thought. Boston, Little, Brown.
Wrong, Dennis H.
1961 The oversociologized conception of man. American Sociological Review, 26(2) (April): 183–92.
Zum Felde, Alberto.
1954 Indice crítico de la literatura hispano-americana: el ensayo y la crítica. Mexico City, Guaranía.

4

History and the Social Sciences
in Latin America

Permit me to begin by recalling two personal experiences which, strictly speaking, never occurred. Although these experiences never went beyond the intention stage, recording them will help me to make a point I regard as important, namely: My views on the great subject which all of us are to examine are not of recent origin; on the contrary, they were formed a long time ago and have grown stronger with the passage of years.

It was in 1961, I believe, that I had the honor of being invited to address the Latin American historians of the United States, who were then meeting in Chicago. I accepted the invitation gladly, and immediately proposed as the subject of my speech the debt of gratitude which we, the historians of Latin America, owe to our North American colleagues. In the end, I was unable to attend, and I never wrote my speech. However, a year ago I was to have given a series of lectures at the University of Buenos Aires, and I did write the first of these lectures, on political life in Latin America. It began with some pages which have not appeared in print and may be pertinent now:

The United States has been and is today the only place in the world in which Latin America is the subject of constant concern and study. Matters have gone so far that a Latin American who wants to study any aspect of Latin America not only cannot possibly ignore the United States literature on the subject, but often is obliged to take it as his starting point. This is due to a large extent to the blind prejudice of the Latin American, which has caused him to amuse himself by studying whatever is foreign, and to disregard what is his own, to take his lamp out into the street and leave his own house in darkness. To some extent, too, this state of affairs must be attributed to the special point of view usually adopted by the United States scholar. For him, Latin America is an entity, and he therefore studies it as a whole.

This means that he generally turns his attention to those elements which are common to the twenty nations composing Latin America. The Latin American, on the contrary (provided, of course, that he decides to do any work at all) concentrates on the differences, whether he is concerned with his own country or is comparing it with another, usually also a Latin American, country. The result is comic, but significant: whereas a citizen of the United States listening to various Latin Americans talk jumps to the conclusion that all of them speak Spanish, a Mexican would conclude that, except for himself, no one was really speaking Spanish, or at best that each one of them spoke it very differently from himself. He would notice, for example, that an Argentine's speech was harsher, that the Chilean's had a singing lilt to it, and that the Cuban liked to swallow the letter "s," so that he pronounced both *"fósforo"* (match) and *"fósforos"* (matches) as *"fóforo."*

The two approaches, however, are not to be regarded as a thesis and antithesis, nor is it claimed that either one of them is the better working method. They are now looked at as different but equally valid ways of attacking a task. Even so, the matter is worth raising, if only to conclude that both methods are equally legitimate, since each of them corresponds to an undeniable and daily demonstrated fact— that all Latin American countries have a common denominator, and that each one of them has its own special features.

Here, however, two points should be made. The first is that both the generalizing and the differentiating approach should be used with caution; otherwise, there would be a danger of seeing Latin America as one single nation, like France, for example, or of taking the view that every Latin American country is as different from the rest as, for example, the United States is different from India. A rather more important point is this: in some aspects of Latin American life the similarities count or weigh more than the differences; this is true, for example, of geography, the language, religion, the legal structure and the general history; in other aspects, on the contrary, differences are not only more noticeable but appear to have special significance. As examples of the latter, one might cite political life, its general organization, the parties or groups active in it, the programs they seek to implement, and so on.

The United States scholar sees Latin America as a whole for reasons of economy; but also because, concerned with understanding that which exists today and with visualizing what might be tomorrow, he has begun by studying the entire history of Latin America. And there can be little doubt that many of the differences which today seem to us tremendously striking, with time, which is to say when they have become history, will lose much of their stature, thereby confirming the observation that there is more movement on the surface of the sea than in its depths.

I should like to comment on a few of the points in this quotation, since they lead me into my present subject.

First, I readily admit that the United States is still the only country which is concerned with Latin America and studies it; moreover, it has done so continuously. Second, I drew attention to the logical consequence of this sustained effort: United States studies on Latin America are so varied and numerous that the Latin American would find it difficult or impossible to disregard them if he decided to make a study of his own. In fact, I said that in some cases, whether he wished to or not, the Latin American would have to take them as a starting point for his own work, with the qualification that he may regard his own conclusions as more accurate. I then remarked that the opposite approaches of the United States scholar, who looks for similarities, and of the Latin American scholar, who digs up differences, offered an unequaled opportunity for mutually complementary collaboration.

But the most important thing about those pages, in fact the only thing of real interest, was the purpose for which they were written. By organizing a program of public lectures, the University of Buenos Aires wanted to awaken the interest of students, professors, and public authorities in the study of Latin America, that is to say, of the questions common to some or all of the nations composing it. As the first speaker on the list, I was responsible not only for my own lecture but I also had to serve as an *aperitif* and arouse the appetite of the audience. And I could find nothing better to say than, on the one hand, that the Latin Americans had neglected that field of study and, on the other hand, that it was now largely occupied by foreigners and, worse still, by scholars of the United States. The Latin American was forced to conclude not only that he owed a great debt of gratitude to the studious North American but also this: If he decided to devote himself to the study of Latin America, he would need all the intelligence and diligence at his command.

Well, it turns out that I was mistaken and that those pages, expressing an old conviction of mine, a conviction confirmed by what I deemed to be a solid experience, my own and others', are entirely unfounded. The Latin American scholars of the United States are now telling us of their own accord, over and over again, that they have worked little and badly and that nearly everything is still to be done.

I do not know how they arrived at this conclusion, but I suppose that at some point one of these Latin American scholars had the idea of comparing the startling boom in Asian and African research with the progress in Latin American research, which then looked to him hesitant and unimpressive. That sensitive man shared his doubts with his closest colleague and the two of them decided that the situation not only appeared to be atrocious, but really was atrocious. Those two coopted a third in order to discuss why things were so bad. These three, plus four others who joined them without delay, discovered reasons which struck them as convincing. Latin America was not a "critical area" and therefore did not attract the attention of the all-powerful governments and of the opulent foundations, which were intoxicated with the remote, exotic, and endangered. The consequence was obvious: No funds were available to stimulate Latin American research. The slogan "publish or perish" became truly maddening; as a result, the student of Latin America was compelled to repeat himself or to repeat his colleagues, thus dulling the sharp edge of discovery. As if that picture were not dark enough, it was further discovered that publishers, including the universities, were increasingly reluctant to give serious consideration to anything that was not at least a potential best seller; in consequence, there had been a sharp drop in the number of heroes willing to write books that would be read only by their own families.

The snowball had rolled a good distance down the mountainside, but it was fated to grow to gigantic proportions before it came to a stop. These discoveries and the doubts they had engendered had to be communicated to the entire body of area specialists on Latin America, not haphazardly, but in a planned and systematic manner. Consequently, the geographers were convened to deliberate in one locality, the historians met somewhere else, later in a third spot the anthropologists gathered together, and they were followed by the economists, the sociologists, and the jurists. Finally, they all met together at what might well be called a General Assembly of Latin American Scholars.

At that assembly and at the sectional meetings complaints inevitably abounded: "Latin America has . . . been neglected by our scholars. . . . As much as Africa, Latin America has been in many ways 'a dark continent' " [Wagley (Editor) 1964: 3]. Typical, too, was the ironic and bitter remark that by having converted Latin America into a "critical area," Fidel Castro had become the patron saint of United States scholars concerned with Latin America (Naylor 1962: 352).

The participants repeatedly expressed doubts of the very usefulness of the studies in which they were all engaged:

Our studies are addressed primarily to students and scholars, but perhaps they may be of interest to policymakers, administrators, technicians, and others who are eager to learn more about Latin America—and perhaps even the public at large [Wagley (Editor) 1964: 4].

Worst of all, even at the sectional meetings, some very harsh things were said, such as the following: "In very *general terms,* the *entire* social history, the *entire* economic history, the *greater part* of the political and intellectual history of 19th and 20th century Mexico still has to be written" (Naylor 1962: 353–54). Indeed, it should be added that Professor Naylor, rapporteur of that meeting, remarked that this statement met with little or no objection.

As was only natural and inevitable, there was an outpouring of examples and long lists were made of important subjects or areas for study and research as yet unexplored, and others already dealt with, but so inadequately that to review them would mean doing everything all over again.

It is not easy to bring myself to say this, but say it I must: Can all this self-criticism have been a kind of collective madness? If the word "madness" seems too strong, let us substitute a gentler one; let us say skepticism, discouragement, or collective uncertainty. We know that such phenomena do occur, perhaps more often in our epoch than in earlier ones. We know that sometimes collective madness takes the form of the group's identifying itself with its visible leader, conjuring him to react for it, personally and individually, as a separate entity and not as one small particle of the mass that carries him along.

Of course, it is not only moral, but "seemly," *decente* as the old Spanish saying goes, to examine one's conscience now and then. I will say more: It is decidedly more salutary to do so mercilessly; but once it is finished, it would be wisest to follow the advice of the great French chefs: Allow the dish to *rest* a little before serving it . . . and then enjoy it!

Everything that the North American students of Latin America have said about their own studies and everything they have said or omitted to say about the studies being made by ourselves, the Latin Americans, is true—very true. These studies are not as yet very numerous; their quality is unsatisfactory; many of the subjects, in addition to being banal, are taken up over and over again without apparent need; there is an oversupply of intelligent and brilliant but unsubstantiated generalization, as there is of studies on certain subjects—such as political history—while there is a lack of studies on other subjects, such as the social sciences. And the suggestions that we should explore new fields, some of them indeed virgin, are extremely attractive, not to say fascinating. None of this is in doubt; but the real problem is not to determine whether it is true, but the exact point at which truth ends and exaggeration begins. For example, of all the factors given as reasons for the stagnation of Latin American studies the only one which applies to Latin America alone is that prior to Fidel Castro it had not been a "critical area," and even this is not entirely true, since there had been abundant literature in the United States on Latin America before Castro, and it had been produced in a steady stream. The other two factors, the idea that one must "publish or perish" and the determination of publishing houses to accept only what they can sell, are applicable to any study, on any subject of limited interest, whether good or bad.

Another case in which allowing the dish to "rest" would have improved it is the statement I quoted before by Professor Naylor, which is, if not crushing, certainly wounding. If the statement were taken literally, it should plunge us into desperation and despair. Fortunately, there are certain correctives to be applied. One of them might relate to the personal style of the author who might well be a very severe judge of the work of other historians. Consequently, when Naylor says that the *entire* social history and the *entire* economic history is yet to be written, we common mortals should understand that what he means is a good deal of it. And when he says that the *greater part* of the political history has not yet been written, it should be clear to us that he means "some." Second, we should remember that the blow of the axe was preceded by the following words: "In very *general terms,* the *entire* social history. . . ." The terms, in fact, are so general that any exception that anyone—but certainly not I—would like to make can assuredly be made.

It was also said that the first works on Latin America by United States scholars date back barely a hundred years, and strictly speaking, the first studies appear only in the present century (Stein 1964: 87).

First, we might well ask whether the tradition of Asian and African studies is any older and, second, what the word "studies" is intended to mean, although I suppose it means "research." As far as I am concerned, however, what must be taken into account is the whole of historical literature and not one of its branches, such as "studies" or "research," although that is its latest and therefore most valuable product. Consequently, for the moment I am more impressed with other facts.

In a recent attempt to assemble a bibliography on "The Question of Texas" I collected a total of 504 entries; of these, 335 were by United States authors and only 162 by Mexicans; the remaining 7 were by writers of other nationalities. This means that 66 percent of the literature on this subject has been penned by United States scholars and only 32 percent by Mexicans. To these ugly figures, two facts must be added: The Mexican lot includes a good many short official publications which ought to be deducted from the total. What is still more significant is that the question of Texas is a hundred times more important for Mexico than for the United States. The same point could be made with regard to the formal academic book; we would have to admit that so far no Mexican has written in Spanish a work comparable with that of Justin H. Smith (1919) although we have had forty-six years to equal or surpass it.

Let us now consider, not Mexico or any one of our countries, but Latin America as an entity, and let us exclude the literature on the political and economic relations of Latin America with the United States, since unless we do so, the weight of the United States literature will be crushing. Let us confine ourselves to Latin America considered as a whole in its relations with the outside world, always excluding the United States.

We shall find that there is a bibliography of 1,818 "studies" in the form of books, learned articles, and official publications which are not mere verbiage but contain some of the elements of a "study." Very well—of these 1,818 works, 726 or 40 percent are of United States origin, 572 or 31 percent are by Latin Americans, and 510 or 27 percent are from other sources, among which are included, in addition to authors of other nationalities, the international institutions—especially the United Nations, the Organization of American States, and their respective specialized agencies. Even so, as we have seen, the greatest contribution has been made by the United States.

Of these 1,818 works, 776 are about the legal problems of Latin America and 1,042 about its social and economic problems. This fact is interesting in itself, since it contradicts the generally accepted idea that there has been far more concern with political and legal matters than with social and economic affairs.

Of these 776 political and legal studies, 364 are by United States authors, so that the total contribution of the United States is 47 percent. Latin American authors have contributed 38 percent or 295 studies; 103 studies are from other sources.

It is only when it comes to social and economic literature that the United States is relegated from first to second place, with a contribution of 364 studies, comprising 34 percent of the total. Even so, the Latin Americans trail behind with 277 studies, or 26 percent of the total. The first place is occupied by the "others," with 403 studies, representing 38 percent. This is clearly due, as I have already said, to the great work being done by the Economic Commission for Latin America, the Secretariat of the United Nations, and to a lesser degree, the Organization of American States.

These figures and what they stand for give the impression that in reviewing their output, in both quantitative and qualitative terms, the United States students of Latin America mentioned above were thinking solely of academic "studies," in other words, they disregarded those studies produced by men and institutions outside the college and the university.

We must now mention the last, and perhaps the most interesting point which led our United States colleagues to search their conscience, namely: the list of topics, and even of entire branches, which it is now considered urgent or very necessary to investigate in order "truly" to understand Latin American society.

Taking these topics one by one, I find them not merely appropriate, for that would be saying too little; I find them admirable, fascinating, so much so that I dare say many a Latin American would wish to be twenty, twenty-five, or thirty years younger in order to throw himself into the stimulating task of investigating some of these suggested topics. For example, many a Mexican would be eager to study the *hacienda* as the backbone of his country's political, economic, and social history in the nineteenth century, and thus meet a "crying need."

Nevertheless, even here, it would have done no harm to stop and think. A second and a third reading of the list of suggested topics might have resulted in a number of them being discarded, some because they are, strictly speaking, of secondary importance, and others because the reply to the question that must be asked in every piece of research is altogether too obvious.

Here is one of the many topics suggested: What was the long-term influence of U.S. government policy upon the course and duration of agrarian reform and indeed upon the Mexican Revolution itself (Stein 1964: 97)? I should think that there is and can be no other reply than the following: The influence delayed and limited agrarian reform, and in general revolutionary change as such. I may be told that the problem is not to give an immediate answer to the question, especially in vague and general terms, but to adduce facts and proof in establishing the manner, the time, and the place in which this influence was applied. Moreover, and possibly most importantly, the problem is to describe the magnitude and weight of this influence not only in absolute but in relative terms, that is to say, in relation to other factors which, while each operated independently, combined to set the Mexican Revolution on the course it has pursued to this day.

Then the more important subject, dealing not only with the particular case of Mexico and the Mexican Revolution, but with all of Latin America, would be that mentioned by an English Latin American scholar: "What really attracts the historian's attention in Latin America is not so much the political instability as the extraordinary stability of the social institutions" (Humphreys 1965: 15–16).

To turn back to the original question of agrarian reform and the Mexican Revolution, a Latin American might be tempted to propose another version on the grounds, *inter alia,* that the answer would be of greater interest to the United States scholar than to himself. The version would be this: Why did the United States government decide to exert this influence, or to put it in another way, why did the United States decide to oppose the Mexican Revolution? Or, to come closer to the heart of the matter, we might even phrase our question: Why did the United States government fail to evaluate correctly the nature and the regenerating force of the Revolution?

The United States government opposed the Mexican Revolution for obvious reasons; that is why the original question is not particularly attractive. After the complete peace and stability attained under the rule of Porfirio Díaz, after an exceptionally prolonged period during which foreign capital and technology and the foreigners themselves were cordially invited to come to Mexico and were welcomed without any reservations, this neighboring country of Mexico plunged into a veritable political and administrative chaos which unwittingly destroyed much of the previously created wealth, including the wealth of United States citizens. Mexico then started to introduce measures which hurt the financial interests of United States citizens and also their social position in the country.

However, faced with this visible and tangible phenomenon, the United States government had two alternative courses. They were equal in that they both inevitably aimed at the same goal—the goal of opposition; but they were very different in degree and in form. The United States government chose the course of bringing Mexico back to a political condition essentially the equivalent of the Díaz regime; the course it rejected was that of helping to channel the regenerating force of the Revolution in such a way as to make it as little destructive as possible in the short run, and to enable it in the long run to build a better society for Mexicans and, at the same time, for the United States. When Woodrow Wilson asked Victoriano Huerta and Venustiano Carranza to appoint between them an "impartial" temporary president, i.e. one who would be *au-dessusde la mêlée,* who would call elections and install a constitutional president, Wilson wanted to take Mexico back to the condition prevailing under Díaz. If, on the contrary, Wilson had attempted not to restore the status quo ante, but to establish a new status quo, which could have been brought about only by the political and military victory of the revolutionary forces, he would have favored Carranza.

It is now time to consider the other half of the problem—the problem as it concerns ourselves, as scholars in Latin America. We must naturally assume that there is a long, an interminable series of reasons which prevent our own contribution to the history of Latin America from being more voluminous, produced at a more constant rate, or of a better quality. But as it would be impossible to go into each one of these reasons in detail, there is no point in merely listing them, and I shall therefore limit myself to the major ones.

The fact which I myself find most striking is that the Latin American by far prefers inventing history to studying it, and therefore he is decidedly inclined to invent such history as he writes himself and to regard with respect and admiration such history invented by others. On the other hand, the Latin American barely tolerates history based on actual study. Charles Gibson has recently expressed a similar idea, although in a gentler and more courteous form: "Partly because history in Latin America is not yet thoroughly professionalized its popularity remains high" (Gibson 1964: 38). William J. Griffith expresses a similar view when he remarks that, apparently, the study of the period between Independence and the dissolution of the Confederation is used by Central American authors to escape from a frustrating present and to take refuge in the glorious past of the Great Central American Nation (Griffith 1960: 553).

One must agree that this preference of the Latin American is not as capricious as might at first appear. For where study represents an effort and a discipline which of necessity cause pain, invention has always been regarded as an inexhaustible source of pleasure and satisfaction. Let us recall that to create out of nothing has always been deemed to be an attribute of God alone.

Moreover, the Latin American has put in so much work and shed so much blood to attain even the little personal and civil freedom which he enjoys today, that he is instinctively and perhaps irrationally enraged by anything which, in fact or in his imagination, curtails or threatens to curtail his freedom. Again the contrast could scarcely be more impressive: To invent means to shake off all bonds; study and discipline impose certain limitations which, by definition, may not be exceeded and still less arbitrarily and freely disregarded. Where the poet—that creator par excellence of the world of letters—writes with his eyes closed so that reality will not interfere with his inspiration, the historian must write with his eyes fixed on the inexorable index card which contains the facts of a name, a date, or an event. The historian must not twist such facts unless he has decided not to invent, but simply to lie.

If this should not seem enough of a complication, it may be apposite to refer at this point to another remark of Professor Gibson's, namely that in Latin America, in addition to its "scholarly" function, history serves a great variety of purposes, all of which, or almost all, are respectable: patriotic purposes, partisan purposes, literary purposes (Gibson 1964: 38).

It is scarcely necessary to say that such invented history has its faults, which I shall examine briefly. Naturally, history neither is nor can be invented totally from start to finish. The result is that invented history lacks both the flight of imagination of a work of fiction and the anchored stability that comes from study and reflection. Therefore it readily becomes a tissue of reality and invention, of truths and lies or, what is even more unfortunate, of half-truths and half-lies. Some facts are recognized and respected, but these are generally the less significant ones, such as names of persons, places where they were active, and dates. Two or three strokes thus suffice to situate, in space and time, the scene in which the historical narrative will develop; but all the rest is left not merely to the imagination, but to the creative power of the inventor, his whims and his prejudices, which are often gratuitous. From that point on, the sequence of events, the changes brought about by time, and certainly the motives which might alter the original position of the actors in the historical drama, are of no importance.

Hence these stiff cardboard marionettes of Latin American history, who even before their birth are fated to follow one straight path, which they then undeviatingly pursue in disregard of wind or tide—of all the winds and all the tides of time and space. Our history is thus peopled with these monotonous and single-minded beings who were conceived by their mothers as heroes or villains, who were born as heroes or villains, who lived day in and day out as heroes or villains, who died as heroes or villains, and who, two or three hundred years after their bodies have turned to dust and ashes, continue to be heroes or villains.

Is there a remedy to this situation? One occurs to me, although I doubt that it can be quickly or easily applied. To describe it, on the other hand, is extremely simple: The Latin American would somehow have to be convinced that outright invention is the death of history, but that talent and imagination are not. Curious and surprising as it may seem, basically the Latin American fears that study and discipline will shrivel his talent and his imagination to the point where imagination will perish and talent will become purely conventional. That is the true reason why the belief survives among us that United States scholars would write better histories of Latin America if they studied less and invented more.

Perhaps a way might be found to dispel this conviction by referring to what some Latin American scholars regard as one of the few libels invented by their United States colleagues to avoid facing the problem of understanding the unnecessary complexity of the Latin American mentality. I refer to the theory of what the Mexicans call *machismo* and what the Argentines and Uruguayans call *prepotencia*—maleness or virility.

The maleness or virility of the Latin American man does not, as the United States Latin American scholar thinks, manifest itself solely vis-à-vis a woman, but vis-à-vis all the beings, things, and natural or moral forces that may cross his path. If this theory is true, the Latin American historian should be told that to write history on the basis of serious study takes more courage than simply to invent his material. Perhaps when his manhood is thus challenged, he may decide to study more and invent less whether concerning himself with the history of his own country or that of other lands.

The basic remedy for this situation, as for so many others, should be supplied by the Latin American institutions of higher learning. It is in these institutions that one can acquire in an organized way that cultural background which is the hallmark of a university education; it is in these institutions that the more advanced techniques of research can be learned; and, in the last analysis, it is these institutions which, bringing to bear the weight of their academic and moral authority, should succeed in gaining greater public esteem and recognition for the student of history. The universities and colleges should also give a more rounded training to the historian so that there will be people qualified to continue research on political history, which has indeed been the most favored subject so far, and to begin research on economic, social, and cultural history, the inadequacy of which we all rightly deplore.

Unfortunately there is not much to be expected from this quarter, for if there is a fundamental component of Latin American society which has failed lamentably in these ill-fated times, that component is the university, whether government-run or private, secular or religious, old or new. Why this should be so, however, is a question irrelevant to this paper.

That this is the actual state of affairs is borne out by the persistent presence in Latin America of the self-taught historian. We all know, of course, that among the misfortunes that have afflicted history in all times and places is its easy invitation to the attention of any casual passerby, in the same way that a woman with attractive curves invites compliments. (For this reason someone has irreverently called history "the Mae West of the Humanities.") Nevertheless, this pheonomenon is of such frequent occurrence in Latin America that one might say with justice on the one hand, that the self-taught historians always outnumber the professionals (so-called), and on the other hand, itself highly revealing, that the scholars have not always been the best historians of Latin America. In any event, we are fairly safe in adding that the self-taught historian who, as may be logically supposed, is driven by an entrancing and all-absorbing interest, works more steadily and produces more, and therefore is responsible for a disproportionate share of his country's historical literature at any given moment.

All of this indicates that the Latin American university has in some way lacked and continues to lack the necessary appeal to attract men with inquiring minds and intellectual predilections, as is certainly the case with the self-taught historian and the critic who evaluates his work in the public press.

There remains one last consideration, and our picture will be complete.

The university has failed to take cognizance of the changes brought about by the times and to adjust to them; it would be too much to ask it to have foreseen them. For the past sixty or seventy years at least, courses in economics and sociology have been given in Latin American universities. It is true that these courses were elementary, intended purely to supplement what was regarded as a desirable general culture, and also poorly placed, since usually they were part of the programs of the law schools, although some of those schools were called schools of law and of the social sciences.

The teaching of sociology, to say nothing of research, has become almost completely stagnant so that it would be no exaggeration to say that the little sociological work being done in Latin America today is being carried on either by self-taught sociologists or by professionals who have been well trained, but trained in related subjects such as social anthropology. However, the teaching of economics and economic research have made notable progress, so that it may be said that there exists in Latin America today a substantial group of qualified, well-trained economists, with professional experience and interests. However, almost without exception, these economists received a significant part of their training outside Latin America; they are still a small group, and since a good many of them are working full time for governmental and private institutions, those who are engaged in basic research are few indeed.

The most neglected of the social sciences, however, is what is called in English "political science" and what in Spanish ought to be called *politología*. It has never been taught as such and I know of no research of any importance in this field. Consequently, it may be said that political science either does not exist in Latin America or is the old charlatanism of bygone days.

Our main question, however, is not the present state of the teaching and research of the social sciences, particularly economics, sociology, and political science, in Latin America. We are concerned with determining to what extent the progress, stagnation, or retrogression of history depends on the present state of teaching and research in the social sciences. For the moment, the only thing that can be said is that to the extent that its progress depends on the social sciences, history in Latin America will proceed at a speed which no one would call vertiginous.

Let us suppose that the teaching of social sciences and social research attained a level comparable to that which economics has reached in England, sociology in the United States, and political science in France. Would Latin American history become one of the wonders of the world? There can be no doubt that it would benefit greatly from this splendor; nevertheless, it is to be feared that it would benefit only indirectly. Let us take the case of economics as an illustration.

It is, of course, a rare thing for the same man to combine the talents and the training of the historian and the economist. An historian turned economist may discharge his own task well; he may describe the economic changes that have taken place in the course of time, and he may be expected to do so clearly, and occasionally brilliantly, but—and this is a very serious matter— he may overlook the internal mainsprings of the changes he describes and their more remote consequences. The economist turned historian, being naturally sure of his science and its techniques, may readily confound economic analysis, by definition a static task, with economic history, which is essentially dynamic. He may find it difficult or impossible to stop using his jargon, which is sometimes unnecessary, at other times incorrect, and always irritating.

I therefore feel that if we are to witness the miracle of a new and more substantial Latin American history, it has to be brought about by the historian himself and not by the laborer in the field of social science. But the historian's training will have to be drastically reformed. According to what ideas and what methods? This is a question for the wise to ponder.

REFERENCES

Gibson, Charles.
    1964 History: Introduction. *In* Handbook of Latin America Studies, no. 26. Gainesville, University of Florida Press, pp. 38–42.
Griffith, William J.
    1960 The historiography of Central America since 1830. Hispanic American Historical Review, 40: 548–69.
Handbook of Latin American Studies.
    1964 No. 26. Gainesville, University of Florida Press.
Humphreys, R. A.
    1965 Tradition and revolution in Latin America. London, The Athlone Press.
Naylor, Robert A.
    1962 Research opportunities in modern Latin America: Mexico and Central America. The Americas, 18: 353–65.
Smith, Justin H.
    1919 The war with Mexico. New York. 2 vols.
Stein, Stanley J.
    1964 Latin American historiography: Status and research opportunities. *In* Social Science Research on Latin America, edited by Charles Wagley. New York, Columbia University Press, pp. 86–124.
Wagley, Charles (Editor).
    1964 Social science research on Latin America. New York, Columbia University Press.

The Social Sciences

VÍCTOR L. URQUIDI

5

Further Observations on Economic Research in Latin America

One of the most striking aspects of the Seminar on Latin American Studies held at Stanford, California, in 1963 [Wagley (ed.) 1964], is the extraordinary preoccupation of all branches of social science with the economic development problems of Latin America.* This concern of anthropologists, historians, geographers, political scientists, sociologists, and even jurists poses a fundamental problem whenever one attempts to comment on economic research activities. Much is said about improving interdisciplinary studies, and it is obvious that there are wide areas of contact and that the different specialties are complementary. However, the studies included in *Social Science Research on Latin America* [Wagley (ed.) 1964] reveal that the field of economics has been invaded by the other specialists. On the other hand, as Dr. Carlos Massad (1964: 214–42) correctly states in his excellent essay, the economist must be conversant with the other branches of the social sciences if he is to be able to do what is asked of him, namely, to advise on the economic policy which should be pursued; he therefore finds himself compelled in his turn to encroach on the domains of his social science colleagues whenever they cannot help him.

Some thought must therefore be given to what is meant by economic research, what is meant by research in the other branches of social science, and what interdisciplinary studies really are. For example, much of what Dr. Massad regards as the subject of economic research actually relates to sociological,

* The present essay was written in response to the request of the Social Science Research Council for a comment on the earlier essay by Dr. Carlos Massad mentioned in this first page.

juridical, administrative, institutional, and political aspects of problems of general interest such as those mentioned by him, namely, land reform and fiscal reform. Dr. Karst (1964: 290–333), on the other hand, in examining research on law and legal institutions offers a long list of topics, referring again to land reform, in which little juridical material is to be found and in which attention is centered rather on sociological and economic aspects.

In the introduction to the book, Dr. Wagley (1964: 16, 28) points out that it was only when the economics of development became an important factor in the lives of the Latin American peoples that a vast field was opened up for social science research. Each specialist focuses on the problems which he identifies as the most serious obstacles to development or on those which governments, owing to circumstances and various forms of pressure, are compelled to deal with. However, a serious attempt to achieve a relative delimitation of the various fields would appear to be necessary, because it will otherwise prove difficult to bring about an understanding among the different specialists and there is a danger that specific problems will be approached without the proper analytical tools.

Despite the headway made in economic research in Latin America in recent years, the inadequacy of such research, and in some cases its virtual nonexistence, may be what has induced the other specialists to encroach on the domain of economics. Actually, economic research in Latin America has advanced very slowly. In the past, research activities were mainly of a short-term nature, generally sponsored by government offices or departments which felt the need for information and criteria that would be useful in taking more or less immediate action in the field of economic or financial policy. At first, much of the research was undertaken by the central banks. There was an obvious need for systematic information that would enable them to deal with the problems created by the economic and trade depression of the thirties; they also had to cooperate in adjusting the Latin American economies to new conditions in which the beginnings of an industrialization policy were faintly discernible. That was an era in which no very useful experience of other countries was available, no personnel were capable of adapting or applying such experience in the Latin American countries, and the teaching of economics had not yet been modernized to the point where it could provide the few research institutions with the requisite technical staff. This situation existed throughout the thirties and most of the forties. It is significant that, when the Economic Commission for Latin America (ECLA) was established in 1947, it was not easy to recruit even a moderately experienced group of Latin American economists for its secretariat.

In addition to these difficulties which confronted governments and universities alike, there was a paucity of adequate statistics, a relative dearth of country studies, and a total lack of comparative studies. It is surprising that studies of economic history have never flourished in Latin America and that today there are very few economic historians. If economic history had been a field of interest in the past, greater attention would surely have been devoted, in due course, to the quantification of growth phenomena and even to the proper preparation of censuses and other data which could have served as a basis for initiating analytical studies of Latin America as a whole, studies which were subsequently undertaken by ECLA under more favorable auspices. ECLA was confronted at the outset with obvious difficulties in assembling statistical material which would enable it to evaluate the condition of Latin America in the years immediately following the Second World War (United Nations: ECLA, 1949). No effort had even been made to collect information on external trade or monetary experience except for an initial attempt, in the latter field, by the Banco de México (1946), when it convened a meeting of central bank experts.* The Latin American economists were virtually unknown to each other except for the brief contacts that some of them were beginning to make at the postwar international conferences designed to establish international monetary and agricultural agencies. There was no practical contact between the universities and, then as now, there was little or no interchange of the few books, pamphlets, and periodicals containing the studies or ideas of the Latin American economists.

Economic studies were in relatively small demand. Govern-

---

* Since 1946, seven meetings of central banks have been held in different capitals. In 1952 the Latin American Center for Monetary Studies (CEMLA), largely maintained by the central banks, was founded.

ments had not yet realized the gravity of the problems that would confront them after the war, and development in the various countries had not yet reached the stage where decisions of economic policy could be implemented with adequate technical support. The influence of leading figures of the "old school" was still to be reckoned with. Consequently, the supply of economists was also limited in the sense of both current graduates from modern schools of economics and persons firmly established in their profession and abreast of the theories and research methods developed abroad. It is common knowledge that for a long time the teaching of economics in Latin America formed part of law or accounting curricula in which the point of view of the lawyer or the accountant prevailed. The economist, whose services were rarely required, would have found it difficult to make a living as such if, at the same time, he had not possessed other professional knowledge to guarantee him public or private employment.

It should also be noted that the few economists who managed to go abroad to study often returned completely ignorant of their own country and of its problems and with no clear idea of how to apply their knowledge to the situation prevailing either in their own country or in Latin America. In a nutshell, economic research lacked the incentives required to transform it into a systematic and scientific activity based on a continuing search for information and employing adequate instruments. It was caught up in a vicious cycle in which a weak demand for research duly led to a poor supply.

Postwar readjustment and especially major changes in the economic policy of various European countries, and above all of the United States, confronted Latin America with the need to adapt the structure of production to a new pattern of aggregate demand. Meanwhile the rising rate of population growth began to reveal the existence of economic development problems that were deeper-rooted than had previously been imagined. Some early material was available, particularly in the studies initiated by Raúl Prebisch in the late twenties in Argentina and when the Central Bank of Argentina was founded in the thirties, on the unsuitability of traditional economic policies (Prebisch 1943;

Banco de México 1946: 25–33). Attention was then drawn to research needs relating to policies for safeguarding the economy and offsetting cyclical fluctuations.* Nowadays, when a wide range of statistical tools is available and professional contacts are maintained throughout the world, it is easy to forget that the qualitative importance of those first attempts at research and analysis were the forerunners of many other subsequent studies both by Dr. Prebisch, before and during his service in ECLA, and by economists from various other Latin American countries.

Consideration of postwar problems and the first awareness of the difficulties, and at the same time the possibilities of economic development were the main factors which caused ECLA to direct its efforts, to a marked extent, toward formulating some general ideas on development policy. When ECLA was set up, it may have been regarded in some quarters as only a technical body concerned with compiling statistics and submitting a few more or less conventional studies on economic conditions. But the nature of the problems and the challenge which they held out for a small group of economists, not to mention the extraordinary personal influence of Dr. Prebisch himself, laid a special imprint on the secretariat's activities which distinguished them considerably from, for example, what was being done by other regional commissions of the United Nations and even by that organization's own central technical services. Whether or not one agrees with much of what ECLA has advocated or with its research methods, it must be acknowledged that thanks to ECLA's efforts a body of ideas has been emerging in Latin America consistent with the long-term interests of Latin American economies. Policies based on this gradually evolving framework of ideas were originally considered completely wrong by people outside the area, but have in the end been largely accepted as effective solutions. ECLA's studies, which have been widely circulated and whose methods have been presented and explained on various occasions, have not only been of service to individual countries and have prompted studies and research by national economists and institutes, but also form part of the important background ma-

* Cf., for example, the *Revista económica* of the Banco de la Nación Argentina, 1928–1934, and the publications of the Central Bank of Argentina from 1935 to 1943.

terial of the Alliance for Progress and even of many of the topics discussed in 1964 at the United Nations Conference on Trade and Development. The somewhat adverse evaluation of ECLA's work made by Dr. Massad in his essay therefore does not seem quite justified. I would even venture to say that Dr. Massad somewhat simplifies some of the arguments and conclusions set forth in ECLA's studies, and also ECLA's analytical explanation of the crucial problems of Latin American economic development, inflation, and other subjects.

But this is not the place to discuss whether the work of this or that organization is good or bad; my aim is to evaluate the condition of economic research in Latin America and to suggest in what ways it could be improved or on what aspects attention might be focused.

Some stress should perhaps be laid on the fact that economic research is becoming increasingly costly. The days of the individual study by an economist capable of using statistical data to support a certain hypothesis or theoretical position are no more. Nowadays economic research requires the compiling, revising, adapting, and processing of a vast amount of statistical material; it must rely on sampling and on the use of electronic computers (which brings the economist not only into the field of applied mathematics but also into that of computer programing). Economic research also involves building up large libraries which must include not only the enormous output of books in various languages but also a considerable array of specialized academic periodicals, the publications of financial and technical bodies, statistical yearbooks, the unpublished memoranda and documentation of international agencies and research institutes in other parts of the world, and other source materials. Research now costs more, economists' scales of remuneration are much higher, and the expenses of building up libraries and accumulating reference material grow heavier every day.

The foregoing shows that it is difficult for universities and private groups to undertake research on an adequate scale unless they have financial support from the public sector or outside sources to guarantee the specialized staff a certain security of tenure and to underwrite the expenditure required for research. Where research work is thought to be not yet sufficiently comprehensive or thorough, it will be found that this is largely due to a lack of resources. The accomplishments of recent years by various institutes in Argentina, Brazil, Chile, Colombia, Venezuela, as well as the beginnings of systematic research in Mexico, show that possibilities exist for improving economic research; and to the extent that something is being achieved, it has had favorable repercussions on the methods of training economists. There are already some postgraduate schools with reformed curricula and a mounting number of fellowships for sending the best students to complete their training abroad. In addition, many international organizations have launched special training programs and recruited Latin American economists who have thus been able to acquire wider experience, and compare problems and methods of analysis with what is being done in other countries; this enables them to engage in new activities when they return to their own countries.

Nevertheless there is still no adequate evaluation of economic theory, i.e. the theoretical and analytical tools on which much research is based. The Latin American economist brought up on foreign textbooks or trained in foreign universities, even though he may reach high levels of skill, necessarily cannot have been able to devote enough time to considering whether or to what extent the theoretical concepts he was learning could be applied to actual conditions of production, demand structure, social change, and the stage of political evolution prevailing in his country. I am not attempting to revive a debate on the universality of science versus the so-called development of a particular theory applicable only to a given area. I simply wish to point out that a high proportion of the theoretical knowledge of any Latin American economist is a combination of ideas and analytical tools that can be applied only in economies which have already reached an advanced stage of development, or which have evolved in specific conditions in which private enterprise plays a much larger role and sociopolitical situations of another order prevail. Even in the matter of economic development, the Latin American economist often learns the little he knows through the more or less systematic attempts of United States or European economists to cope with this problem area, and it goes without saying that there are few foreign economists who have understood the problems of development as phenomena distinct from mere economic growth. The borrowed tools used by Latin American economists need to be extensively overhauled and this may be one of the fundamental tasks of economic research in the wider sense.

Without theory, without a clear picture of a body of ideas and overall concepts, it is difficult for basic research to have any real meaning; this is just as true in economics as in the other branches of the social sciences. It would not be an exaggeration to state that in many cases, an adequate theoretical concept, for example, of Latin American economic development, would have to be largely based on a study of history. As Dr. Stein (1964: 113–14) points out in his chapter of *Social Science Research on Latin America,* many important aspects of the history of Latin America have been neglected and its economic history in particular has suffered. If the economist searches historical experience for an explanation or a series of concepts that will help to explain why there was a given pattern and rate of growth in a given country or in the area as a whole, he will find enormous gaps like those mentioned by Dr. Stein. Historical studies, particularly if some economists collaborate in them, may lead to a better formulation of ideas with a better appreciation than exists at present of the nature of economic evolution and social change.

Pending such studies, it seems to me legitimate that the economist should make certain assumptions, even though they may not be clearly demonstrable, which will provide a context of consistent ideas within which he can place his analysis of growth or development. If intuitive aspects and perhaps even some prejudices intrude, I do not think that this is altogther objectionable, given the present circumstances, provided the door is always left open for discussion and, where applicable, for refutation on the basis of further research. It is rather difficult to accept the position that in all this the economist is acting superficially and without objectivity. There may be such studies, but looking at the picture as a whole it seems to me that the serious and objective studies are more in evidence, although they may suffer from the aforesaid drawback of insufficient information.

The same can be said of certain criticisms directed at ECLA's work to the effect that much of what it has done is based on a priori reasoning and on ideological positions (Massad 1964: 221). Without necessarily sharing Dr. Wagley's fears that social science is drawn inevitably into politics and may therefore lose its objectivity (Wagley, ed. 1964: 28) it must be recognized that economic development, on which the intergovernmental organizations focus their attention, has both national and international political aspects, and that it would be unrealistic for an international organization to devote itself to a simple neutral examination of the facts and to refrain from offering the information that would enable the very governments which constitute the organization to deal with the problems and embark on the policies requiring technical guidance. One may disagree with many of ECLA's studies, but I do not think that one can go so far as to deny their objectivity.

Even though I agree with many of the general remarks made by Dr. Massad, I do not regard the examples he selects and develops as important areas of research, or the series of questions he asks, as the real crux of Latin America's economic research problems. For example with respect to land reform, apart from the need for more information and descriptive and comparative studies, I believe the basic purpose of economic research is not to try to evaluate the different ways in which land reform can be carried out, or to advise on partly juridical and partly social aspects, but to go to the heart of the problem, about which I find no clear idea in Dr. Massad's proposals, which is the following: What role does Latin American agriculture play in economic development? Since Latin America's agriculture accounts for a large proportion of its economic activity, since Latin America's rural inhabitants still constitute two-thirds of the total population, and since agriculture is recognized to be the sector in which productivity is lowest in overall terms, there is every good reason for not only the economist but indeed all other specialists to ask what has led to this situation and what can be done to remedy it—not just as a social phenomenon but because agriculture should, we assume, form an integral and dynamic part of the economic development process. I am not contending that agriculture must be the main element in a faster and perhaps better-balanced development process; I am only advocating the need to understand fully the role of agricultural development in overall development, how agriculture absorbs modern technology, how it becomes flexible (or, from another standpoint, why the factors of production employed in agriculture become rigid). It is in this connection that I would be concerned with land reform, that is, with the pattern of ownership and land tenure systems, to the extent that these are important for an economic solution to the agricultural problem. It seems to me that relatively little has been done in the matter of research; in particular there has been a shortage of economists with adequate training in agriculture or capable of grasping sufficiently the very diverse historical, technical, legal, and social aspects of agricultural development which would enable them to form more educated opinions.

Similarly, I think that Dr. Massad's concern with fiscal reform is secondary to the basic issue, namely, the importance of the public sector in economic development, or more precisely, the activity of the state as the direct promoter of economic activity as consumer and as an agent of national capital formation. Whether economic development can or cannot take place without considerable activity by the state as a producer or consumer is a question which should be investigated in the light of other countries' histories and of Latin America's own history. If the conclusion is that the economic activity of the state and of what would now be called the public sector is fundamental, the problem of financing then arises. This would, of course, lead to inquiries into the past and present role of a country's saving capacity and its division into private and public savings. Economic research on taxation should center largely around the matter of public savings, but taxation is, of course, only one part of the state's economic power. Nowadays many of the state's functions are performed through producing or distributing agencies which operate sometimes as enterprises, in the same way as private undertakings, but may also be guided by a deliberate policy of subsidy or be unable to muster sufficient financial resources, or be placed under restrictions to do so. The distributive aspects of the fiscal system and of public expenditure in Latin America should be studied more fully. But these are only secondary aspects of a much more basic consideration of the importance of the public sector.

The problem of economic integration, which Dr. Massad mentions as an important subject of research, also seems to be somewhat ouside the mainstream of basic economic research. It can be argued that Latin American integration is actually only a somewhat broader aspect of national economic development problems. As integration is achieved in the industrial field as part of the general progress of industrialization, it must also be considered simultaneously in the context of the overall development policy of each country and of Latin America as a whole. It is unrealistic to approach integration as if its problems were distinct from those of a nation's internal development, because development problems exist both within a country and between one country and another. The only difference is that, in the latter case, other monetary systems operate and there are barriers and obstacles to trade in addition to the effects of policies which may not be similar. To me the essential thing is to focus economic research on the problems of industrialization within the context of overall economic development, given the demographic conditions and extraneous factors which influence the Latin American economies, and, as a result of such research, to consider integration as an extension of industrialization problems to a multinational geographic area.

These brief critical observations bring me to a much more general problem. The great dearth of economic research in Latin America is in the study of the determinants of production from the standpoint of the importance of real capital formation, expansion of the labor force, use of technology, and other growth factors. So far as the structure of demand is concerned, substantial progress in research has been achieved in recent years thanks mainly to recognition of the important role played by the growth of external demand and its transmission via various channels to the internal economy, i.e. through direct expenditure and through the fiscal system. As more has become known about external demand and its apparently declining future role, a thorough study has begun of the import-replacement process and the factors influencing domestic demand. Thus, studies have been made of the effects of income distribution, and the impact of industrialization on the generation of purchasing power and the absorption of surplus manpower from the rural sectors; sample surveys have led to a clearer identification of consumption functions and the trends of consumer demands. The efforts made to analyze public expenditure and to evaluate its importance as a factor offsetting the shortcomings of external demand may also be included in the studies of demand.

All this has been of value and has revealed one side of the operation of the Latin American economies, but it has not provided an answer to the other fundamental question: What has made it possible, historically and at present, to increase production and productivity in Latin America and gradually to change their pattern in the light of changing demand? Or what has prevented productive capacity and the factors influencing supply from adjusting themselves adequately to the ever-changing conditions of demand? Demand and supply is certainly the field in which statistical information is scarcest not only in Latin America but also in many other countries; but there are many examples of important research carried out in the United States and Europe on the role of real capital formation and technological advance, and on the implications of population growth, resulting from natural increase or immigration, and its gradual transformation and greater productivity through education and the absorption of technology, both imported and national.

The three fields of research specified by Dr. Massad (land reform, fiscal reform, economic integration) could be studied from these angles: What determines the agricultural production function? What determines the productivity or the productivity effect of the public sector in a country's economic development, i.e. how can we evaluate the influence of the public sector on supply, and hence, of course, derive a host of conclusions on economic policy? What, from the supply viewpoint, determines the Latin American countries' capacity to produce manufactures and make effective use of technical resources, both natural and human, in the proper combinations required to boost production and productivity? These questions refer to the three subjects selected by Dr. Massad, but they could be applied to many others. Our Chilean colleague enumerates other very interesting topics, which he mentions only incidentally, on which research might be undertaken in order to emphasize the forms of structural change, and the determining and conditioning factors of growth in output.

In this context it is curious to note the way in which the Latin American economist has dealt with demographic problems.* Assuming that demographic information has been deficient—although the same can be said of any basic information—there is no justification for the economist considering population growth simply as a figure, a rate of increase which is to be deducted from the rate of expansion of output, or a numerical factor which has to be taken into account and applied to various overall figures. Demographic analysis is, of course, complex and involves many statistical and intrinsically demographic techniques which the economist either does not know or finds it difficult to find the time to master. But again it may be the economist's scant experience of historical events which prevents him from realizing that the labor force is not just a cipher but a number of people combined with a productive capacity determined by institutions, the educational system, the standard of health and hygiene, and a series of other conditioning factors.

Thus many economists, because they fail to take these problems into account or do not know how to analyze them, tend to project population as if it were a homogeneous mass incapable of changing its productivity or its adaptability to new techniques. So long as Latin American development tended to conform to the conventional pattern of the international division of labor without requiring much participation from its population, and the means of communication did not make this any easier, there might have been some justification for neglecting the labor force as a factor of growth; but as the pattern of development has changed and industrial growth has been called upon to play a much larger part, and as social and other phenomena have led to massive migration from rural to urban areas in Latin America in the last twenty or thirty years and medical advances have brought a marked drop in the mortality rate, the role of population growth obviously has begun to change. The population is

---

* Demography was not discussed at the Stanford Seminar; there are short and incomplete references to it in the chapters by James J. Parsons (1964: 53–59) and Rex Hopper (1964: 262–65) on geography and sociology, respectively.

far from homogeneous: Levels of education vary considerably, and the capacity to absorb techniques is not the same in the different population sectors. Clearly it is no longer valid to assume that part of the population is incapable of improving its productivity or that another part, because it has become urbanized and educated, can raise its productivity indefinitely. Nowadays both assumptions are simplifications without an adequate basis, and what seems to be missing is a reconsideration of the relationships between economic growth and demographic growth, and especially of the role played by certain sectors of the population as elements which absorb technology and productivity increases.

This would also be a different way of viewing, from the reverse side so to speak, many of the problems that are apparent from the studies on income distribution. These studies simply deal with the purchasing power of various segments of the population, but it is assumed that within each income level there is an entirely homogeneous population with the same potential (or lack of potential) to raise its productive capacity. Some thought should be given to the desirability of statistical surveys which would reveal the characteristics of the population at different levels of income as factors of production, and relate the educational level, occupation, and other aspects to the income level.

The actual distribution of income as an economic and social phenomenon is also usually studied very superficially. Distribution is related to the concentration of ownership, to the social structure (which permits positions of monopoly), to the nature of the tax system, and so on. If traditional economic theory teaches anything which constitutes a modicum of fundamental truth it is that income distribution is influenced, on the one hand, by the relative shortage of capital (not of savings) and the attitude and expectations of those who have the opportunity of using such real capital for productive purposes and, on the other hand, by the educational level and technical skill of the majority sectors of the population. The majority sectors in particular, for historical reasons, have had no other role to play than that of providing their labor; they have lacked bargaining power, and they have been faced with conditions not enabling them to acquire a larger share of the product without impeding a continuing growth of productive capacity and productivity. In other words, income distribution will not be improved through changes of one kind or another in the tax system or by various social welfare measures, but by acting, again from the supply side, on the processes of production and productivity and on the attitudes of those who are in a position to contribute, as entrepreneurs or labor, to productive activity. This statement leads once again to the fundamental problem of the role which the state itself has to play, or has played in the past, as entrepreneur and as an instrument in a country's real capital formation.

Once these fundamental problems of economic research are taken care of, studies on demand and the analyses of the distributive machinery and on the effects of different methods of changing land or tax systems will be a net gain. I am not disparaging the importance of the great variety and range of research work which may provide the answers, on a limited scale and with reference to a specific issue, to many of the questions without which it is difficult for the public or private sector to make rational decisions. Nor do I deny the desirability of making comparative and historical studies of what economic policy has been on various specific matters. I am only stressing what I regard as fundamental, and where, in the long run, the emphasis should perhaps be put.

Dr. Massad's contribution to the general survey of the condition of economic research in Latin America is very valuable. I am convinced of the positive nature of his position, and, if I have not agreed with some of his evaluations, this does not mean that from other points of view and possibly from the standpoint of many of my colleagues they may not be correct.

REFERENCES

Banco de México.
1946 Memoria [de la] primera reunión de técnicos sobre problemas del banco central del continente americano. Mexico City.
Hopper, Rex.
1964 Research on Latin America in sociology. *In* Social Science Research on Latin America, edited by Charles Wagley. New York, Columbia University Press, pp. 243–89.

Karst, Kenneth L.
 1964 The study of Latin American law and legal institutions. *In* Social
       Science Research on Latin America, edited by Charles Wagley. New
       York, Columbia University Press, pp. 290–333.
Massad, Carlos.
 1964 Economic research in Latin America. *In* Social Science Research on
       Latin America, edited by Charles Wagley. New York, Columbia Uni-
       versity Press, pp. 214–42.
Parsons, James J.
 1964 The contribution of geography to Latin American studies. *In* Social
       Science Research on Latin America, edited by Charles Wagley. New
       York, Columbia University Press, pp. 33–85.
Prebisch, Raúl.
 1943 El patrón oro y la vulnerabilidad económica de nuestros países.
       Jornadas 11, El Colégio de México.
Stein, Stanley J.
 1964 Latin American historiography: Status and research opportunities.
       In Social Science Research on Latin America, edited by Charles Wag-
       ley. New York, Columbia University Press, pp. 87–124.
United Nations, Economic Commission for Latin America.
 1949 Economic survey of Latin America, 1948. Lake Success, New York,
       United Nations.
Wagley, Charles (Editor).
 1964 Social science research on Latin America. New York, Columbia Uni-
       versity Press.

VICTOR FLORES OLEA

6

On Political Science
in Latin America: Viewpoints

We must acknowledge that Merle Kling (1964: chapter V) has provided us with a very good survey of Latin American studies. I doubt if there is a single North American publication of any value dealing with political research on our countries that he has overlooked. However, when it comes to studies by Latin Americans (and, occasionally, Europeans), of direct or indirect interest to students of Latin American politics, I consider that the list of publications could be considerably expanded. It is true that the vast majority of these publications fall far short of the minimum standards required of political science in the strict sense of the term; they belong more to the field of "traditional" political studies, as Professor Kling calls them. But it is also true that these publications often provide us with valuable data, comments, and analyses. Political scientists in and on Latin America should not neglect them, for they help to shed light on the causes and aims of the major social and political movements in Latin America, their basic characteristics, their methods and tactics, the processes of their organization and institutionalization (or disintegration), and are an undeniable source of ideas and incentives for concrete political research.

In addition to this literature there are a large number of essays, articles, dissertations, and reports (published in periodicals, newspapers, and pamphlets) which, although they do not aspire to academic standards, do record trends of opinion, the extent and prevalence of problems, the ways in which power is actually exercised, the political influence of various groups or personalities, the ideological platforms of parties and other organizations, and the changes they undergo. Even when it is impossible to reach scientific conclusions from the study of these documents, they still serve as indicators and direct the specialist's attention to political processes that are underway and show him the historical forces at work in the area he is studying. We should remember that the social scientist needs continual points of reference since, however "realistic" and "down to earth" he may be, he is always condemned to work at a certain level of abstraction and is in danger of forgetting certain vitally important phenomena. Need we mention the cases in which specialists, on the eve of a violent political unheaval, have not had the slightest idea of what was brewing?

I am not proposing to enlarge on the bibliographical and documentary aspects of our theme; first because, given the size of Latin America, this could only be done by one or more teams of specialized research workers. I shall merely confine myself to emphasizing their importance and expressing the hope that one day we may have a systematic index of useful books and documents in the field of political science.

We must also acknowledge that Kling is right in referring to the generally low level of Latin American political science. The use of modern research techniques and methods is extremely limited and recent. As Kling points out, most of our works in this field are of the strictest "traditionalism"; their approach is inadequate to the present needs of the discipline and contributes little to its future development. Again, quite rightly, he mentions our weakness for formal research on the constitutional and legal structure of the Latin American countries (it is true that this research sheds some light on the rules of the political game and the values which apply or have applied historically, but it tells us nothing about our real political life), generalizing without systematic observation beforehand, prescribing formulas and advice for rulers, and evolving "broad theories" which are purely doctrinal and speculative and do not even purport to be original. Indeed, these studies are no substitute for political science in the strict contemporary sense of the term.

There is no doubt that many features of our theoretical "traditionalism" can be explained on historical, cultural, political, and economic grounds. The methods and techniques of political science research are comparatively new, even in the United States and Western Europe. And they have reached us, or are beginning to reach us, very late in the day. Moreover it is not the first time that this has happened. Our political and economic dependence is also reflected in the cultural sphere. In the nineteenth century we assimilated the ideas of democratic liberalism and, subsequently, of positivism after these trends had already become quite widespread in Europe. In this century some of the German philosophical trends, mainly those which describe the social sciences as "sciences of the spirit," which have had a definite influence in many of our universities and academic circles also reached us at a late stage, even when it was obvious that they were on the decline in their place of origin. In the case of modern political science, history is now repeating itself with the aggravating circumstance that its belated arrival in our midst is confronted by a cultural tradition which, in more than one respect, is opposed to it. Our university and academic system has had on occasion to be thoroughly overhauled to accommodate institutions which are beginning to operate on modern lines in the field of the social sciences. Until very recently—in Mexico for example—sociology and political science occupied only a small part of the curriculum in the faculties of law and philosophy. Much of the traditionalism in our political science is due to the presence of those cultural influences, which are still remarkably strong, and to the subordination of this branch of learning to others which are considered more universal.

In addition to these causes, one could point to others arising out of the very nature of political science itself. The progress of political science depends less on the efforts of isolated research workers than on one or more organizations with the necessary human and material resources. Unfortunately we nearly always find ourselves faced with a shortage of one or the other. Experts are in short supply or still undergoing training; funds are notoriously inadequate for any worthwhile research in the field. Until progress is made in solving these aspects of the problem political science in Latin America will, to a large extent, remain entrenched in its traditionalism. Its modernization will be neither rapid nor easy. The situation in Mexico is particularly serious since there is not a single institute or center for political research within Mexico's university and academic framework. We should not be surprised at the dearth of specific studies on many key phenomena in our political life or at the fact that, in more than one sense, the North Americans have done more than we to bridge certain gaps in this field.

I have mentioned several cultural, technical, and economic factors which help to explain the reasons for the traditional nature of Latin American political studies. But it would be unfair to stop there. To my way of thinking there are other causes which we cannot overlook, are possibly more profound, and lead us to the crux of the problem: What function does political traditionalism in Latin America fulfill? Why this marked tendency to make value judgments and generalizations? Why the frequent references to the classics of political thought? Why the profusion of advice to the authorities? On the other hand: What significance and application should traditional political science have in our countries? Can we and should we use political science in the same way as it is used, for example, in North America? What connection is there between our political and economic development and the progress of political science from traditionalism to modernism? For my part, I am convinced that satisfactory answers to these and similar questions will depend largely on a proper understanding of our political problems and the future trend of political science in Latin America. These questions deserve frank and honest consideration.

We must first understand that conditions in our countries have forced Latin American political thinkers to seek solutions and alternatives rather than to furnish descriptions of behavior and quantifications. Is it possible to conceive of an analytical and neutral scholar in countries in which coups d'état occur in rapid succession, in which force is the rule and law the exception, in which instability and *caudillo* governments are often the keynotes of the system? It is not easy. By force of circumstance political theory has become inextricably entangled with political practice. Thinking has had mainly to be devoted to problems and their possible solutions and it has, in many instances, been partisan and frankly militant, concentrating on the best means of waging the campaign. Hence political thinking immediately became political action, an affirmation and an effort to find and produce solutions.

The permanent crisis in our political systems (with exceptions, such as Mexico during the past thirty years) has been all-pervasive, its causes affecting the entire organization of Latin American society. This is why Latin American political science has also viewed its problems in the widest possible dimension. The chief aim has been not to correct the odd deficiency or minor defect in a system which, on the whole, was considered acceptable but to radically correct the entire system. Hence the Latin American tendency to elaborate broad theories, to quote the classics, to make value judgments, and openly adopt ideological positions. It is true that a *weltanschauung* type of political thinking could, in the light of recent advances in the discipline, be considered obsolete and dysfunctional. However, I insist that this traditionalism has not been gratuitous and, what is more, that today it still has a reason for existing in most parts of our continent. I think that we should bear these facts in mind when analyzing the past and future development of political science in Latin America.

At the same time we should not forget that the committedness of Latin American political thought has too often given rise to excessive and unscientific generalization and to vague subjectivist rhetoric. Unfortunately the scientific value of most of the literature is very slight and the gaps in our political knowledge are alarming. What Latin America needs is to produce better conditions for political science: to assimilate modern research techniques, increase the number of specific studies, and to ensure, insofar as possible, that they are tested experimentally. This is a most pressing need, because this is the only way to establish an effective and realistic policy for tackling our problems as distinct from dependence upon rhetorical pronouncements and statements of good intentions. I am sure that rational men will not object to this much needed transition from traditionalism to modernity in political science.

These reflections lead to others which we cannot escape. The fact is that progress in political science, and the social sciences in general, has been made chiefly in the industrialized countries. Is this progress due exclusively to the greater cultural and organizational development of these countries, to their abundant resources and adequate technology? Can the significance and method of operation of modern political science be the same in an advanced society as in countries like ours? Is there not a close connection between the general development of a society and the concrete application of a science, especially when its subject is human behavior? Is it not true that the social sciences have a definite ideological importance deriving from their very existence as social phenomena? My answer to these questions is in the affirmative.

The industrialized countries of the West are now enjoying a political and social stability that is not to be found in the Latin American countries. The possibility of a sudden change in their structure, if not to be ruled out entirely, is very remote. The integration and organization of those societies is extremely solid. Radical solutions and structural alternatives are of concern to minorities; in all events they are not generally regarded as serious problems which should receive attention in academic circles. I would even go so far as to say that the cultural environment and the mass media are at great pains to dispel any such notions. All the resources of collective influence are employed to divert attention from fundamental questions about society and from all attempts to criticize its foundations and organization. Instead, the aim is to represent the society as a model of unimpeachable rationality. Of course the social and political organization of the industrialized countries is not entirely free from problems. But the problems are considered secondary and subordinate, simple problems of adjustment and control, and not crucial problems of structure. Stability (even if only relative) has given them an extraordinary amount of security. This situation is particularly apparent in the case of the United States and is even reflected in some of the assumptions of North American political science. For example, the particular connotation which Merle Kling gives to such terms as "traditionalism" and "modernism" is revealing.

We have already seen that traditional political science is considered to be fraught with normative elements and value judgments, and limited to a high critical content regarding the foundations of society. Modern political science is supposed to be characterized by an essentially empirical and descriptive concern with political phenomena. Normative and critical judgments are out of place, since they are considered prescientific and dysfunctional. What is important is to think not of historical alternatives but of knowledge which conscientiously distinguishes between values and facts, between theory and practice, between means and ends. In this sense, modern political science is supposed to be strictly acritical, not as regards deficiencies but as regards the foundations of the system, which is implicitly or explicitly accepted as the supreme historical incarnation of reason and technique. And what is this system? In the West it is the political system of the industrial society and, ultimately, of North American democracy.

Obviously this type of political science is very different from traditional political thinking. In the eighteenth and nineteenth centuries social theories had played an eminently *critical* role; they sought alternatives and courses and were not afraid to maintain ideological positions or suggest new patterns of organization. Even the United States was not untouched by this revolutionary experience of social and political theory in the nineteenth century. For their part, Europeans fought for a long time to break down aristocratic privileges and introduce representative democracy, to destroy the feudal economic system, and to develop a market in which all men might compete on a free and equal footing. Can there be any doubt that political theory played a decisive role in this fight, that it was characterized by evaluative elements, and that it acted as a tremendous creative force and stimulus on a world in the process of transformation?

Making the necessary allowances for certain differences, the disparity between our level of development and that of other countries, the international balance of power, the fact that there now exist organizational patterns different from those which were available as alternatives to the developing countries a century and a half ago, and even at the risk of oversimplifying slightly, I would venture to say that the Latin American situation is now parallel to that experienced by those countries in the last century. We, too, are seeking alternatives and solutions which will result in a comprehensive and revolutionary political theory. We must understand this: Social research in Latin America, the analysis of facts and factors, the elaboration of hypotheses, and the empirical definition of concepts, in short, the modernization of political science, *cannot* be divested of all ideological and evaluative content. In a stable and well-organized society such "objectivism" can be set as the ideal standard for political research—we shall see later on whether it is achieved or not; in countries like ours it cannot even be taken as an ideal. In my view, any Latin American political science which purports to purge itself of all critical judgments and reference to the total structure of society is doomed to sterility, fated to be no more than a laboratory experiment of no social significance. For us, as for the better North Americans of the nineteenth century (and of today), political science cannot isolate facts from values or theory from practice. In our situation, all these terms are necessarily interrelated and mutually complementary. I must emphasize once again that the modernization of our discipline in Latin America depends on the strict application of its most advanced techniques. However, as its legacy from traditional political theory modern political science must retain at least the lessons of an acute critical sense and the imaginative and historical capacity to find solutions to our problems.

I think it no exaggeration to say that many specialists in Latin America would agree with this view. I feel that it would be extremely useful if North Americans also looked into the differences between their scientific preoccupations and ours, between their way of practicing political science and our main concerns in this field.

But there is another question that we cannot sidestep. Is a political science devoid of all evaluations really possible? My answer is in the negative. In my opinion the difference in this respect between traditional and modern political science is that while the former openly upholds its beliefs and normative judgments the latter does so implicitly and without confessing its ideology. However this does not mean that modern political science is politically indeterminate. On the contrary, practical and partisan interests can be discerned even when it employs the most elaborate conceptual notions. I therefore believe that all discussion of the "neutral" character of the social sciences should be abandoned once and for all. It is simply a waste of time. The real problem is to ascertain how the scholar can maintain the maximum objectivity in spite of his ideological convictions, professed or unprofessed. In short, how can one be scientific despite the inevitable ideological commitments? This is not the place to discuss such a weighty problem, about which so much has been written. I shall simply point to its existence and illustrate it with some examples taken from *Social Science Research on Latin America,* and from Merle Kling's contribution in particular.

Samuel P. Huntington (in Kling 1964: 194–96) states that: "Political development—from traditionalism to modernization—seems to offer the best framework for analyzing Latin American politics. Political development, however, is a complex process. At a minimum, it takes place through four channels." The first of these channels is said to be *mass mobilization* (including increased communications, national identifications, integration, socialization, participation—all dealing with the attitudes and behavior of people-in-the-mass). The second is *interest articulation,* including both the forms and methods of interest group organization and the substance of the interests articulated; are these interests modern or traditional? The third, *elite broadening,* including the expansion of the number and type of political activists and the assimilation of new types of individuals into leadership roles, their methods of operation, and their origins. The fourth, *institutional development,* including the generation and growth of political organizations and ideologies: parties, executives, legislatures, judicial bodies, the rules of the game among political leaders, autonomy of these organizations, their attitudes and practices as distinct from those of other groups in society.

Huntington's statement is certainly very interesting. But I wonder: Are not the features he notes, strictly speaking, mainly characteristic of the industrialized societies of the West, and particularly of the North American political system? And then, are we not being offered this system as the ultimate criterion for defining political development per se? And is not this system being presented as a sort of paradigm or ideal that we ought to pursue and attain? Huntington might disagree, and say that it is a question not of paradigms or ideals but only of a conceptual device useful for the study of political development problems; that it is not a question of channeling political action in a particular direction, but merely of knowing and describing and being rigorously scientific. However, after touching briefly on the difficulties involved in "unbalanced" political development when it occurs in one or more of those four channels but not in all of them, Huntington asks:

> In policy terms, should the United States aim for a "balanced" political development across the board in all four channels? If so, perhaps a most scholarly and yet directly policy-relevant use of resources would be to analyze each Latin American society in terms of its developmental progress in each of the four channels. Where gross imbalances are discovered, American efforts should be devoted to pushing development in the channels where it has lagged the most.

Is it not perfectly clear that Huntington, too, uses concepts to advocate concrete political measures? And is it not also clear that what he is proposing is a predetermined model of political development to which we should aspire in absolute terms? And does not all this imply a frankly evaluative and ideological approach, even if it is not openly proclaimed and appears to be confused with the conceptual device of the scholar?

To my mind, the problems deriving from such an approach are obvious. Can political development be said to have taken place only when progress has been made in the four directions listed by Huntington? Are these criteria the only ones which we can apply in order to detect any political development? How flexibly should they be applied? Can they also be used to determine the degree of political development, let us say, of societies such as the Soviet or the Cuban? And supposing we discovered that apart from Western society there are other models (such as the socialist society) which aspire to a kind of political progress which would be hard to assess by Huntington's standards? Should we define political progress in terms of democratic progress? What would happen if we found that mass mobilization is induced and manipulated by the great power centers, economic, political, and cultural, whose aims are not exactly democratic? What if substantial interest articulation is achieved for the purpose of maintaining the dominance of one section of society over the others? What if the process of elite broadening caters essentially to the needs of those partial and minority interests? What if institutional development ultimately serves only to sanction the authority of these power centers and to consolidate a dominant status? In such an event could we still speak, without stretching the meaning of the terms too far, of real "political development" and "democratic development?"

Should we not say that genuine political progress is possible only when the integration and participation of the masses aims to achieve democratic control of the economic, political, and cultural machinery by the majority? When we have, not the articulation of pressure groups but the articulation, expression, and satisfaction of the interests of the community as a whole? When elite broadening is carried out in a community which affords identical opportunities to all its members? When institutional development is aimed at achieving not merely political democracy but economic democracy, as an essential prerequisite for the former?

If these questions are legitimate, I think some observations can be made on the basis of our brief analysis of Huntington's statement. First, the statement contains value judgments and prescriptions for political action which need to be examined critically. Second, his four channels of political development cannot be applied universally, still less without explicit reference to the actual structure of society. Third, the conceptual categories of political science are inevitably linked to political movements and to certain basic considerations, such as what a genuine democracy should be. Fourth, the purely functional use of these categories, without critical judgments concerning the structure of societies causes us to lose sight of the substance of the problem. Furthermore, is it possible to assess Latin American political development in terms of the United States model? And is that model sufficient justification for devoting American efforts to pushing development in the channels where it has lagged the most? Does not this imply that these efforts are also exerted to hamper or destroy aspirations or movements which do not conform to that model? Must we regard the forces in our countries which oppose the American model as necessarily dysfunctional and disruptive? Unfortunately, within the limits of this study I can only call attention to the entire complex of political and evaluative problems to which modern political science gives rise, emphasizing that ideological questions are not rendered obsolete by it and that, on the contrary, they form a constituent part of political science as such.

There is therefore no qualitative difference between traditional and modern political science. Both have definite political interests and take ideological stands. But while traditional political science has profoundly critical and revolutionary aims, modern political science is of an eminently acritical and conservative nature. However, we need go no further. The passage I have quoted from Samuel P. Huntington sheds sufficient light on these questions. Nevertheless, we could reinforce this statement by quoting some further sentences from *Social Science Research on Latin America*.

In the Introduction for example, the editor, Charles Wagley (1964: 1–4), frankly admits:

Never before has knowledge of Latin America societies been so important to the United States. . . . The future of these Latin American nations and of these rapidly expanding peoples is crucial to our way of life. . . . The future of Latin America is important to our own security. . . . More than ever before, we need their votes and their support. . . . In many ways, Latin America is no less important to us than Asia, Africa, or even Europe. We should maintain our financial aid and technical assistance programs to the area. We must support those forces in Latin America which promote economic, social and political progress by peaceful and democratic means. . . . Knowledge of Latin American societies should be available to our decision-makers on the many levels of government, of business, and of private foundations. . . . Many advanced graduate students and mature scholars have "discovered" Latin America and are now preparing to carry out research and teach on this highly strategic and interesting area.

One does not often find such a clear admission of the self-interest inherent in North American social research on Latin America. Can we still maintain that no ideological elements have entered into this research? However, we should not be shocked. We have already said that a neutral political science is a virtual impossibility. In fact, we should welcome a frankness that can prevent a great deal of misunderstanding on both sides.

In political terms, this self-interest consists in "pushing our political development" (Huntington), and in "promoting effective democratic procedures" (Kling). An initial difficulty stems from the fact that, apparently, these goals are identified with North American patterns of democracy and political development. Does this identification mean that, in the eyes of the American scholars and decision makers "on the levels of government, of business and of private foundations," on whom "financial aid and technical assistance" to Latin America ultimately depend, any political process which deviates from these patterns is unacceptable? Does it mean that the political process will automatically be branded as disruptive and dysfunctional? Last, does it mean that in the opinion of the United States our interests must necessarily coincide with United States interests in this area? To put it differently, must our political and democratic development follow a course that will not prejudice North American interests in Latin America?

The theoretical and practical importance of adequately answering these questions must be obvious. They affect our political relations with the United States, and we cannot fail to recognize the decisive importance of these relations to our history, past, present, and future, and the ability of North American and Latin American scholars to understand the nature of these relations and of our political movements. What if our political backwardness should prove to be due, in part, to the way in which North American interests operate in our countries? What if it were clear that our political, economic, and social progress can only be achieved at the expense of United States interests in Latin America? Would the political scientists of that country be capable of admitting it openly to the decision makers in government, business, and private foundations? To what extent could the scholars and decision-makers help in the matter? Would they be able to comprehend the underlying reasons for the radical political movements in Latin America and state those reasons? Would they be able to explain the real reasons for our radicalism to their own public without attributing it to propaganda, subversion, or communism, thus helping to dispel the ignorance and correct the misconceptions which are widespread among the American public about events in our countries? Would they be able to explain the causes and the forms of Latin American nationalism? I hardly think there is any need to stress how extremely important it is to elucidate these questions, first, insofar as our political relations with the United States are concerned, second, as regards the theoretical understanding of our problems and the development of political science in and on Latin America, and third, as regards the social function and significance of political science.

The other alternative would be to aim at a Latin American political development and democracy that would be strictly acceptable to the United States; a political development and democracy that not only did not conflict with, but essentially coincided with the scale of values on which that system is based. The practical purpose of such a political science would, I think, also be quite clear: first, to condition and gear Latin American political behavior (through mass media?) to certain symbols and values, and second, to perform the "therapeutic" function of eliminating dysfunctional tendencies which resist acritical acceptance of certain values. Why, for example, does Merle Kling ask how Latin American political values can be changed, and how the techniques of "governmental engineering" can be employed to promote effective democrative procedures? (Kling 1964: 193.) Would it be a matter of organizing a party life, a democracy, a public opinion, and a community of interests from which all opposition to and radical criticism of the system were eliminated? Would it amount, ultimately, to organizing a political life in which the first requirement was unconditional respect for established interests?

I feel that the implications of this alternative should be made clear, and some of its consequences pointed out, not only because it is a real historical alternative which students of Latin American politics are faced with, but also because Kling's work does not deal with the question directly and contains certain ambiguities.

For example, there is his insistence on the nonevaluative character of modern political science, the reference to Huntington's four channels of political development, without considering the content or structure of the community which is to achieve this progress, and the use of a term like "governmental engineering." This term and, more generally, the term "social engineering" is a concept of technocratic origin which implies a definite analogy between the control of nature and the control of society. Technological rationality and man's growing control over nature thus have their complement in a political rationality which aims at man's increasing control over man. Is this the "rationality" toward which modern political science is leading us? And should we not inquire into the content and ethics of this "engineering"? To be sure, Merle Kling tells us that this governmental engineering is designed to "promote effective democratic procedures." In that case should we not find out whether this technique of social conditioning or control is in flagrant contradiction to the democratizing goal that is being pursued? Should we not start by defining the content of democracy? For we cannot overlook the fact that nowadays the most disparate and even conflicting systems are regarded as democratic. Are we aiming at a process of democratization which would encompass Huntington's four points concerning political development? If so, could not "governmental engineering" mean controlled mass mobilization, minority interest articulation, the recruitment of an elite which would make authoritarian decisions, the development of institutions which would serve to safeguard and legitimize established privileges? Is it not true that in such an event "governmental engineering" would be promoting a decidedly undemocratic procedure?

I have taken the liberty of raising these questions because I feel it is most important to stress that the functional application of political concepts and their techniques is not enough. The phenomena under examination must be analyzed basically and structurally. Moreover, if we lose our historical and critical perspective, the operational concepts of political science end by being "therapeutic" and defending the status quo, limiting the political universe to what already exists, rejecting the critical choices and failing to see the underlying causes of social tensions and their dynamics, atomizing facts and viewing them in isolation without perceiving their role in the overall development of society. A bare description or quantification of phenomena gives us a false notion of the concrete, which is isolated from its origin and development and loses its true historical dimension.

Kling has compiled a very interesting list of possible topics for political research in Latin America. The list does not purport to be exhaustive, and the topics are only enumerated, but there is no doubt that a plan drawn up on these lines should contribute enormously to our knowledge of political realities in Latin America. I am sure that I am not alone in hoping fervently that we may one day have a sufficient number of monographs dealing scientifically with all the questions raised and with other questions which might, perhaps, be pertinent. However, I must repeat that if a genuine contribution is to be made to political science in Latin America the contribution will depend largely on the perspective of the proposed studies. Is it enough to establish typologies, behavior patterns, and correlations? Why is consideration not given to the economic basis of political power and the contending classes, the interests which are being defended and attacked in the political struggle, in short, the dynamic and contradictory, and therefore real, image of our societies? Is it right to be so concerned with describing and classifying political phenomena and relations in Latin America without showing the same interest in their working and developmental processes and their social significance? I shall try to illustrate what I mean by mentioning a few of Kling's specific points.

Kling proposed that we should study "the recruitment and socialization of elites, rigidity and flexibility among elites, a taxonomy of political leadership" (1964: 192). But are we to give the false impression that Latin American elites and leaders are the outcome of a natural and objective process of selection, and that their "rigidity and flexibility" is a style of conduct which needs only to be classified and described? Is it not our duty to point out the relationship that exists between political power and economic power and the fact that in general the ruling classes select their own leaders? Does not the very concept of *elite* conceal an underlying reality: the political and economic power exercised by a particular class? Should not political scientists look into this question thoroughly? Why is mention not given to one of the decisive facts about political power: that it implies domination by one group over others? And should there not be a specification of who dominates whom, by what means and for what purposes? Should not this be a central topic of political science research on Latin America?

In some of his other points Kling uses terms like "cohesion," "consensus," "national integration," and "unification." Here too, unless one is specific the impression could be given that we are invariably confronted with a process of rationalization and progress in our political life, a harmonious picture of the whole. A study of these topics, however, would have to show us the political, social, and economic significance of these phenomena. Is "cohesion" or "national integration" imposed? If so, by whom and for what purpose? Is "consensus" conditioned? By whom and for what purpose? Are the procedures democratic or authoritarian? Again it is important not to overlook the power conflicts and the social and economic contradictions.

In other points the lack of reference to social antagonisms seems to lead Kling to level off the conflicts, which are converted into formally definable behavior patterns. For example, when one proposes the construction of "theoretically oriented typologies of political actors and regimes in Latin America" or establishment of "relationships between the type of violence employed and the nature of a political system," does not one run the risk of setting forth purely external and formal identities and presenting the phenomena as something contingent and accidental, which does not tell us much about their real causes?

I wish to stress these aspects of our problem (the methodological aspects relating to the assumptions and the political and social consequences of research) because they are not always sufficiently apparent. Need I repeat that they merit careful attention and require definite attitudes on the part of political scientists, that they affect the outcome of our studies and constitute a sort of backdrop and frame of reference which we must keep in mind when conducting a specific investigation? From the standpoint of general methodology, and summing up the foregoing in one sentence, I would say that modern techniques of political science can only provide a true knowledge of phenomena if grounded in a wholly dialectical understanding of society and of the political and social significance of our discipline (Marcuse 1964: 106).

Merle Kling's essay is not only a fine work of bibliographical synthesis but, above all, a source of very valuable suggestions on

Latin American political topics and on the application to our problem of the conceptual and technical machinery of modern political science.

There is no doubt that it is extremely important to conduct experiments in quantification, if possible, particularly in matters of electoral behavior, attitudes and public opinion, and relationships between distribution of income and political participation. There is also a pressing need to describe as accurately as possible a number of concepts which are frequently employed in political studies on Latin America. Merle Kling uses terms like "instability," "violence," *"caudillismo,"* "dictatorship," and there are others that could be added to the list, such as "oligarchy," "nationalism," "radicalism," "subversion," "imperialism," "paternalism," *"continuismo."*

It should be stressed that the use of more general categories such as power structure, leadership, political parties, pressure groups, democracy, elections, political development, consensus, authoritarianism, social classes, trade unionism, and the construction of types or models for analysis require particular caution and strict adaptation to Latin American conditions. For example, should we study political parties, pressure groups, or trade unions in Latin America on the basis of European or North American models? Have not these institutions a special political, social, economic, and human significance in our countries? Is the function of parties in countries which have no parliamentary life comparable to that which they fulfill in truly representative systems? What is the relationship between the parties and the social classes in Latin America? What part does the one-party system play in our countries? What specific techniques are used by the Latin American parties to win their clienteles? How do our archaic forms of organization influence the actual structure of the parties? What are the relevant factors in Latin America which cause political parties to change or new ones to emerge?

In regard to pressure groups, is there not a radical difference between these groups when they are organized into lobbies, as happens, for instance, in the United States and France, and when they are not recognized institutionally, as is nearly always the case in Latin America? How do pressure groups operate in Latin

America? Which powers, executive, legislative, or judicial, do they chiefly work on and why? What basic interests are pressure groups designed to promote—economic, political, military, or professional? What connection is there between the pressure groups and foreign political and economic interests? To what extent do pressure groups influence crucial political decisions, military and police operations, economic policy, and international policy? What are the exact links between pressure groups and the authorities?

With respect to trade unions, how does the fact that they are generally made up of a new proletariat without traditions affect their character? What connection is there between the particular features of trade unions and the migratory trends within the country from rural areas to the towns? What are the ideological sources of trade unions and what influences have they received from abroad? What is the economic and cultural level of members compared with other sections of the population? How dependent or independent are trade unions of the authorities? What are the methods of government control over the trade unions, the relations between the trade union leaders and the authorities, the most widespread means of corruption? To what extent do trade unions function democratically and what are the usual means of undermining trade union democracy? How important are the trade unions politically? What are their relations with the political parties? How far do they promote social integration? Do the trade unions give their members opportunities for political and professional training?

There are many other topics that could be listed. However, I shall only stress that the structural features of Latin America make it practically impossible to automatically apply general concepts of political science in studying our countries. That is why I have said that real political knowledge can only come from a thorough understanding of the historical dynamics and concrete structures of the country under consideration.

Moreover, there is a pronounced tendency to generalize and to speak of Latin America as if it were a single homogeneous unit. The actual situation is just the opposite. Despite their common historical, cultural, and ethnical bases, the problems, stages of development, and types of organization—in fact the structural features—of the twenty Latin American republics are very different. Students of Latin America should avoid hasty and superficial generalizations. In fact, I would go so far as to say that before studying Latin America one should systematically determine which regions can be covered by the same assumptions and hypotheses. We may have to concede that the thorough study of a series of political and social problems requires specialization in a particular country. The growing complexity of our social life may make specialization a necessity in the near future.

As well as proposing experiments in quantification, Kling suggests using comparative methods, specifying the dependent and independent variables of phenomena, employing new techniques to investigate the nature and origin of political attitudes and values prevalent in Latin America, conducting surveys of public opinion, and even examining literary works and other documents which can provide a clue to the underlying political motivations of certain groups and persons in our countries. We agree with these proposals. And we unreservedly support his belief that Latin American political science can mature only within this framework, adding once again that we cannot lose sight of the critical and dialectical dimension of our discipline and the series of problems which we mentioned at the outset. These problems are fundamental, and we repeat that unless they are fully understood, political science runs the very grave risk of falsifying the facts, failing to see the real historical trend, serving a reactionary cause instead of being an effective instrument for the advancement and betterment of the peoples of the continent.

In conclusion, I shall consider two questions which I consider to be of interest.

First: Mexico has been studied more intensively by foreign political scientists, economists, anthropologists, and historians than any other Latin American country. Kling briefly mentions a few hypotheses that might form the basis for an "empirical theory" of the Mexican political system (1964: 199–201). Unfortunately it would take us too far afield to discuss his interesting theories in any detail. Instead, and purely for the sake of interest, I think it would be useful to list in summary form a few topics which might become the basis for specific studies of Mexican political life. Some of these topics already have been studied systematically. Others, perhaps the majority, afford the student an unexplored and fertile field for research. Needless to say the list does not claim to be exhaustive.

1. *The 1917 Constitution:* basic principles. What political forces were responsible for the inclusion of "socializing" articles (article 27, on private property and original and direct ownership by the nation of lands and waters, mineral resources and fuels, and land reform, article 28 prohibiting monopolies, article 123 on workers' rights)? The present validity and significance of the Constitution, and particularly of these articles.

2. *Presidentialism in Mexico:* from *caudillismo* to the institution. What factors helped to bring about this change? How is it connected with the country's economic development? What archaic elements still exist and what influence do they have? Bossism and paternalism.

3. *The power of the President:* supremacy of the executive over the legislature and the judiciary. Centralism within the Federation. Control over the army. Objective and subjective limits to the power of the President including political groups, economic groups, other real power factors, presidential arbitration, the need for stability, support for revolutionary principles.

4. *The presidential succession:* how is it decided and by whom? Are there any objective principles or rules governing the six-yearly change? What factors are taken into account in deciding the succession? So-called *tapadismo* and the behavior of public figures and political groups in connection with the succession. The attitude of popular organizations. Public opinion regarding the change of president.

5. *The power elite:* political figures and ex-presidents. Captains of industry, banking, and commerce. The national bourgeoisie and the pro-imperialist bourgeoisie including their influence and methods. Leaders of workers', peasants', and bureaucratic organizations. Military and religious leaders. Interdependence of all these groups. Is there a new class of technocrats with its own place in the Mexican power elite?

6. *Pressure groups:* political, finance and banking, industry and commerce, workers' and employers' unions, professional associations, the universities and other cultural institutions, the army, the church, the press, the monopolies which run television,

radio. The National Liberation Movement and the Centro Cívico de Afirmación Revolucionaria. How do pressure groups operate in Mexico? Does the key to their strategy lie in influencing the President of the Republic? What interests do they represent?

7. *The political bureaucracy:* stratification and mobility. The process of selection and rotation. Are there any discernible patterns? The economic importance of the upper class and its links with finance, industry, public services, trade, agriculture, etc. Is the political bureaucracy a homogeneous or a heterogeneous stratum? The extent and solution of its conflicts.

8. *Political symbols:* the figure of the President. Non-reelection. Nationalism. Invocation of the principles of the Mexican revolution: rhetoric or reality? To what extent? For what purpose and with what results? The charismatic prestige of power. National unity and the revolutionary family. The rejection of "exotic" ideas and the original exclusiveness of the Mexican revolution and its ideology.

9. *The official party:* the history. The various periods, including ideological and organizational variations. Political party or election bureau? Dependence on the state and especially the executive. A one-class or a multiclass party? What interests does the party represent? Is the party a stability factor? Conflicts within the party, their extent and their arbitration. Recruitment of members. Degree and forms of militancy. Party branches, their size and effective representation. Is there bureaucratic authoritarianism or democracy within the party? The actual method of selecting leaders and candidates. The political career available within the party. Party discipline. Operation of the party during election periods and regular activities. Regional structure and concrete action at the state, district, and municipal level. Propaganda.

10. *The opposition parties:* the PAN, PP, PCM, and PARM.*
Platforms and ideologies. The interests the parties represent. The actual strength of the parties in different regions. The social origin of their members. Activity at election and other times. The propaganda media of the parties. The leadership and sources of finance. The position of the parties regarding presi-

* PAN: Party of National Action; PP: Popular Party; PCM: Mexican Communist Party; PARM: Party of the Mexican Revolution.

dential changes. The real content and scope of the parties' opposition. Are they really parties or pressure groups? The relations of
the parties with government circles and degree of integration in
the system. Have they the potential means of changing the
regime?

11. *The elections:* the electoral law. The opportunities and
difficulties the law affords for free interplay between the parties
and a democratic electoral procedure. What fraudulent practices
have been most frequently employed at elections? Relation between election participation and economic development, living
standards, and education. Geographical distribution. The main
propaganda lines and dissemination media. Personalities or
programs? Consensus or manipulation? Intervention by parallel
organizations, including the Church.

12. *Public opinion, mass media, and integration in the system:* How is public opinion shaped and by whom? How important is it in Mexican politics? The press, including means of
financing and content. What interests does it represent? Censorship
and self-censorship. The relations of the press with the government, including dependence and critical processes. The right-wing
and left-wing press, their political symbols. Modern propaganda
and public relations techniques, including their content and
political influence. Conformism or criticism? The extent to which
these techniques reach the various sections of the public.

13. *The social classes:* political relevance and attitudes. Have
the social classes a definite ideology? Their main organizations.
Relation between income and political values and attitudes. Social
mobility and stratification, including political effects. Population
pressure, the industrialization process and its impact on political
life. The middle class, its interests and political symbols. The
social classes and the parties. Class consciousness and its main
manifestations.

14. *The trade unions:* ideological and fighting traditions.
How did article 123 of the 1917 Constitution come about in a
country which had no industrial proletariat at the time? The
part played by the workers' movement in the Mexican Revolution. Are the trade unions a creation of the state? The workers'
unions and their political importance during the Cárdenas period. The participation of the workers' unions in the nation-

alization of oil. The new course of trade unionism since 1940 and its political effects. So-called *charrismo* and trade union corruption. Official control of the trade unions. Is the organized and dependent workers' movement the real basis of the regime's stability? Prospects for trade union independence and democracy, including political consequences.

15. *The intellectuals:* participation in political movements. Their influence on public opinion. Their political attitudes, including entry into government machinery and independence. Ideological trends of the intellectuals and their expression. Conformism and criticism. Political positions of scientists, technologists, and liberal professionals. The attitudes of university students and how attitudes change when the students enter a profession. Present significance and future prospects of the intellectuals. The social origins of the Mexican intelligentsia.

Naturally, this type of empirical investigation means carefully formulating advance hypotheses and, above all, endeavoring to arrive at principles or explanatory theories which cover an increasing number of political phenomena, without losing sight of the dialectical link between the various sectors studied and, ultimately, the dialectical and dynamic interplay of the various fields of research in the social sciences. The object is to try to promote a thoroughly realistic and scientific political science in Mexico, based on concrete research and capable of grasping fully the historical processes of Mexican society in all their complexity and variety. The ultimate objective would be to win greater respect for our different countries and, insofar as possible, for the Latin American world as a whole.

Second: Kling tells us that he omitted consideration of international relations, international law, and international organization, as they impinge upon the study of Latin American political processes (1964: 169). It is a pity that in such an interesting paper no mention is made of this crucial aspect of Latin American politics. This is especially to be regretted, since our foreign policy is unquestionably important particularly as regards the United States, whose actions in connection with our countries, both governmental action and that of private economic interests, are not without their effects on the development and characteristics of Latin American political life.

Merle Kling suggests that we should study "the impact of United States policies, international politics, and international institutions upon decision-making in Latin America," and, without specifying further, refers to the "problems of diplomatic and military intervention." Personally, I am sure that a proper understanding of a great many Latin American political phenomena would require a frank and thorough study of our relations with the United States and its influence on our political processes. If we were to overlook this aspect of our political life we would be refusing to understand a key factor in our development, our current problems, and our future prospects, and we would be betraying the intellectual integrity which should underlie any scientific research project.

Once again, I am going to propose summarily a set of topics that have to do with the international side of our politics, particularly as regards the United States, and which should figure prominently in Latin American political science.

1. The change from Latin American dependence on European powers to dependence on the United States. The Monroe Doctrine.

2. Correlation between the increase in United States investments in Latin America and the intensification of its influence in this region. Is that influence directly linked to the sum of United States economic interests in each country?

3. A documentary and historical study of United States military and diplomatic interventions in Latin America. Their causes and their consequences. Which regions have been affected most by such interventions and why? Can we form any general hypotheses to explain these interventions?

4. What is the connection between political instability and violence in Latin America, and United States interventions and pressures? How is the United States connected with coups d'état?

5. What forces and what interests have been supported by United States interventions in Latin America? For the sake of what symbols and principles were they undertaken? What practical results did the interventions achieve in the matter of de-

mocracy and the political and institutional development of Latin America?

6. According to what criteria has the United States acted in providing military, technical, and economic assistance to Latin American governments? What connection is there between this assistance and Latin American dictatorships, between this assistance and the way in which our governments vote in international organizations? What guarantees do United States investors require from our governments?

7. What has been the attitude of the government, business leaders, and press in the United States toward revolutionary movements in Latin America? The cases of Mexico, Bolivia, Guatemala, and Cuba. The counterrevolution in Latin America. What connection is there between this change of attitude and the decline of radicalism in some of these revolutions?

8. Who decided on these interventions? What political, economic, and military forces had a share in the decisions? What connection is there between the interests of the United States interventionist groups and the "protected" interests in Latin America?

9. Variants of United States interventionism: the "Big Stick," the good neighbor policy, the Second World War, the cold war, and the Alliance for Progress.

10. The problem of the Cuban revolution. Why does Charles Wagley say that "Cuba illustrates dramatically the danger, both real and mythical, which a neighboring unfriendly government under an avowedly Communist regime represents to the people of the United States?" (1964: 2.) Effects of interventionism and United States pressure on the internal and external trend of the Cuban revolution. United States assistance to counterrevolutionaries. Outlook for Cuban-United States relations. The impact of the Cuban revolution on Latin America and its influence on the continental policy of the United States.

11. Coups d'état in Latin America during the last five years, and the policies of the United States Government.

12. The structure of the Organization of American States and the origins of its decisions. The political symbols which determine its attitudes. Its importance in the international balance of power and the global strategy of the United States. Its future prospects.

13. Reform and revolution in Latin America. Possibilities and scope of each of these alternatives. Attitudes of the United States toward them. The importance of guerrilla warfare in Latin America and counterguerrilla warfare. The tolerance of the United States toward changes in the structure of our countries.

14. Independent economic development in Latin America, the conflict with United States interests, and its political consequences.

Conclusion

In more than one respect this article has been deliberately polemical, not only in an attempt to highlight some of the key problems of our discipline, which tend to be neglected, but also because I think that at a conference a provocative exposé can be more stimulating and profitable than a mere "neutral" report. However, I would not wish the essentially positive purpose of this contribution to be overlooked.

1. We have acknowledged the generally low level of political science in Latin America. The intensive application of modern research methods and techniques cannot be delayed. I believe, however, that Latin Americanists (particularly in the United States) should pay more attention to, and show greater understanding toward much of the work that has been and is being done in Latin Ameirca and which, even if it is far from meeting the strict requirements of modern political science, is a rich source of information and reference on our problems.

2. In this connection I should say that North American specialists should make a greater effort to understand our frames of reference, our main preoccupations, our purposes and goals in undertaking political research. Very often their research projects and programs do not relate to matters that are of vital concern to us or that are decisive at a particular stage of our development. An inside view of our problems, greater harmonization, and intercommunication with Latin American specialists are essential to the progress of our discipline throughout the continent. The main difficulty is that where Latin Americanists see our problems from the outside, we are to some extent, whether we support or oppose them, involved in the power structure and political processes of our countries. For North Americans, Latin America is

an area of strategic importance and a sphere of interest, that is, something basically alien and extraneous to the things that we on the inside consider vitally important such as political and economic development (with social justice), the political integration and participation of the various sections of the community (with genuine democracy), political and economic independence (the affirmation of national sovereignty). We must grasp the implications of this different situation. While the North Americans may claim to view our politics as disinterested and impartial observers (although we have seen that this is not so), for us, political science and its promotion cannot be without practical and political consequences. Does this mean that we must abandon all attempt at scientific objectivity in social research? On the contrary, it simply means that we must in Mannheim's sense, rigidly control our conceptual apparatus, and at the same time it means that we are in an ideal position to understand the meaning, the genesis, and the development of our political and social structures. It is a matter of life and death for Latin Americanists to get inside our problems.

3. The distinction between traditional and modern political science is not clear. There are, indeed, advances in technique and equipment which should be made use of by contemporary research workers, and the topics and approaches of our discipline have shifted to some extent, especially under the influence of sociology. But this does not mean that traditionalism can be viewed unilaterally as a primitive stage from which we must move on as rapidly as possible. Modern political science cannot afford to forget some of the fundamental teachings of classical political thought, particularly the capacity for analyzing the genesis and development of structures, comprehending the social scene as a whole, and, above all, examining the economic and social bases of political systems in a critical and even revolutionary light. Without these general concepts and criteria the concrete research required by modern political science cannot be undertaken profitably or meaningfully.

4. We must not lose sight of the connection between economic and political development and the progress and social function of political science. In Latin America we are now experiencing a situation parallel to that of the European countries and the

United States in the nineteenth century. Our problems are not merely problems of adjustment and control of secondary aspects of a system which, on the whole, is considered acceptable and complete. On the contrary, they are problems which to a large extent have to do with the foundations of the system, with the organizational bases of society. Hence our tendency to seek sweeping and radical alternatives, to pass value judgments. A political science without normative postulates might be considered ideal in a stable and rational society. But I do not think such a thing is possible in our case. Political science would be insignificant, a laboratory pastime whose utility and social import would be of no account. On the other hand, it seems clear that even modernism in our discipline has failed to rid itself of value judgments and ideological considerations, although they may not be quite so evident as in the past. Modern political science both in Latin America and in the United States would do well to reconsider some of the "old" themes of the sociology of knowledge.

5. I believe that it is most essential to bear this type of problem in mind, not only because of its importance when it comes to securing solid and scientific foundations for our discipline, but also as regards the social significance and role of the scholar. Are Latin American specialists only to be concerned with reinforcing the status quo and, ultimately, with defending and justifying an order that is unsatisfactory for the majority of the people, and, at times, unjust all around? Or will they be able to concentrate systematically on finding solutions and alternatives to our problems? Will they adopt a critical, or a conformist attitude? Will they be capable of presenting the results of their research in an objective manner, without hasty or demagogic judgments and at the same time without concealment or distortion? Will North American scholars be capable of confronting public opinion at home and leading circles in the government and the economy, and explaining satisfactorily and objectively the nature of our problems, their causes and effects, and the meaning of our revolutionary movements? Is their academic interest in this part of the world merely a reflection of their own country's economic and military-strategic interests? In short, will the social function of political science in and on Latin America be conservative or progressive? Will it promote the human and social development

of the various countries of our continent or will it be an obstacle and a barrier to our progress on all fronts? Will the technical and conceptual apparatus of political science help us to understand, promote, and suggest or will we, instead, use it for "therapeutic" and "operational" ends, to combat innovating trends in our society and to manipulate the masses undemocratically? These dilemmas have to do with the extent and depth of the development of political science in Latin America, and not only for reasons of substance, but also of form.

6. Let us consider the organization, cooperation, and personal contacts which are necessary to promote the advancement of political science in Latin America and which can be achieved in universities, institutes, and public and private research centers. I believe that a fruitful collective effort would require a minimum of agreement on, or at least an open discussion of, the points I have mentioned. The possibilities and the difficulties of setting up one or more centers for specialized political research on Latin America should be given careful thought by all who are interested in the development of our discipline in the hemisphere.

7. In applying research techniques and the conceptual apparatus of modern political science we cannot overlook the structural features of Latin America and the dynamics of our political, social, and economic processes; that is to say, they will only yield truly scientific results if based on a fully dialectical understanding of our societies. Experiments in quantification and behavioral studies, the intensive and extensive study of attitudes, the study of the dependent and independent variables of political phenomena, the use of a large number of general terms and concepts in political science, all require strict adaptation to Latin American conditions.

8. Similarly, it is not enough to be concerned purely with description and classification, establishing typologies, behavior patterns, and merely external correlations. Reference must be made to the real content of political and economic power and class dynamics. Moreover, the use of concepts like elite, integration and cohesion, consensus, and *governmental engineering*, require explicit and ample reference to the social structure and a strict definition of their real meaning. Without that definition they became exclusively operational terms which convey nothing

about the actual historical process—in fact they served to conceal or dissemble the true facts of rule by a few men over others, which needs to be investigated with the help of a scientific political theory. Both the content of the concepts of our discipline and the content of the facts to which they refer need to be determined at all times. Last, a careful investigation of political procedures in Latin America cannot disregard the central and sometimes decisive problem of our relations with the United States, of the influence of the United States Government and United States economic interests on our countries, United States interventions, and the ways in which these interventionist activities have shaped or distorted our political development. This field cannot be neglected by Latin American political science, one of whose major efforts must be to determine, as accurately as possible, the causes, characteristics, and at least the most visible results of our relations with North America.

REFERENCES

Kling, Merle.
    1964   The state of research on Latin America: political science. *In* Social Science Research on Latin America, edited by Charles Wagley. New York, Columbia University Press, Chapter V: 168–213.
Marcuse, Herbert.
    1964   One dimensional man. Boston, Beacon Press.
Wagley, Charles (Editor).
    1964   Social science research on Latin America. New York, Columbia University Press.

Additional Bibliography *

Bassols, Narciso.
    1964   Obras. Mexico City, Fondo de Cultura Económica.
Beteta, Ramón.
    1961   Entrevistas y pláticas. Mexico City, Ed. Renovación.
Cabrera, Luis.
    1934   Los problemas transcendentales de México. Mexico City, Ed. Cultura.
    1937   20 años después. Mexico City, Ed. Botas.

* By way of example, I am venturing to suggest a few works and publications, which, in the case of Mexico, are not only of exceptional historical interest, but are compulsory reading for those who need to understand a number of topical political phenomena, linked, naturally, with the Mexican revolutionary process.

Ceceña, José Luis.
1963   El capital monopolista y la economía mexicana. Mexico City, Cuadernos Americanos.
Fuentes Díaz, Vicente.
1954   Los partidos políticos en México. 2 vols. Mexico City, Impresiones Perfectas.
González Casanova, Pablo.
1955   La ideología norteamericana sobre inversiones extranjeras. Mexico City, Universidad Nacional Autónoma de México, 1.
1965   La democracia en México. Mexico City, Ed. Era.
González Pedrero, Enrique.
1961   El gran viraje. Mexico City, Ed. Era.
Iturriaga, José.
1951   La estructura social y cultural de México. Mexico City, Fondo de Cultura Educacional.
Lombardo Toledano, Vicente.
1954   El drama de México. Mexico City.
1955   La perspectiva de México: una democracia del pueblo. Mexico City.
1958   Democracia y partidos políticos. Mexico City.
1961   Teoría y práctica del movimiento sindical mexicano. Mexico City, Ed. del Magisterio.
Madero, Francisco I.
1960   La sucesión presidencial en 1910. Mexico City, Ed. Los Insurgentes.
Millón, Robert P.
1964   Vicente Lombardo Toledano. Mexico City.
Molina Enríquez, Andrés.
1937   La revolución agraria de México. Mexico City.
1964   Los grandes problemas nacionales. Mexico City, INJM.
Moya Palencia, Mario.
1964   La reforma electoral. Mexico City, Ed. Plataforma.
Palavicini, Félix F.
1948   Política constitucional. Mexico City, Beatriz de Silva.
Pani, Alberto J.
1948   Una encuesta sobre la cuestión democrática en México. Mexico City, Ed. Cultura.
Peña, Moisés T. de la.
1964   Mito y realidad de la reforma agraria. Mexico City, Cuadernos Americanos.
Poblete Troncoso, Moisés.
1946   El movimiento obrero latinoamericano. Mexico City, Fondo de Cultura Económica.
Portes Gil, Emilio.
1954   15 años de política mexicana. Mexico City, Ed. Botas.
1957   La crisis política de la revolución y la próxima elección presidencial. Mexico City, Ed. Botas.
Revueltas, José.
1962   Ensayo sobre un proletariado sin cabeza. Mexico City.
Silva Herzog, Jesús.
1941   Petróleo mexicano. Historia de un problema. Mexico City, Fondo de Cultura Económica.

1959 El agrarismo mexicano y la reforma agraria. Mexico City, Fondo de Cultura Económica.
1960 Breve historia de la revolución mexicana. Mexico City, Fondo de Cultura Económica.
Sol, Arguedas.
1962 Que és la izquierda mexicana. *In* Encuesta. Mexico City.
Various authors.
1962 50 años de revolución. Mexico City, Fondo de Cultura Económica.
Vasconcelos, José.
1958 Obras completas. 4 vols. Mexico City, Librero Mexicanos Unidos.
Yañes, Agustín.
1962 La formación política. Mexico City, Ed. Justicia Social.
1964 Conciencia de la revolución. Mexico City, Ed. Justicia Social.
Zea, Leopoldo.
1955 América en la conciencia de Europa. Mexico City, Ed. Los Presentes.
1957 América en la historia. Mexico City, Fondo de Cultura Económica.

Reviews and Periodicals

BIP [Buró de Investigaciones Políticas].
1944– Director: Horacio Quiñones, Mexico City Weekly.
Ciencias Políticas y Sociales.
1955– Director: Pablo González Casanova. Mexico City, UNAM, 19. Quarterly.
Comercio Exterior.
1962– Director: Francisco Alcalá. Mexico City, Bancomex, Monthly.
Cuadernos Americanos.
1942– Director: Jesús Silva Herzog. Mexico City. Bimonthly.
El Día.
1962– Director: Enríquez Ramírez y Ramírez. Mexico City. Newspaper (Sección "Testimonios y Documentos"). Daily.
El Espectador.
1959–60 Mexico City. Monthly.
El Trimestre Económico.
Director: Oscar Soberón. Mexico City, Fondo de Cultura Económica. Quarterly.
Foro Internacional.
1960– Revista Trimestral publicada por el Colegio de México. Director: Rafael Segovia. Mexico City. Quarterly.
Política.
1960– Director: Manuel Marcué Pardiñas. Mexico City. Bimonthly.
Problemas Agrícolas e Industriales de México.
Director: Manuel Marcué Pardiñas. Mexico City. Quarterly.
Siempre.
1953– Director: José Pagés Llergo. Mexico City. Weekly.

OCTAVIO IANNI

7

Sociology in Latin America

If it is true to say that there is reciprocity between scientific thought and the social patterns of life, the principle is especially true in regard to the social sciences, particularly sociology, political economy, political science. Whether we are discussing basic problems, or are concerned with the outlook underlying the contributions made by these disciplines in a specific country it is clear that there is at all times a correlation between sociological thought and the conditions of social life.

The intellectual disquiet of social scientists meeting in institutions, seminars, and conferences to study the prospects for and contributions to scientific work in Latin America amply confirms the above-mentioned principle of the sociology of knowledge. The work entitled *Social Science Research On Latin America,* which consists of a number of papers on studies in geography, history, political science, political economy, and sociology carried out in the Latin American countries, shows definite signs of involvement. "Never before has knowledge of Latin American societies been so important to the United States. . . . The future of these Latin American nations and of these rapidly expanding peoples is crucial to our way of life" [Wagley (ed.) 1964: 1]. The same sense of involvement is evident in the *Report of the Expert Working Group on Social Aspects of Economic Development in Latin America,* prepared by economists, social scientists, and political scientists, under the auspices of UNESCO, ECLA, and OAS (1960). The theoretical and practical concern of social scientists is always to a certain extent bound up with the conditions and trends of social life; but the link and the reciprocal influence are distinctly more evident the moment the social patterns of life reach a critical stage. It is in periods of internal disturbance that scientific speculation turns directly to the fundamental problems. At times it has to focus simultaneously on the problems raised by social change and on the actual structure of scientific thought. This is what is happening at the present time; indeed it is the subject of the present paper.

Clearly the thesis propounded in the above paragraphs does not mean that the correlation referred to arises only in one direction, nor that the correlation gives rise to one line of thought and one alone. A particular pattern does not involve a single trend only; it implies or makes possible a variety of trends, real or apparent. The significant patterns of society open up different and at times antagonistic trends of thought. However well integrated the social system of a particular country may be, the social system invariably embraces a high degree of heterogeneity and differentiation both in regard to social organization and within the sphere of social action. The diversity of social attitudes in human beings within the framework of the social structure implies a great many ways of looking at the world, ways at times diametrically opposed to one another. The image which social groups and classes create of the society of which they find themselves a part affects the possibilities and trends of thought in varying degrees. Scientific thought is not immune to this:

The world has a right to expect that sociology contribute to the rational basis of the choices confronting mankind. Planners and politicians, technicians and citizens are likely to be impatient with and disrespectful of the practitioners of a science who try to waive this responsibility for contribution to knowledge of the consequences of feasible alternatives and equally inclined to respect those who will assume it (Hopper 1964: 243).

The logic of scientific thought is not immune to the creative stimulus of the social patterns of life. Paraphrasing Hans Freyer, we might perhaps say that anyone who finds himself immersed in the reality of the social situation at a given point can not only grasp it theoretically but is compelled to interpret it scientifically (Freyer 1945: 22). Or rather, in sociology, as in political economy or other social sciences, the actual conditions of social life in the environment of the scientists are fundamental components of his scientific outlook. To a certain extent the present moment is an inescapable criterion or object of scientific speculation. The basic problems or potential interpretations always bear some correlation to the cultural environment of the scientist. This is true with regard both to a large proportion of the works of the pioneers of sociology, as well as to the works of Latin American scholars like Florestan Fernandes, Gino Germani, L.A. Costa Pinto, Pablo González Casanova, and others.

The False Dilemma of the Underlying Theories

When we start from these premises, it is evident that sociology has never lost the connotation of a technique of scientific self-awareness in regard to the social milieu (Freyer 1945: 13). Apart from this connotation, sociology is found at times to be an ivory tower science, at other times to be part and parcel of reality. According to the trend of thought, sociology is found to be either a way of knowledge or a way of action. In other words, it is a branch of knowledge on which techniques of action are based, and a branch of knowledge which is at the same time an element essential to the crystallization of reality.

If we follow this line of thought, certain theoretical problems with which sociology in Latin America is faced are seen to be false. The theoretical dilemmas confronting sociology are various. Owing to the many and contradictory influences to which sociology is exposed, to the variety of the problems and themes requiring investigation, and to the heterogeneous and conflicting nature of the social interests involved in scientific research, sociology in the Latin American countries has to cope with a number of theoretical dilemmas of great importance. The following may be mentioned: ivory tower science and science for action, quantitative induction and qualitative induction, description and interpretation, Comte and Marx, microsociology and macrosociology, *ensaismo* (essayism) and science. Of course, not all these problems are typically Latin American. Many have spread through Latin America, but originate in highly respected scientific centers in Europe and North America. In some instances, the dilemmas are badly stated, and in other instances they are false.

Probably the main theoretical question with which sociology is concerned in Latin America has to do with the opposition between quantitative induction and qualitative induction. This question is constantly cropping up in writings on the trends, limitations, and advances of sociology in the countries of Latin America. This antithesis may be found under a large variety of names. Studying the structure of Latin American sociological thought, Rex Hopper distinguishes the "institutionalization of sociology" phase from the "scientific sociology" phase (Hopper 1964: 250–56). This distinction follows closely the formulation adopted by Gino Germani, who distinguishes the "university sociology" stage from the stage of "beginnings of scientific sociology in Latin America" (Germani 1959: 440–53). A phase corresponding to the essay period of social philosophy is that of speculative reflection and general interpretation. "Teaching was not linked up with research. Very little research was undertaken in the context of university sociology programs. There was writing, of course, but there was little writing that resulted from research in any technical sense" (Hopper 1964: 252). A number of critics find a relationship between this general tendency and movements of ideas of a nonpositivist type, and some regard it as a manifestation of an antipositivist reaction. In this connection mention may be made of Dilthey, Rickert, Weber, Scheler, Freyer, Sartre:

Actually, sociology based on these philosophical views has been unusually sterile as regards actual works produced; most of these have emerged independently. It was in the main a "professorial" type of sociology, concerned almost exclusively with authorities, with methodological problems, or with the interminable discussion of previous questions. It is not surprising that in the places where this prevailed, it discouraged a really scientific approach; indeed it discouraged research altogether (Germani 1959: 448).

As we see, the tendencies which grew up during the period of "institutionalization of sociology" have a predominantly negative outlook. However, neither Hopper nor Germani brings out satisfactorily the positive aspects of the period. When they examine the other currents of sociological thought from the angle of positivist empiricism, they reject or minimize the relative importance of the theoretical and methodological contributions of scientists and philosophers who furnished other bases of reference for sociology in Latin America. Moreover, it should be emphasized that, looked at in the light of the formation and development of scientific thought, these tendencies helped to broaden the bases and the scope of sociology in Latin America. There is no denying that the recent expansion of scientific thought on the Latin American continent is attributable to the contacts which the various generations of intellectuals were able to establish with Dilthey, Weber, Freyer, Marx, Mannheim, Sartre, Lukacs, Merton, Parsons, and others. It might even be argued that there are certain problems which only arise in the presence of given theories, or that it is only on the basis of a given theory that a particular type of problem can be properly solved.

The other phase or trend implies the strict observance of the canons of the scientific method. It implies the use of the natural sciences as paradigms for the social sciences, so that scientific monographs are produced or their production is encouraged. The main feature of these monographs is the use of techniques of sophisticated, scientific observation. In other words, they favor the statistical treatment of data and the production of quantitative inferences. In this process of modernization of sociology "institutes and schools have been growing up in a number of countries which have incorporated or tried to incorporate recent trends, in an attempt to approximate the international level (Germani 1959: 449). According to this interpretation, the culmination of this process of creating a truly scientific outlook in Latin America is the establishment of teaching and research institutions by UNESCO in Santiago and Rio de Janeiro:

There is rapidly emerging a new generation of sociologists who have been the leaders in the reorganization of old establishments and in the organization of new institutes and schools in which training in sociology is being introduced. Two international institutions have been formed to train social scientists and to promote social research. The Latin American Center for Social Science Research (CENTRO) in Rio de Janeiro is primarily a research agency. The Latin American Faculty of Social Sciences (FLACSO) in Santiago, Chile is a teaching and training institution. Both were established in 1957 under the joint sponsorship of UNESCO and the respective governments and function under the supervision of the same Board of Directors. Certainly they may well become focal points of the new sociology (Hopper 1964: 256).

As teaching and research institutions they are in line with the most up-to-date developments of scientific thought in Latin American sociology.

In our view, however, the two salient trends, as defined above, are not always isolated and antithetical. They meet on a number of points; they overlap, and there is continuity between them. Moreover, the links between these two trends are positive, if we take the currents of thought at the level of the most general process of elaboration and development of science. And at times empiricism is quite sterile as far as abstract speculation is concerned. What is more, the notions of totality and historical orientation worked out by the system of trial and error are as a rule elements without which monographic research amounts to no more than mere description—a static snapshot of social phenomena.

Actually, FLACSO itself does not make any pretense to a unilateral approach:

The introduction of a strictly scientific methodology calls not only for the transmission of a body of knowledge and technical know-how, but also for a mental training which will give great facility in the manipulation of abstract concepts so as to speed up the assimilation and absorption of sociological knowledge; will help to overcome the tendency to reification of concepts and reliance on stereotypes; and which will both impart a certain independence in regard to the "authorities" in the particular branch of science, and will develop a universal outlook as a prerequisite for a high degree of receptivity and flexibility. . . . (Escuela Latinoamericana de Sociología).

It might be more correct to say that FLACSO is open to the use of observational techniques and interpretative methods. When it is pushed to extremes, empiricism does not produce new knowledge. The subtleties of quantified observation techniques are inadequate for carrying out original studies. Frequently the monographs do not attain a sociographic level. The importance of descriptive reconstruction of social phenomena does not mean that research must be interlarded with sociological description at the analytical level. It must be treated interpretatively, as a synthetic whole:

In Latin America speculative sociology and social philosophy have predominated during a more or less prolonged period. When modern sociology is introduced the first reaction is often to consider all theorizing as suspect and to reject it consistently, a reaction which may lead to a crude and unreflective empiricism. There appears a strong preference for some kind of survey which is neither preceded nor followed by any theoretical consideration, i.e. a preference for merely descriptive inventories without explanatory value or predictive power. But modern sociology is conceived as an empirical as well as a theoretical science (Heintz 1962: 3).

The question does not become completely clear, however, if we interrupt the discussion at this point. The idea persists in the minds of Latin American sociologists that there is a radical difference and antithesis between quantitative induction and qualitative induction, between monographs and general interpretations. Yet it may be observed that there is a high degree of congruence between the results of studies carried out on the basis of these methods. The reflections of Gino Germani and Glaucio Ary Dillon Soares, for example, on political radicalism in Latin American countries, far from being contradictory, overlap in many points. This might also be said of Guillermo Briones. According to Germani, "Whereas the popular masses tend to veer towards the parties and ideologies regarded as 'leftist,' the middle and upper classes incline towards the opposite pole, in other words, to parties and ideologies regarded as 'rightist'" (Germani 1962: 131). Dillon Soares states that "both the members of the lowest strata and those identified with the lowest classes favor reformist and leftist parties, whereas the higher strata and classes favor political conservatism" (Soares 1961: 150 and Briones 1963: 376–404). Yet these views derive from different interpretative processes, since the latter bases his conclusions on quantitative induction. In the same way, the interpretations of Sartre and Adorno and his colleagues on the relationship between personality structure, social structure, and racial discrimination likewise do not negate one another (Sartre 1960; Adorno and others 1950). Following the same order of thought, it may also be said that there is a considerable parallelism of interpretation in the researches of Warner and Low, Centers, and Marx regarding the process of becoming aware of the conditions of social life on the part of the proletariat (Warner and Low 1951; Centers 1949; Marx 1956).

The fact is that scientific thought is not a rigid and exclusive system, as those sociologists maintain who are opposed to any investigation not based on the exclusively quantified manipulation of variables. Quantification is of course one of the devices open to scientific reflection. Another is comprehensive hermeneutics, the term used by Dilthey; another is "explanatory comprehension," according to Weber's theory.

We have to resort to empathy or vicarious experience to capture the content, the possibility of manifestation, and the meaning of actions. The fact is that sociology is not merely reflection external to social phenomena. In addition to external, manifest structures, sociology can and needs to apprehend internal structures, and volitional states, which cannot always be reduced to quantified variables.

As we see, the stages in the development of sociology in Latin America and the distinction made between the presociological period, the institutionalization of sociology, and scientific sociology proper, are descriptive devices which at times oversimplify and demean the significance of creative thought in science. If we observe them closely, these stages involve various types of relationships between Latin America and the United States and Europe. Furthermore, the phases in question correspond to various stages not only of acquisition of scientific knowledge but also of absorption of the different currents of sociology. Not only this—in Latin America there are not only distinct periods when the influences of Spencer, Comte, Marx, Durkheim, Weber, Tonnies, Simmel, Mannheim, Freyer, Parsons, Gurvitch, Merton, and others were paramount; such influences exist side by side and intermingle, so that we can observe the dialectical method and the functionalist method existing side by side and influencing each other in much sociological research on the Latin American continent.

It should be pointed out that the various approaches do not necessarily imply different phases of recourse to scientific method.

The gulf which some critics find between overall interpretations and monographic studies is often just perceptible. Not infrequently the research overlaps, new vistas may be opened up, and the one lays the foundation for the other, or they complement each other reciprocally.

The Sociologist and the Technician

The false dilemma of theoretical studies of sociology in Latin America is not fully clarified until we have carried out the metamorphosis of the sociologist into the technician. The fact is that the roles of the scientist undergo change and renew themselves, thus giving new meanings to science itself.

There is no doubt that sociology, like political economy, political science, history, and anthropology, is continually pulled in two directions. There is indeed a certain duality of aim in the scientific activities of the sociologist. On the one side, the small group of specialists sets up targets and patterns of scientific activity, in conformity with the cumulative character of the science. Historically and in their theoretical development, the various systems select concepts and problems, techniques and approaches, implying the constitution of a body of theory to which the sociologist needs to apply himself. Obviously the problem of objectivity and neutrality arises. One of the problems which most exercised Weber was precisely this. In Latin America it is to be found in the observations of many sociologists. Florestan Fernandes (1963: chapters 1–6), Rex Hopper (1945 and 1964), Peter Heintz (1962). Gino Germani (1962; 1961) and others, for example, in discussing the history and the theoretical and practical problems of sociology on the Latin American continent, found themselves obliged to focus on this. Their works constitute contributions to the development of scientific thought in Latin America. In a sense they are discussions whose object is to utilize and expand original research on the basis of empirical investigation.

In some instances, certain students of history and of the problems of theoretical speculation and research in Latin America emphasize the value of one model and ignore or reject other models. Clearly this is a matter of prejudice, or to say the least a cavalier attitude. What certain critics label mere "speculation," "social philosophy, or "essayism." is frequently interpretation of a pioneering type which opens up new prospects for thought and research. Furthermore, the condemnation of certain interpretative models as outmoded, prescientific, or parascientific, has the negative effect on young sociologists of intellectual intimidation, scaring them away from the intelligent use of the sociological imagination. "Science does not destroy the imagination, rather it exercises and disciplines the functions of the imagination" (Pearson 1909: 36). The art of scientific discovery is an act of creative imagination. The sociologist cannot fail to recognize the value of the interpretations or the suggestiveness of works like *Facundo,* by Domingo F. Sarmiento or *Os sertões* by Euclides da Cunha.

The sociological imagination enables us to grasp history and biography and the relations between the two within society. That is its task and its promise. . . . No social study that does not come back to the problems of biography, of history and of their intersections within a society has completed its intellectual journey (Mills 1959: 6).

But there are requirements of other kinds. It must be remembered that society as a whole, or certain spheres of influence, call for special studies from sociology, focused on a number of practical problems. The sociologist finds himself faced with the social phenomenon filtered through particular or general interests according to the circumstances. In the last analysis, the scientist is called upon to validate or invalidate a given social structure, by studying either the present situation or past history. When UNESCO encouraged and subsidized studies on race relations in Brazil, its interest was to discover the model features of "racial democracy," with a view to making them known in other nations. In the same way it was practical necessities, i.e. the seriousness and the deep-rooted character of social tensions in rural society in Brazil, that led CENTRO and the Inter-American Committee on Agricultural Development (CIDA) to program and direct the execution of studies on the system of ownership and use of land.

These are the two constantly active trends in the work of the sociologist. Inevitably, they affect both the selection of themes and the degree of intensity of their treatment. Whether they are handled in a simple, descriptive manner or interpretively, analytically, or synthetically, monographically or comprehensively, will depend on the intensity and direction of the influences at work. There is no doubt, however, that sociology has made progress, as a rule, when involved in direct or indirect investigation of the actual conditions of social life. The two works *De la division du travail social* by Emile Durkheim (1947) and *The American Soldier* by Samuel A. Stouffer and others (1949), both represent the outcome of the need to throw light on the contemporary scene as seen by the scientist. The same might be said of works by Pablo González Casanova (1962), Rodolfo Stavenhagen (1964), J. A. Silva Michelena (1963), Germán Guzmán Campos, Orlando Fals Borda, Eduardo Umana Luna (1963–64), Octavio Ianni (1965), Torcuato S. di Tella (1964), Marialice Mencarini Foracchi (1965), and others. Underlying the ideals and demands to which sociology is subject are the reciprocal relationships and the interplay between scientific thought and the social patterns of life.

This is the broader context of the changing roles of the sociologist and the practical possibilities of scientific thought in relation to the social sciences. Here the scientist becomes technician. Science always retains the connotation of a technique of social self-awareness. The instrumental character of sociological knowledge is something which society neither desires nor is able to dispense with. And this need occurs not only over the broad field of the interplay and correlation between social conditions and the structure of scientific thought, but also in the particular sphere of the practical, immediate, institutionalized use of scientific knowledge. Here the technician comes into the picture. It is the technician who will have to work directly on the formulation of governmental and private programs, and on their administration and execution. The relationship between subject and object, in the process of sociological knowledge, is a phenomenon basic to this question. In the last analysis, the fact is that there are various types of integration of subject and object.

The growing complexity and internal differentiation in the social and economic systems in Latin America, the more and more frequent demands made by the masses as they steadily drift into rapidly changing urban and industrial centers, and the swift social changes occuring in certain agricultural and mining areas, tend to aggravate the social problems facing employers and workers, administrators and politicians, social scientists and educators. The need for working out sectoral, regional, and even national plans, as well as the emergence and wholesale increase of social tensions and problems of group and class relations, have led the authorities, employer groups, and trade unions, to promote the training of technicians in social matters. The transformation of the sociologist into a technician arises in this context. Little by little, sociology assumes the character of a technique for smoothing out tensions or channeling them into nondestructive directions.

In the context of Latin America taken as a whole, FLACSO and the Latin American Institute for Economic and Social Planning reflect this trend. Since the universities of Latin America have not fully realized the need to modernize their programs of training and research so as to train technicians for public and private organizations, the institutions in question were set up for this purpose:

An institution like FLACSO which professes to be a center where social science can be given a new look and which thus prides itself on being at all times alive to the demands of the moment, cannot fail but take note of the "Latin American theme" of the present time and make it one of its declared and primary concerns. The experience of the large industrialized countries has brought out the growing importance of the part played by the social sciences in solving these problems and in acquiring experience of the machinery of economic and social development. It has been shown that no capital investment can be productive in the long run without a parallel human investment, if possible antedating it. As in other domains, the human factor is still the decisive factor in development in the Latin American countries. Consequently, one of the priority tasks in this part of the world is to establish rapidly a reserve panel of well-trained social science specialists capable of undertaking scientific research—the only type which enables action to be taken on the basis of knowledge (FLACSO 1959).

The document from which this is taken contains the essential observations made in this paper. Among the themes are the following: the close relationship between scientific thought and the conditions of social life, principally when the latter appear and must be treated as problems, sociology as a technique for scientific self-awareness of the social milieu, and the metamorphosis of the sociologist into technician.

A still more specifically practical purpose was served by the creation of the Latin American Institute for Economic and Social Planning which includes both economists and sociologists. It was resolved:

1. To establish the Latin American Institute for Economic and Social Planning, which will be responsible for providing, at the request of the Governments concerned, training and advisory services to the countries and areas within the geographical scope of the Economic Commission for Latin America (ECLA) and for undertaking research on planning techniques, in accordance with the following aims and functions:

(a) To raise the technical level of government officials and specialists through training programs in the form of courses and in-service training;

(b) To assist Governments in establishing the institutional and technical organization required for the more efficient programing of their economic and social development policies;

(c) To assist Governments, at a purely technical level, in preparing their economic and social development programs;

(d) To carry out the theoretical studies required for the improvement of planning techniques used in Latin America (*Economic Bulletin for Latin America*: 1962).

The activity of the technician is institutionalized on a continent-wide scale. The tasks of economic development and its social implications mobilize both economists and sociologists. Again, we find the concern for the neutrality and objectivity of scientific work. It is taken for granted that "at a purely technical level," the scientific activity of the economist and the sociologist is impartial. We are in the sphere of the intelligentsia sociology of Karl Mannheim.

A similar process is in progress in the various Latin American countries. In Brazil, it is already well under way. The formal description of the profession of sociologist, which is under discussion at the present time, provides for a definition of the technical activities of the sociologist. With the progress of rationalization seeping through into the social system as a whole, science is becoming a vital factor in social organizations and social action. The patterns handed down by tradition are being replaced by patterns worked out by scientific methods. Human acts are translated into variables.

It is obvious that these transformations entail serious problems in the field of scientific knowledge. As the sociologist is gradually changed into a technician, his research instruments and his thought tend to become more refined. We see again quite clearly the imperious need for organizing intellectual activity on the basis of manipulation of variables. Practical necessity demands that research be carried out within a predetermined period of time, that it depend on financial and human resources established in advance, and that it reach precise and summary conclusions. Often these conclusions must be in a form enabling them to be compared with results obtained by parallel studies carried out at the same time in other communities or countries. All this implies the use of quantifiable variables as landmarks for observation and interpretation.

The Social Milieu and Sociological Problems

As we have seen, there is a very close relationship between the involvement of the sociologist in his period of history, the transformation of the role he plays, and the tremendous increase in the expectations arising out of his work and the contribution he makes. We find that the very argument as to forms of induction is related to these factors. All these questions point invariably toward a parallelism between the social patterns of life and scientific thought.

But the peculiar position of sociology in Latin America can only be thoroughly clarified in the light of the problems with which sociology is faced. The complexity of the tasks given to the sociologist and the scope of the contribution he makes depend in the last analysis on the topics placed before him by society.

If we examine sociological literature in Latin America from this angle, we find a number of phenomena which are important for determining the conditions, positive and negative, governing its progress: Preoccupation with the "exotic," the inadequate formulation of research problems, and the lack of interest in basic questions of methodology of research and interpretation—these are relevant factors for an understanding of some of the distortions undergone by sociology in the region. In analyzing the value of contributions by sociologists in Latin America, it is essential to grasp certain interventions in the relations between the social milieu and the selection of topics. Let us look more closely.

First, we find that there has been and still is a transference, pure and simple in some cases, of the problems of other countries to Latin American nations. Certain studies on race relations, for example, betray this tendency. Regardless of the exceptional quality and importance of some of the works produced on this topic, there is no denying the fact that the problem was formulated in reference to factors and approaches which were found satisfactory in other countries. Some of the disappointments, from a logical and theoretical point of view, found in *Brancos e pretos na Bahia* (Pierson 1945), drive from the unthinking and inappropriate transference of a particular empirical and theoretical view of the subject.

At one time, UNESCO sponsored studies on race relations (Klineberg 1949: 11–12). In Brazil, some of these studies were encouraged on the assumption that the Brazilian nation was a racial democracy. However, as the results came to light and this hypothesis turned out to be untenable, UNESCO lost interest in the subject.

These facts raise a fundamental problem. Much harm has been done to the process of elaboration and development of scientific thought in Latin America because of the fact that its assimilation and utilization have not been matched by a satisfactory formulation of the problems. In other words, social scientists, whether native or foreign, involved in programs concerned with the development of sociological thought in the Latin American countries are not always careful in their choice of the topics vital to a particular society. In regard to the study of the Negro in Brazil, Roger Bastide, Florestan Fernandes (Bastide and Fernandes 1959), and L.A. da Costa Pinto (1953) put sociological thought back on a proper footing (Ianni 1962; Cardoso 1962).

It should be noted, however, that the same dilemmas are arising in regard to the analysis of the social background of economic development. The problems posed on the basis of the outlook of industrialized nations are not always restated in the light of the different approach suggested by the peculiarities of underdeveloped nations. Here, more than anywhere else, the lesson taught by C. Wright Mills has been forgot. There is research concentrated on the formation of attitudes favorable to innovation, or the formation of managerial elites, but it fails to take account of the historical context and the overall social structure which is indispensable to the initiation and execution of creative social policies and relationships.

Second, another important aspect of the matter must be considered. This aspect has to do with the connection between the social situation and the set of problems selected by sociology. We are on another level here. Contrary to what certain critics maintain, sociological literature in Latin America pays scant attention to theoretical questions. Most of the activity of sociologists in the theoretical field is concerned with the assimilation and dissemination of studies made in the United States, France, and Germany. The manuals, dictionaries, and articles in specialized journals are of this nature.

Such an outlook places sociology in a position of inferiority in relation to economics. For reasons which need not be expounded, Latin American economists began long before the sociologists to make a critical appraisal of the key concepts in their discipline. In particular, the economists tried to elucidate the prejudices inherent in those theories. The criticism leveled at the theoretical basis of political economy by Gunnar Myrdal (1955; 1960), as well as by Marxist economists, gained new impetus after 1945. Economics developed enormously during the succeeding years, side by side with the establishment and functioning of ECLA and of national planning organs and technical advisory services of governments, private undertakings, and economic groups. The relevant problems facing the economic systems in Latin America and the Latin American economy as a whole were brought into the limelight for discussion, and at the same time doubts were raised about some of the postulates of the various currents of liberal economic policy. The work of Juan F. Noyola Vázquez, Aníbal Pinto Santa Cruz, Jorge Ahumada, and Celso Furtado, among others, bears witness to the trend of this critical appraisal.

In sociology this phenomenon is merely in its infancy. Not until a few years ago did we see the beginnings of a somewhat isolated movement aimed at a critical appraisal of the contributions and achievements of sociology in Latin America. It is an attempt to reduce the negative consequences of the demonstration effect in the fields of theory, research methodology, and the thematic aspect of science. This movement is proceeding on two levels. First, in the sphere of criticism of research methodology and interpretation (Stavenhagen 1962; Ianni 1961), the process is in its initial stages. Starting from the teachings of sociologists of past generations, national and foreign, a number of recent schools of sociological thought in Latin America are beginning to apply constructive criticism to accumulated experience and perpetuated errors.

On the other hand, the critical appraisal has already gained a distinctly firm footing in regard to practical research work. In this field, not only interpretative theories but also the practical problems of science are being reviewed. The most up-to-date trends of sociology in Latin America are characterized both by their concern for innovation on the theoretical side and by the real contribution the trends have made to our knowledge of the situation as it is. In large part, Latin American sociology is taking up the challenge of today.

Naturally, the major themes of sociology in Latin America are only just beginning to be tackled. The programs being carried out by FLACSO, the Latin American Institute for Economic and Social Planning, the Department of Sociology in the Faculty of Philosophy, Science, and Letters of the University of São Paulo, the Institute of Sociology of the Faculty of Philosophy and Letters of the University of Buenos Aires, the National School of Political and Social Sciences of the National Autonomous University of Mexico, the Research Institute of the Faculty of Economics at the Central University of Venezuela in Caracas, and the National University of Colombia in Bogotá indicate a strong tendency to focus on a series of essential problems, bypassing themes of lesser importance, practical and theoretical. In keeping with this focus, problems are being studied such as *getulismo, peronismo,* violence in relation to the structure of domination, the social conditions of industrialization, the tenacity and reform of the agrarian structure, the sociology of revolutionary processes, class relations and economic development, political power and economic power, the formation and structure of wage-earning classes, the formation and ideologies of managerial groups, and urbanization and industrialization.

Naturally, there are subjects which have not been touched upon at all, or have been treated only in a fragmentary manner, or in cryptic language. Typical examples are: Latin America and the world wars, Latin America and the political and economic systems of the world, the situation and prospects of Latin America in the "third world," the sociology of the coup d'état, the armed forces and the church as social and political forces, national intelligentsia and the demonstration effect in the scientific field, democratic order and economic progress, the sociology of inflation. These are themes which call for treatment, since they are the outcome of the dynamism of social phenomena in Latin America and they allow for the scientific play of the sociological imagination.

The Reintegration of the Social Sciences

When we look at the more recent developments of sociology in Latin America, we perceive that sociology is constantly renewing its contacts with political economy, history, political science, and anthropology. The major themes of Latin American societies, by the very fact that they are basically related to overall structural change, demand of the social scientist an expansion in terms of the contribution made by each individual discipline. The problems which appear when we investigate social change, for example, depend on a thorough grasp of the economist's reflections on the economic processes taking place in these nations. The social change now under way in the northeast of Brazil, for example, can only be understood if we are familiar with the economic structure of the region, internally and in its external manifestations, the various aspects of technical and social organization of production, and the programs and activities of SUDENE and other organs. The same might be said of agrarian reform in Mexico and Bolivia, or of the social conflicts in rural society in Venezuela and Colombia. These entail economic processes which the sociologist cannot afford to ignore.

In another direction, analytical studies of *peronismo,* for example, cannot dispense with the cooperation between sociology and political science. The peaceful and violent phenomena of the Mexican revolution involve political, social, economic, ecological, demographic, and other processes, making collaboration between the various specialists essential.

The same thing is true in economics. Economists have been forced constantly to turn to the work of sociologists in order to make headway with their studies. Otherwise, economists themselves produce reflections of a sociological character. This condition is true of the analytical and interpretative studies carried out by the staff of ECLA, and the theoretical treatises of Aníbal Pinto, Noyola, Ahumada, and Celso Furtado.

Furtado's *Dialética do desenvolvimento* symbolizes some of the principal dilemmas of the social scientist in the nations struggling to combat underdevelopment. On the one hand, the work reflects the conflict between the intellectual and political demands which surround the activities of the scientist, by combining interpretation and planned intervention in regard to economic processes:

The responsibility of the intellectual has never at any period been as great as it is today; and it is being brought about by commission in some cases and omission in others. . . . But there is no ignoring the fact that the intellectual has a special social responsibility, since he is the only factor in a society which not only can, but must, surmount the immediate social conditions of individual behavior (Furtado 1964: 87–88).

This conception is very close to the sociological theory of the intelligentsia formulated by Mannheim. It reflects the intellectual decision to respond objectively to the demands of practical and urgent problems. But this conception is also a political option. On the other hand, the first part of Furtado's book, from which the title is taken, aims at formulating an overall conception of the social milieu in which the economist and the politician appear in man-to-man relationships. In particular, the problem of tensions between the classes is reappraised, in the light of the growth of industrial capitalism:

Today, the behavior of the urban and rural working masses is of basic importance for the economic and social development of the country—which means that this development must become part of the political process. This broadening of political bases is essential if the process of social change which is already in process is to be carried out with the least possible cost to the community (Furtado, 1964: 87–88).

The social scientist is working within the framework of the over-all historical process, where an integrated view of the social sciences is indispensable. In April 1964 the political rights of the author of these reflections were withdrawn by the new Brazilian government.

Time and time again, as we see, the problem of the links between the social sciences crops up; or rather, the subject of the reintegration of these disciplines crops up. In a sense the social sciences were integrated in a single comprehensive view in works such as those of Adam Smith, David Ricardo, and Karl Marx (Lukács 1959: 471–73); since then, owing to the trend toward division of labor in scientific activities and the practical, theoretical, and ideological need for the fragmentation of the social phenomenon, the social sciences have become self-contained disciplines. Today however, in the countries of the third world the question of links again demands an answer, and a comprehensive picture of vast social systems undergoing transformation must be forthcoming. There is constant advocacy, and a constant effort, to return to an overall viewpoint, in other words, to integrate the disciplines. Works like *Social Science Research on Latin America, Las naciones que surgen, Resistencias à mudança,* for example, have this viewpoint [Wagley (ed.) 1964; Millikan and Blackmer (eds.) 1961; Centro Latino Americano de Pesquisas em Ciências Sociais 1959]. The same trend may be seen in the seminars of social scientists concerned with formulating unified series of problems and working out cooperative programs. For example, the governments of Latin America, in studying and working out economic development plans or social policy plans should bear in mind the interdependence between economic and social factors

(UNESCO-ECLA-OAS 1960: 251; Round Table . . . 1961). Social scientists are beginning to recognize that sociological truth does not always conflict with the truth of political economy, political science, anthropology, or history. There are aspects of reality, there are manifestations of the processes of reality, which only become intelligible when the scientist grasps their various nuances, trends, and composition. Social factors frequently turn out to be economic or political factors and vice versa. In other words, there are manifestations of social phenomena which are only fully expressed at the level of political action or economic behavior. The problem of the metamorphosis of social events from, say, the economic sphere to the political, is a phenomenon which escapes the observation and interpretation of the sociologist who is blind to the various dimensions of reality. It is obvious that again we are in the sphere of the theory of knowledge.

There is no doubt that these are expressions of an epoch of crisis in the social sciences as they are developing in Latin America and in other nations of the third world, of a moment of creativeness which could produce notable results, but undoubtedly a crisis as far as the theory and the problems of sociology are concerned. The fact is that two fundamental theoretical viewpoints are confronting each other. First, sociology is seen as a scientific discipline which can supply knowledge useful for practical action. Second, sociological knowledge arises as a dimension of reality, not merely as a juxtaposed dimension but as an element which forms part of the reality itself. In the one case, sociological knowledge is external and independent of the object. In the other case, it fuses subject and object, knowledge and existence. In both cases, however, it appears in the makeup of reality. It is at this point that science and social consciousness meet.

We have been concerned merely with a number of fundamental questions which face sociology and the sociologist in Latin America today. Other important aspects of sociology that have already been amply discussed in well-known works, dealing particularly with questions such as the following are: the periodization of the development of teaching and research, the transition from social philosophy to science, the relationship between literature and sociology, the predominant influence of positivism, the antipositivist schools, cooperation between countries or their teaching and research institutions, the rigidity and shortcomings of teaching and research institutions, the intellectual evils inherent in the institution of the professorial chair, and narcissism and the sociologist in intellectually mediocre surroundings.

REFERENCES

Adorno, T. W. and others.
    1950   The authoritarian personality. New York, Harper & Brothers.
Bastide, Roger, and Florestan Fernandes.
    1959   Brancos e negros em São Paulo. 2nd ed. São Paulo, Companhia Editora Nacional.
Briones. Guillermo.
    1963   La estructura social y la participación política. *In* Revista Interamericana de Ciencias Sociales, Vol. 2, no. 3. Washington.
Cardoso, Fernando Henrique.
    1962   Capitalismo e escravidão, no Brasil meridional. São Paulo, Difusão Européia do Livro.
Centers, Richard.
    1949   The psychology of social classes. Princeton, New Jersey, Princeton University Press.
Centro Latino Americano de Pesquisas em Ciências Sociais.
    1959   Resistências a mudánça. Annals of the International Seminar held at Rio de Janeiro in October, 1959.
Costa Pinto, L. A. da.
    1953   O negro no Rio de Janeiro. São Paulo, Companhia Editora Nacional.
di Tella, Torcuato S.
    1964   El sistema político argentino y la clase obrera. Buenos Aires, Editorial Universitaria.
Durkheim, Emile.
    1902   De la division du travail social. 2nd ed. Paris, F. Alcan. English translations 1933 and 1947.
Latin American Institute for Economic and Social Planning.
    1962   *In* Economic Bulletin for Latin America, vol. VII (2) (Oct. 1): 116.
Escuela Latinoamericana de Sociología.
    n.d.   Su objetivo y orientación. Santiago, Chile, No. 3.
FLASCO (Facultad Latinoamericana de Ciencias Sociales).
    1959   FLACSO, El papel de la FLACSO en los estudios sobre el desarrollo económico. Working paper submitted to the seminar on Resistance to Change, held at Rio de Janeiro, October 19–25, p. 2.
Foracchi, Marialice M.
    1965   O estudante e transformação da sociedade brasileira. São Paulo, Companhia Editora Nacional.

Freyer, Hans.
1945 Introduction to sociology, translated by Felipe Gonzáles. Madrid, Ediciones Nueva Epoca.
Furtado, Celso.
1964 Dialética do desenvolvimento. Rio de Janeiro, Editôra Fundo de Cultura.
Germani, Gino.
1959 Desarrollo y estado actual de la sociología latinoamericana. Instituto de Sociología, Buenos Aires.
1961 Algunas condiciones para el desarrollo de la investigación en la América Latina, Memoria of the Sixth Latin American Congress on Sociology. 2 vols. Caracas, Imprensa Nacional, vol. 1: 113–20.
1962 Política y sociedad en una época de transición. Buenos Aires, Editorial Paidos.
González Casanova, Pablo.
1962 México: El ciclo de una revolución agraria. *In* Cuadernos Americanos.
Guzmán Campos, Germán, Orlando Fals Borda, and Eduardo Umaña Luna.
1963–64 La violencia en Colombia. Bogotá, Ediciones Tercer Mundo. 2 vols.
Heintz, Peter.
1962 "Research models" for Latin America. Second Inter-American meeting of sociologists. Princeton, N.J. Sept. 10–12. Mimeographed.
Hopper, Rex.
1945 The status of sociology in Latin America. *In* Intellectual Trends in Latin America. Latin American Studies: I. Austin, Texas.
1964 Research on Latin America in Sociology. *In* Social Science Research on Latin America, edited by Charles Wagley. New York, Columbia University Press, pp. 243–89.
Ianni, Octavio.
1961 Estudo de comunidade e conhecimento científico. *In* Revista de antropologia, vol. IX (1–2): 109–19. São Paulo.
1962 As metamorfoses do escravo. São Paulo, Difusão Européia do Livro.
1965 Estado e capitalismo (Estrutura social e industrialização no Brasil). Rio de Janeiro, Editôra Civilização Brasileira.
Klineberg, Otto.
1949 The UNESCO project on international tensions. *In* International Social Science Bulletin, vol. I (1), Paris.
Lukács, Georg.
1959 El asalto a la razón. Translation by Wenceslao Roces. Mexico City, Fondo de Cultura Económica.
Marx, Karl.
1956 O 18 Brumário de Luis Bonaparte. Rio de Janeiro, Editorial Vitória.
Millikan, M. F. and D. L. M. Blackmer (Editors).
1961 The emerging nations: their growth and United States policy. Boston, Little Brown. Spanish edition: Las naciones que surgen. Translation by Florentino M. Torner. Mexico City, Fondo de Cultura Económica.
Mills, C. Wright.
1959 The sociological imagination. New York, Oxford University Press.

Myrdal, Gunnar.
1955　The political element in the development of economic theory, translated by Paul Streeten. London, Routledge & Kegan Paul.
1960　Teoria econômica e regiões subdesenvolvidas, translated by Ewaldo Correia Lima. Rio de Janeiro, Instituto Superior de Estudos Brasileiros, Ministério da Educação e Cultura.
Pearson, Karl.
1909　La gramática de la ciencia, translated by Julián Besteiro. Madrid, Daniel Jorro Ed.
Pierson, Donald.
1945　Brancos e pretos na Bahia. A study of racial contact, with an introduction by Arthur Ramos and Robert E. Park. São Paulo, Companhia Editora Nacional.
Round Table on Culture Shock and Social Change.
1961　Report and recommendations, Mexico City, December 19–23, 1961. Portuguese translation by Instituto de Ciências Sociais, Bahia.
Sartre, Jean-Paul.
1960　Reflexões sôbre o racismo. São Paulo, Difusão Européia do Livro.
Silva Michelena, José, and others.
1963　Venezuela 1°. Instituto de Investigaciones, Facultad de Economia, Caracas.
Soares, Glaucio Ary Dillon.
1961　Desenvolvimento econômico e radicalismo político. *In* Boletim, Centro Latinoamericano de Pesquisas em Ciências Sociais, Rio de Janeiro, Ano IV, no. 2, Maio.
Stavenhagen, Rodolfo.
1962　Estratificación social y estructura de clases. *In* Revista de Ciencias Políticas y Sociales, Ano VIII (27): 1–30. Mexico City.
1964　Essai comparatif sur les classes sociales rurales et la stratificacion dans quelques pays sous-developpés. Paris.
Stouffer, Samuel A., and others.
1949　The American soldier. Princeton, N. J., Princeton University Press.
UNESCO, ECLA, OAS.
1960　Report of the expert working group on social aspects of economic development in Latin America held under the joint auspices of the UNESCO, U.N. Bureau of Social Affairs and Bureau of Technical Assistance Operations, and Economic Commission for Latin America at Mexico City, December 12–21, 1960. Portuguese translation: Relatório sobre os aspectos sociais do desenvolvimento econômico na América Latina. *In* Revista Brasileira de Ciências Sociais, vol. II, No. 1 (1962): 251–73. Belo Horizonte.
Wagley, Charles (Editor).
1964　Social science research on Latin America. New York, Columbia University Press.
Warner, W. Lloyd, and T. O. Low.
1951　The social system of the modern factory (The strike: a social analysis). New Haven, Yale University Press.

Additional Bibliography *

Arboleda, José Rafael.
1959 Las ciencias sociales en Colombia. Rio de Janeiro, Centro Latino-americano de Pesquisas em Ciências Sociais.

Azevedo, Fernando de.
n.d. A antropologia e a sociologia no Brasil. *In* As Ciências Sociais no Brasil. São Paulo, Edições Melhoramentos, pp. 353–99.
1950 A sociologia na América Latina e, particularmente no Brasil. *In* Revista de História, 1 (no. 3). São Paulo.

Barnes, Harry E., and Howard Becker.
1945 Historia del pensamiento social: translation by Tomas Munõz Molina. Mexico City, Fondo de Cultura Económica, vol. II: 314–27.

Bastide, Roger.
1947 La sociologie en Amérique Latine. *In* La sociologie au XXè siècle sous la direction de Georges Gurvitch et Wilbert E. Moore. Paris, Presses, vol. II: 621–24.

Berlinck, Cyro, and A. T. Ferrari.
1958 A Escola de Sociologia e Política de São Paulo, 1933–1958. São Paulo.

Bernard, L. L.
1953 Latin America. *In* Encyclopedia of the Social Sciences, edited by Edwin R. A. Seligman and Alvin Johnson. New York, The Macmillan Co., vol. 1: 301–20.

Bulletin International des Sciences Sociales.
1952 Documents relatifs à l'Amérique Latine. Paris UNESCO. Vol. IV, No. 3.

Cândido, Antonio.
1958 Informação sobre a sociologia em São Paulo. *In* Ensaios Paulistas. São Paulo, Editôra Anhambi pp. 510–21.

Costa Pinto, L. A., and Edison Carneiro.
1955 As ciências sociais no Brasil. Rio de Janeiro, Campanha Nacional de Aperfeiçoamento do Pessoal do Nível Superior. Série Estudos e Ensaios, no. 6.

Donoso, Luiz V., and Alejandro Zorbas D.
1959 Estado actual de las ciencias sociales en Chile. Rio de Janeiro, Centro Latino Americano de Pesquisas em Ciências Sociais, No. 9.

Fernandes, Florestan.
1958 A etnologia e a sociologia no Brasil. São Paulo, Editôra Anhembi. Especially pp. 179–244.
1963 A sociologia numa era de revolução social. São Paulo, Companhia Editora Nacional, pp. 147–75.

Germani, Gino.
1959 Desarrollo y estado actual de la sociología latinoamericana. Instituto de Sociología, Buenos Aires, Universidad de Buenos Aires.
1961 Algunas condiciones para el desarrollo de la investigación en la América Latina. *In* Memoria sixth Latin American Congress on Sociology. Caracas, pp. 113–20.

* Regarding sociology in Latin America and its individual nations.

1964   La sociología en la América Latina. Problemas y perspectivas. Buenos Aires Editorial Universitaria de Buenos Aires.

Hopper, Rex D.
1945   The status of sociology in Latin America. *In* Intellectual Trends in Latin America. Austin, University of Texas Press, pp. 99–110.

Poviña, Alfredo.
1941   Historia de la sociología en Latinoamérica. Fondo de Cultura Económica, Mexico City.

Silva Michelena, J. A.
1960   El estado actual de las ciencias sociales en Venezuela. Rio de Janeiro, Centro Latino Americano de Pesquisas em Ciências Sociais, No. 11.

Solari, Aldo E.
1959   Las ciencias sociales en el Uruguay. Rio de Janeiro, Centro Latino Americano de Pesquisas em Ciências Sociais, No. 4.

Pereira de Queiroz, M. I.
1959   Les études ethnosociologiques au Brésil. *In* Recherches et dialogues philosophiques et économiques. Cahiers de l'Institut de Science Économique Appliquée. Paris, pp. 103–47.

Tropp, Asher.
1964   Report on a visit to Latin American universities and research centers. London, London School of Economics.

JOSÉ HONÓRIO RODRIGUES

8

Brazilian Historiography: Present Trends and Research Requirements

In a relatively recent study (Rodrigues 1958) I tried to summarize the various trends in Brazilian historiography, laying particular stress on the fact that the trends do not relate or correspond to real life. This is no passing phenomenon; it is a permanent, peculiarly antiquated, and backward-looking historical thought-process, factual and not ideological, having its roots in ancient Brazil. Research and its findings seem to be out of tune with contemporary social requirements.

The fault is not due to the predominance of colonial subject matter, because answers to the present challenges can be found, nor is the fault due to disinterested research, which should continue to be encouraged. The fault is basically a result of the complete apathy shown towards contemporary history, especially the lack of response to current appeals and problems.

Modern Brazilian historiography has not made a clean sweep of the problems and themes of the old historiography started by Francisco Adolpho de Varnhagen (1816–1878), and the few departures that have been made are negligible so far as overall production is concerned. No correspondence between historical periods, especially the most meaningful periods, is sought to help us understand the present and serve as a guide for the future. Modern Brazilian historiography is nothing more than the echo of the past and a museum of antiquities.

All these main historical schools of thought fail to understand that, as I have written before:

History belongs not to the dead but to the living; it is a present reality and essential to awareness. Hence it is not extraneous to life. But, unfortunately, history for history's sake, indifferent to life's incentives and stimuli, a dead accumulation of material—when it is not a compendium of names and dates—has dominated historical writing and led to a fight for survival.

My thesis is not difficult to illustrate. The great collections of historical works, such as *Brasiliana* (Companhia Editora Nacional) and the *Biblioteca histórica brasileira* (Editôra Martins) have virtually exhausted their potential; *Documentos brasileiros* (Editôra José Olímpio) survive sporadically when the centenary of some person or city is being commemorated; the *Documentos históricos* of the National Library were discontinued, just as they were becoming more interesting with the publication of the documents of the 1817 revolution; the Brazilian Historical and Geographical Institute and the various state historical institutes have no funds; the periodicals drag on in their humdrum way without leaving any mark or impact; students and researchers have no outlet for publishing their findings and are reduced to blessing centenary commemorations which give them a chance to lecture or publish articles and other material.

Antiquated and backward-looking historiography still has its important moments at centenaries when it is easier to secure funds, not for research but for publicity. The results of such commemorative historiography are usually secondary or inadequate, but nowadays constitute a high percentage of the small historiographical output. University production is on a minor scale and is limited to theses, written by candidates for doctorates or by prospective teachers, which are practically never published.

No attempt to change the situation is likely to be welcomed either by the government or by the academic authorities; the former is completely sceptical about history's function in society, and the latter are indifferent to research activities, since the training of middle grade teachers is their most important function.

This is the main reason for the failure to establish centers of historical research, which we have been lamenting since 1952. Year after year we have witnessed the founding of various university and extramural research centers such as the Brazilian Center for Educational Research, the Latin American Center for Social Science Research, the Institute of Social Sciences, and others dealing with economics or administration such as the Getúlio Vargas Foundation. Not even the University of Brazil, so assiduously administered by its president, a historian, welcomed the idea as it should have done, whereas the University of São Paulo, which has neither a president who is a historian or a historical center, took the initiative of founding an Institute of Prehistory.

The somewhat somber picture I drew in 1957 in my preface to the second edition of *Teoria da história do Brasil* (Rodrigues 1957), and in 1958, in my essay on Brazilian historiography and the current historical process (Rodrigues 1958), has not changed; if anything it has become still more somber. The institutions have either been unable, or have not known how to react to the all-pervading apathy, and the universities have continued to concentrate on their necessary but too limited role as establishments for the training of secondary school teachers.

From 1958 onward, there has been little progress to record so far as history is concerned. The main development has been in the expansion of education, with the spread of faculties of philosophy and arts, which numbered seventy-eight in 1962 and accounted for 22.5 percent of the university student population. Of those who matriculated in philosophy, the sciences, and arts, 60 percent (14,653 students) went on for the bachelor's degree in 1962, mainly in teaching (3,397), Romance languages (1,945), the social sciences (1,536), philosophy (1,347), history (1,313), and English or German literature (1,241)—subjects representing 74 percent of the aforesaid total. In addition, of the 9,517 students who matriculated for training as secondary-school teachers, the largest number took teacher-training courses (1,420), followed by Romance literature (1,120), natural history (868), English or German literature (841), history (650), and social sciences (643) (Brazil: Ministério da Educação e Cultura 1962: 6, 43).

The expansion of education does not therefore imply greater interest in history nor does it respond to social needs, because, among those studying for the teacher's certificate, which confers the right to teach and requires only one year's extra study, there is a drop of more than one-half in the social sciences (1,536 to 643) and in history (1,313 to 650).

Since the great majority want only their bachelor's degree and do not want to train for teaching as a profession, history is becoming for most of this majority, consisting largely of women students, a mere adjunct of general culture, as it became in Britain when it replaced the Bible, as pointed out by G. M. Trevelyan (1919).

Hence, the teaching aspect is not very encouraging; the recipient of the bachelor's degree is not prepared for research because the curriculum and the lack of training do not fit him for it and, even if they did, where would he practice his profession when the public institutes, libraries, museums, and archives have no funds, and the other social institutes are not in the habit of employing historians and researchers for the specific work of historical research and historical reconstruction?

Geographical, economic, sociological, and legal studies, garnished with historical references and gathered at random from superficial research, are common in Brazil. In education, especially in teacher-training, no more than the faintest signs are visible of a renewed and encouraging interest in history.

Actually the one great material success, the greatest of all, is also the best example of the downgrading of history. It is with the textbooks that some teachers, especially in secondary schools, have scored successes which surpass the triumphs of literary bestsellers. One of these, which is in its forty-eighth edition, is yielding a fortune which is only paralleled by major success in industry and commerce. It is keeping alive the tradition that colonial history is more important and meaningful than national history, be it of the imperial or republican era, the latter generally consisting of a list of the names of presidents and information of dubious value. The official nature of the facts selected, the upper-class bias in historical portrayal, with its accent on the importance of the leadership and the unimportance of the people, the total absence of critical sense, bringing everything into unquestioning conformity with the historical deeds of the victors —all this teaches a conformist, subjective, privileged, conservative or reactionary kind of history.

Here again the history which is taught and has a tremendous impact on the education of young Brazilians, who form the majority of the total population (52 percent), reveals the evils of traditional research and historiography, which are directly responsible for its bad quality.

However, since there are over thirty million illiterates and about six million pupils in the primary schools and two million in the secondary schools, and since more teachers and better textbooks are needed, it is understandable that the public authorities and academic institutions should focus their attention on education rather than on research, and on subjective and pragmatic historiography rather than on scholarly and monumental or pioneering historiography.

It may, however, be hoped that research and historiography will eventually serve the cause of democracy and progress in Brazil, which is the only true cause, namely, to provide the people with spiritual nourishment and encourage their freedom of thought.

In this connection, the activities of the Brazilian Center for Educational Research, so long under the direction of Anísio Teixeira, illustrate the efforts to provide both teacher and pupil with improved and more modern textbooks better adapted for teaching children in a changing society, and to build up libraries which help them to broaden and consolidate their knowledge. I do not know to what extent the need for research to engage in such modest tasks ought to be acknowledged in a country which is underdeveloped.

The truth is that the living link between the present and the past cannot be disregarded; otherwise the historian and society may lose interest in each other. This becomes very clear when one realizes that, when publishing houses that produce private historical collections, and institutions that publish collections of public documents stop operating, or reduce their operations to a minimum, or are financed by advertisers, other new collections, brought into existence and inspired by the cultural and social need to respond to current concerns and problems in the light of historical inquiry and reappraisal, have prospered and have been well received.

This happened in the case of the collection started by the Instituto Superior de Estudos Brasileiros (ISEB), and of the *Corpo e Alma do Brasil* collections published by Difusão Européia do Livro, the *Perspectivas do Nosso Tempo* collection of Editôra Fundo de Cultura, the *Retratos do Brasil* collection of Editôra Civilização Brasileira, and the new economic, social, political legal, and historical studies, launched by various publishing houses such as Fulgor and Tempo Brasileiro. All these studies are outcomes of a desire to make an effective contribution to the understanding of the contemporary world.

The new historical studies are based on the principle that history does not belong to the dead but to the living and must serve the latter, and that description in statu nascendi is just as legitimate as reconstruction post mortem.

We wrote, in the aforesaid study of 1958, that the ideological reappraisal initiated by Capistrano de Abreu had gathered momentum and that an attempt had been made to reexamine the course of history in the light of new procedures and theories in order to understand and generalize. This tendency is apparent in various ways, both direct and indirect. In Brazil the Marxist reappraisal has been gaining ground, not just because of the work of Caio Prado Jr., whose *História econômica do Brasil* (1945) is reprinted time and time again unchanged, but also because of the *Revista Brasiliense,* with its wealth of historical studies, because of the popular series *Cadernos do Povo Brasileiro,* the books of Rui Facó, especially *Cangaceiros e fanáticos* (1963), the periodical *Estudos Sociais,* the *História sincera da República* (1958), by Leôncio Basbaum, and Nelson Werneck Sodré's studies, especially the *Formação histórica do Brasil* (1962) and *História da burguesia brasileira* (1964). The latter two are the most orthodox Marxist works, so much so that they constitute, both in their substance and in their description of history, an exposition of Marxist theory.

But the Marxist reappraisal, which is also disseminated by the publishing house of the Brazilian Communist Party in Vitória, is not the whole story. There is another ideological reappraisal to be found in Celso Furtado, with his *Formação econômica do Brasil* (1959) and his explanatory study of Brazilian economic problems which provide much clarification for the historians and political and social analysts of present-day Brazil.

Other reappraisals are emerging, without undertones of doctrine, fostered by a variety of ideas, theories, and methods, capable of rendering better service to a wider human, social, and economic range of several Brazils. They examine the personal or social myths, discuss the role of the leadership and of the people in the historical development of Brazil, try to identify national aspirations, and storm the bastions of official historiography which always lauds the victors, shuns the vanquished, refuses to judge or assign responsibility to the successive upper classes and leaders, and prefers to turn history into a bibliography and the personal chronicles of "statesmen."

The trend toward reappraising ideologies and substance as distinct from reappraising mere facts is nowadays linked with nationalist and evolutionary thinking. Nationalism is a fertile field of study in which the following are particularly noteworthy: Barbosa Lima Sobrinho, in a still provisional study (*Desde quando somos nacionalistas?*) Hélio Jaguaribe, *O nacionalismo na atualidade* (1958), and Cândido Mendes, *Nacionalismo e desenvolvimento* (1963).

For nationalists and advocates of evolution, history can and must be an active influence and an ideal instrument for inculcating political ideas, arousing an awareness of insufficiency, imposing decisions which affect the structure of society, and shaping a new destiny. Thus the past is not banished from the sight of the present generation and, even if the present generation may reject what its fathers did, it wishes to use the past together with its symbols in order to shape the future.

Literature which strives to portray events at the time they occur is influential and effective in creating a keen awareness of the defects of present history and of the need to change it. Chronicling, restored to its old function of describing current events, combines many skills, shows great interest in the contemporary, and enables the historian to gain a better understanding of history in the making. Recent developments in Brazil, especially during the last five years, have produced a vast bibliography.

The gulf between historical thinking and historical events and the efforts to bridge the gulf are indicative of the transitional phase through which we are passing. Throughout its history, Brazil has been a stable country whose institutions have stood firm as a rock against the mightiest efforts to change them. Nothing shakes them and all the crises that occur are settled by juridicopolitical remedies which leave the structures as solid and impervious as ever.

The upper classes and the leadership are strongly antireformist and history, as written by them, has been conservative and indifferent to the problems of the day. This accounts for the gulf and the indifference to historical writing to which I referred. The people, excluded by illiteracy, estranged from the public and political life of the nation, and playing no part in the constitution of government, are completely indifferent to the conflicts and crises which arise among their rulers.

Their apathy is not due to their peaceful nature, as has usually been argued, but to the gulf separating the authorities from society; nor is their peaceful nature so peaceful either, for whenever their existence or liberty was really threatened, the history of Brazil was bloody indeed. And if it was less bloody than other American histories, this may be due, as we suggested in previous studies [*Brasil e Africa: outro horizonte* (Rodrigues 1961), *Aspirações Nacionais* (Rodrigues 1963); and *Conciliação e reforma no Brasil* (Rodrigues 1965)], to our crossbreeding which affects not only racial relationships but also social contacts.

Last, just as the gulf between the authorities and society is the main and most serious aspect of political tension in Brazil, the divorce between historical writing and actual historical events is reflected in apathy toward research and historiography.

This phenomenon—research and historiography which are divorced from life and the people and indifferent to the all-out effort to overcome underdevelopment—is not, I think, peculiar to Brazil. It is widespread throughout impoverished and underdeveloped Latin America, and, leaving aside, of course, the necessary exceptions, both obsolete research and archaic historiography prevail.

The success of ostentatious erudition, the prevalence of the nostalgic colonial curriculum, and the triumph, in national biographies, of upper-class heroes over the people's heroes clearly show that research and history continue to serve the same purpose: to perpetuate the rule of successive minorities who have kept the economic structure of political power intact.

Hence I believe, even without quoting examples, that Latin American research and historiography continue to investigate and reconstruct without the slightest desire to serve the present generation in its pathetic effort to eliminate underdevelopment and move on to the fringes of prosperity and true human freedoms that are unknown to the masses. This does not mean advocating and defending the abandonment of research by researchers or of history—"the cold and pure taste of history"—by historians, but recognizing that historical knowledge must respond to the requirements of life and have a pragmatic potential.

The developed and affluent societies indulge themselves in the luxury of the most refined and erudite research and the most disinterested historiographies. Once Latin America overcomes its stagnation and poverty, it will be able to develop such research and historiography.

History, the most experienced of the social disciplines, is too sensitive not to notice that its state of health reflects the state of health of society, and that, like society it is striving to change. History can and should be an instrument of political change.

The unity of Latin America is now more apparent than ever before. The linking factor was the awareness of its underdevelopedness much more than the so-called "pan-American spirit." Long-standing differences have disappeared, and the old saying of Julio Roca about Argentina and Brazil that "nothing divides us and everything brings us closer together" nowadays expresses both the political truth of Latin America and its peoples' sense of closeness which hopefully excludes the tragic possibility of a war, even if fomented from outside Latin America. Unity was certainly strengthened by the meeting, in Uruguaiana, of President Arturo Frondizi and President Jânio Quadros, both of whom shortly thereafter relinquished command of their countries' historic destiny, voluntarily or by force of circumstance.

To replace the iniquitous idea of a possible war, which nowadays would not have the slightest support of people who are sufficiently intelligent, the insidious idea of revolutionary war has been conjured up to divide the peoples and unite the general staffs of America's armed forces. The doctrine of subversion, which is certainly not native to Latin America, united the sadists against the peoples, impeded the democratic process and imposed upon everyone, not a joint program for eliminating underdevelopment, but an alliance under the exclusive command of a non-Latin American partner—the same mistake that paralyzed pan-American thinking.

This problem, plus the problem of nationalism and the problem of a national, independent, frankly noninterventionist foreign policy, opposed to efforts to impose the will of the strongest or richest in collective policymaking, shows that there are many new fields of action and reconstruction open to a new type of research and historiography.

There is one last aspect that is worth reflecting on: the time element. As Pierre Chaunu has written, the developing nations must not only telescope the different historical stages through which the developed nations have passed but also coordinate the extreme differences in historical time which separate regions and areas in the same society and, I would add, they must act at the proper time and meet historical deadlines so that they eventually triumph and are not condemned to stagnation, death, or subjection for a long period of history.

The New Fields of Research and
Historiographical Reconstruction

The above remarks are intended to clarify and emphasize one point and one point only: Brazilian and, I believe, Latin American researchers and historiographers are concerned with a stationary and archaic society; their main subject matter is therefore divorced from life, ostentatious and erudite, and suffers from a bad and inadequate presentation of problems. The reaction of society is indifference to their findings, apathy toward their publications, and a witholding of resources. An underdeveloped society which is already in economic straits and faces pressing problems in its struggle to survive (especially problems of undernourishment, illiteracy, and high infant mortality and sickness rates) cannot afford the luxury of approving and subsidizing showy studies, which are out of date.

Each culture has to create its own form of history because it is, as J. Huizinga has taught us, a kind of rendering of accounts. The fact is that new fields of research and new horizons of historical reconstruction are opening up that are valuable for their practical impact and for the assistance they can offer to development and democracy.

Once these general premises have been established, a definition or delimitation of the field of research also emerges from the comments called for by Stanley J. Stein's (1964) essay in *Social Science Research on Latin America*. United States interests, United States ideas, and United States methods predominate in these studies, as is only natural and understandable. Sometimes the methods are neither North American, nor Latin American, but merely personal, especially when they disregard certain studies by United States writers themselves, or praise the one and silence the other, in groups that we might call literary coteries.

Comments on Bibliography

Thus, for example, I fail to understand why Professor Stein disregards the works of the Pan-American Geographical and His-torical Institute, especially three series on indigenous, colonial, and national history, and only refers to the final summaries based on partial studies. He has also ignored the national histo-riographies being compiled under the auspices of that Institute. Why? Actually, so far as historiography is concerned, Professor Stein ignores not only the Institute's publications but also those publications issued in Argentina, Brazil, and Europe. The other research material is also picked at random: for example, he quotes the guides by Bolton (1913), Hill (1916), and Shepherd (1907) and does not include references to the great series entitled *Misiones Americanas en los Archivos Europeos,* published by the Pan American Geographical and Historical Institute, and to the new guides, such as those by John P. Harrison (1961) and Lino Gómez Canedo (1961).

Let us not forget the services rendered, and still being ren-dered, by the documentary collections of William R. Manning (1925) or the critical documentation prepared by Sir Charles Webster (1938). I recognize that the author was not trying to be exhaustive but only illustrative, but then he should have referred to the cream of the bibliographical research material available in the United States, Latin America, and Europe, of which the *Manual bibliográfico de estudos brasileiros* [Borba de Moraes and Berrien (editors) 1949] is a good example of cooperation.

No bibliographical criticism of this essay could fail to note the lack of some basic material which has been and continues to be very influential, such as the work of Father Serafim Leite [both the *História da Companhia de Jesus no Brasil,* (1938–50) and the

Monumenta Brasiliae (1956–58)] and, in English literature, the books by John H. Parry (1963), John Lynch (1958), and especially, with reference to Brazil, all the books by Charles R. Boxer (1952; 1957; 1962).

As regards our first century, there is a United States professor of economic history who has exercised and still exercises an enormous influence on Latin American historiography, Earl J. Hamilton (1934; 1948); his work deserves to appear alongside the studies of Clarence Haring (1947), Pierre Chaunu (1955–60), and Frederic Mauro (1960; 1961), and the essay by Francisco Morales Padrón (1955). But Professor Stein does not seem to appreciate Haring's works, of which he quotes only the *Imperio Hispánico en América*, without even referring to *El comercio y la navegación entre España y las Indias en la epoca de los Habsburgos* (1939a) or *Los bucaneros de los Indias Occidentales en el Siglo XVII* (1939b) or *Empire in Brazil* (1958). Actually, *El comercio y la navegación (Trade and Navigation . . .*) was a major contribution and an influential book. On the other hand, Stein (1964: 112) emphasizes the frontier aspect as a unifying factor and quotes the study by Herbert E. Bolton (1939), subsequently referring to the study by Arthur P. Whitaker (1951), without mentioning the seminar on the frontier concept held at the Second International Congress of Historians of the United States and Mexico, the proceedings of which were edited by Archibald H. Lewis and Thomas F. McGann under the title *The New World Looks at its History* (1963).

I am speaking only of basic material and influential authors. Since stress is given to the early days of American history, the books by Florentino Pérez Embid (1948) and Ladislao Gil Munilla (1954) should not be omitted. Seville continues to be an active center of American history which cannot be disregarded any more than can the Historical Commission of the Pan American Historical and Geographical Institute in Mexico City or the Gothenburg Ibero-American Institute, whose publications (more than sixteen of them) constitute an intelligent attempt to understand America, especially the admirable essay by Sverker Arnoldsson, "Los momentos históricos de América según la historiografía del periodo colonial" (1956).

I do not quite understand the criteria of selection, but I think it is impossible to refer to secondary works without mentioning the importance and impact of certain other books and collections. There are, for example, two active centers of historical research in Latin America: the College of Mexico, with which Professor Stein is acquainted, and the Center for Colonial History, in Chile, which he apparently does not know. Two essays produced by the latter and written by Mario Góngora (1962) and Marcelo Carmagni (1963) clearly illustrate the maturity of Chilean historiography.

So far I have kept to the colonial era; I shall now give some examples pertaining to other periods. As regards the period of Independence, no reference is made to the monumental work being done by various American nations, especially the documentary collections of Venezuela, Chile, and Argentina on the Founders; and the activities of the Ibero-American Emancipation Committee of the Pan American Geographical and Historical Institute. And, last, so far as Brazilian intellectual history is concerned, I do not consider the work of Lúcia Miguel Pereira to be the most apposite, nor do I understand why the book by Thomas F. McGann, *Argentina, the United States and the Inter-American System, 1880–1914* (1957), and that of Alan K. Manchester, *British Preeminence in Brazil: Its Rise and Decline* (1933), which is extremely valuable even today, have been overlooked.

Comments on Ideas

Professor Stein's essay also calls for some clarifying comments. I disagree with some of his methodological and philosophical points. When he deals with the colonial period, he speaks of three colonial eras preferred by North American historians, but the fact of the matter is that, in the period from 1570 to 1763, which those historians have neglected, historical events in Brazil were extremely important and gave rise to a vast amount of national bibliography: first, the foreign invasions and colonial struggles for possession of Brazil, second, the conquest of the interior and national expansion. In Brazil no attempts were made to disparage Portuguese colonization; on the contrary, it was praised. Only at the end of the nineteenth and during the present century did colonization become a target of criticism.

In Brazil, Varnhagen began an official historiography which accepted the victorious power without reservation, disowned the vanquished, and excused the victorious minorities; José Bonifácio was rejected from that time up to the present for his innovations, and full support was given to the mailed fist which had subjected Brazil. Varnhagen was so much the apologist of the House of Braganza that he bears the responsibility for starting that version of history that depicts our Independence as bloodless, whereas in Bahia and Maranhão we deployed larger armies than the largest of those commanded by Bolívar or San Martín.

Nostalgic or sentimental historiography, in which the past is always better than the present, is a childish malady which has been prevalent in the past and is still with us.

I appreciate the importance of the *Hispanic American Historical Review* (HAHR), but it should be explained that its influence, like that of the *American Historical Review*, is virtually nonexistent in Latin America, because of the difference of language and the difficulty of purchasing it owing to the dollar shortage. Nor do I need to add that it is in the United States and not in Latin America that interest in recent history is growing, as I indicated above, a point that has been emphasized, in the case of Brazil, by Rollie E. Poppino (1953).

I do not believe that colonial history is easy as compared with modern history. Both are complex; both present problems as regards sources and interpretation; and of each we only know the documented part, the official and the indiscreet version, but there is always a concealed part that remains concealed. Moreover, the modern historian can draw on a whole range of interdisciplinary material, such as the economic surveys of the Economic Commission for Latin America (ECLA), which already cover seventeen years, and of the national economic institutes with their annual studies and periodicals, and the publications of the social science institutes. Thus there is now more and better information for a discipline dealing with overall reconstruction.

Professor Stein's intention, in citing the compilations of modern Latin American history, is to provide examples, since he links didactic histories with interpretative essays, and works covering extensive periods with studies on recent years. The heuristic complexities of modern history are not always specific, since the range of documentation, for Latin America as a whole, spreads over both the colonial and modern eras. The principle of collecting documentary material as a single and indivisible whole is applied by the developed countries, but even among them it is not universally accepted.

The categories into which Arthur P. Whitaker (1961) divided the currents of Latin American history and which are endorsed by Stein are so broad that, except for the last one, they can be applied equally well to all non-Latin American historiographies. In what categories should we classify Jacques Lambert's study *Amérique Latine: structures sociales et institutions politiques* (1963), or Pierre Chaunu's *Historia de América Latina* (1964a) and *L'Amérique et les Amériques* (1964b), and Arnold Toynbee's lectures on the *Economy of the Western Hemisphere* (1962) [see also Potash (1960) and Barager (1959)].

Preferences in the United States naturally do not coincide with those of Latin Americans regarding national subjects for study, especially if we consider that these preferences may be based on the historiographical essays of Potash, Stein, and Barager, who largely disregard national historiographical activities.

After affirming (Stein 1964: 92) that the historical problems of Mexico, Brazil, and Argentina are comparable only in the broadest sense, Stein (1964: 99) states that Brazilian history, unlike that of Mexico, is not characterized by mass movements with far-reaching and penetrating repercussions. The contrast is a fortunate one, because violence was not a prominent feature of our history as it was, for example, not only in Mexico but also in the United States and Colombia. Still, this does not mean that our history was free from bloodshed. Conservatism and compromise, liberalism and conspiracy, are its predominant features. To ask whether our history is therefore "monotonous" is not an objective question, for it is not rendered more amusing by violence or more boring by skill at compromise. Compromise engenders conspiracy because it means gaining, or trying to gain, something without the risk of brutality. Sociologists and political scientists who have studied resistance to change have emphasized current reality without recourse to historical demonstration; the latter would show them how the antireformism of the Brazilian minorities and of the powers-that-be, especially the legislature, has prevailed.

The efforts of the conservative classes to maneuver huge masses of Africans, the most downtrodden in Brazil, were successful and the Africans were largely absorbed through interbreeding, which alleviated racial and social tensions. But to say that the "monotony" (Stein 1964:99) is due to the fact that Brazilians have not produced much historiographical material is to make a serious mistake, for I do not believe that, by comparison, any other Latin American historiography has produced such vast historical collections either publicly or privately.

Contrary to Professor Stein's opinion, there are features in the Brazilian historical process which are visible now that the steel bonds of the historiography emanating from Varnhagen or taken over from Portuguese colonialism and, consequently, from all colonialisms, have been broken. There is also the problem of the bloody and bloodless phases of our history which I recently summarized, as noted above, in *Aspirações nacionais* (1963) and more recently in *Conciliação e reforma no Brasil* (1965).

It is not correct to say that Boxer (1963) is the only opponent of the idea that Brazilian slavery was more humanitarian than others (Stein 1964: 100). Joaquim Nabuco wrote as early as 1883 (Nabuco 1883: 133) in the midst of the abolitionist campaign, that our slavery was said to be mild and the masters kind:

But the truth of the matter is that all slavery is the same; kindness on the part of the masters requires resignation on the part of the slaves. Anyone who undertook to compile statistics of the crimes committed by or against slaves; anyone who initiated an inquiry into slavery and listened to the complaints of those who undergo it, would discover that slavery in Brazil was just as brutal, barbarous and cruel as anywhere else in America.

Boxer's difference of opinion is based on something else; he tries to show, in a comparative historical study, that the Portuguese displayed racial prejudice in their various colonies on the three continents.

The series of questions proposed by Professor Stein, based on Brazilian and United States studies, deserves attention, although it sometimes states the obvious, e.g. that the emancipated Negroes were given the most menial jobs while the better-trained immigrants took the better jobs; and that there is no lack of friction in the South, the region with a smaller percentage of Negroes. Professor Stein also seems to accept the idea of economic cycles of certain products and to reject the idea of fluctuations in short-term economic activity characterized by panics, crises, and depressions that are more frequent than periods of prosperity or recovery. This leads to various other questions, such as the problem of state intervention which is a permanent feature of our history and not just of the past decade; the misuse of the term "revolution," the role of the junior officers (the "lieutenants"), and of the military, the importance of the era ushered in by Vargas, orderly constitutional processes and peaceful evolution, political tensions, and periodic political shifts without any sharing of power by the masses.

I have discussed some of these problems in my new study *Conciliação e reforma no Brasil: um desafio histórico-politico*. The movement of the "lieutenants" of 1954 was a form of conspiracy inspired by indigenous liberalism, aimed at snapping the iron fetters of the Government and using the youngest and boldest in the armed forces to undermine, in the humblest ranks of the officer corps, the military authority of the generals who were in league with the Government.

Indigenous liberalism always meant economic liberalism and hence an export-oriented and antiindustrial economy, and the defense, at least in words, of civic freedoms. Qualified people deserve freedoms and others do not; there is discrimination also in rebellion and nonconformity. Liberalism came into existence in an enslaved society and could not be, as it is not, the stubborn defender of dissenting opinions and non conformity. So it was in the Empire and so it is today. Brazil's historical continuity explains its stability and shows how it is impossible to understand Brazil except in its historic perspective.

Like any form of liberalism, the lieutenancy had deep discriminatory, restrictive, and selective roots. Then, in the course of history, the former lieutenants, now generals, became leaders of a strictly reactionary movement. This explains why there is even a lieutenants' interpretation of history, devised by one of their leaders. The reaction of 1954 is the counterrevolution of 1964.

This is a key aspect bearing on the role of the military in Brazilian politics, a subject that has strongly attracted the attention of United States students, although I do not consider that any of their studies so far shows an understanding of the matter. In *Conciliação e reforma,* as in the preface to the second edition of *Aspirações nacionais,* I try to introduce new data and notes for future elucidation of the problem. The tensions described by Professor Stein are not on target; the frictions are between the executive and the legislature, between the people and the leadership and upper classes. The internal arrangements for the transfer of power, *sub rosa* arrangements, arrangements to avoid breaking the iron chain of successive ruling generations, came to an end, as is apparent from the crises of succession which are not, as politicians think they are, the crux of Brazilian policy but only a reflection of a stable economy's failure to adapt itself to present social requirements. Here Stein hits the mark when he speaks of the economic and social roots of political instability.

Fields of Research

The main fields of research are implicit in the questions formulated by Professor Stein in the section on research projects. He recognizes that Latin America has not achieved its economic freedom even now. This accounts for the importance ascribed to imperialism, colonialism, and interventionism—all topics deserving more research by scholars in the United States and Latin America.

Merle Kling, one of Professor Stein's coauthors, has shown how the contemporary economic patterns of colonialism engender diplomatic loyalty which weakens the power position of the Latin American countries. Economic colonialism generates political instability and reduces the power of the loyal allies of the United States, whereas the elimination of such colonialism would create political stability and increase their power but lessen their loyalty (Kling 1959). This accounts for the disparaging picture of Latin America painted by the newly emerging nations and their fear of so-called "South Americanization," the equivalent of the Balkanization or Mongolization now apparent on a larger scale in the intervention in Southeast Asia.

This raises a problem which is avoided by researchers although vast facilities are available for dealing with it. The study of nationalism is thus a necessity. Latin and North Americans are beginning to study it but what is required, in addition to national studies, is a complete comparative study of nationalism in Latin America similar to the one carried out by Jan Romein (1962), the disciple of J. Huizinga, for Asia. There is also a need to examine United States multilateral and bilateral foreign policy in Latin America, but shorn of the ideas and preconceptions which have predominated in this sector, and to study each country's own independent foreign policy for furthering and expediting its own development, based on nationalism, the idea of progress, and the traditional principle that troublesome alliances should be repudiated and complete freedom of trade established, as I have tried to show (Rodrigues 1962a; 1962b).

The framing of an independent foreign policy, in the face of heavy pressure from large economic and interested groups and extremely heavy pressure from the written and spoken news media, was not an act of despair in the face of foreign economic difficulties but a deliberate attempt to enhance the country's power position. In the nineteen-sixties, when this policy took shape, Brazil's crises were the result of the deterioration in its terms of trade, the fall in the prices of primary commodities, and the heavy burden of external debt, all of which are attributable mainly to our relations with the United States. It is sufficient to say that in the first six months of 1960 alone exports rose 18.5 percent in volume but only 1.4 percent in dollar value. These figures are indicative of Brazil's difficult situation and of its relations with the United States, which the Alliance for Progress is not managing to conceal. The deterioration and gap are growing, as Raúl Prebisch clearly pointed out in his report "Towards a New Trade Policy for Development" (Prebisch 1964).

Thus our independent foreign policy is temporarily obstructed, but only so long as the idea of security prevails in its formulation and so long as the idea holds sway that it is military doctrine and not the will of the people that shapes national policy. The present predominating idea of security is neither national nor Latin American; it obliges all armies to subscribe to the United States military doctrine that we must protect ourselves here and now, not against possible foreign aggression but against subversion and ideological warfare.

Thus the idea of a single front in the underdeveloped world is inconsistent with and conflicts with the idea of the comradely unity of the armies engaged in the cold war, in the fight against subversion. This is an additional factor which combines with the economic factor to jeopardize democracy in Latin America and thwart Latin America's hopes of independence. Here is a field of research that is fundamental today, one in which history, national policy, and international policy merge. Several other projects are also connected with it, especially those relating to economic history, e.g., those projects prepared and published by Wendell C. Gordon (1961; 1962; n.d.).

A serious and objective study of the contribution of private investment, the role of United States enterprises, and the problem of the remittance abroad of profits would make these subjects less emotional and bring them into historical perspective. To continue the series started by William R. Manning, with Spanish and Portuguese translations, would also be a major contribution toward better international relations and would supplement the modern series of foreign policy documents issued by the U.S. Department of State.

To sum up, a priority should be given in general to economic history, political history, and the history of bilateral and multilateral international relations and, more specifically, to the role of the upper classes and leadership, the role of the middle classes, the role of the proletariat and rural classes, their behavior and integration, the groups of vested interests and the economic groups, the part played by violence and conciliation, national aspirations and the formation of national characteristics, the relationship between the stability of economic institutions and political instability, the regular behavioral pattern and its variations in certain popular movements and among the upper classes in the historic process, the structure and dynamism of the three branches of governmental power, the influence and pressure of the United States Government on the policymaking of Latin American national governments, the ideologies, constitutional legal thinking and its impact on the supremacy of the minority and on resistance to change, the role of the church and social change, conservatism and the political parties, the external factors impeding Latin American development, the brake applied by certain political groups, the image of the United States in Latin America and its transformation. In addition, the translation of United States books on Latin America into Spanish or Portuguese and the translation of Latin American books into English would be of great value in fostering mutual understanding between Latin and North Americans.

Now is the time to push ahead with modern research and historiography because it is now that the great battle for modernization is being waged against archaic institutions, their representatives, and their defenders in and out of uniform.

REFERENCES

Arnoldsson, Sverker.
    1956 Los momentos históricos de América según la historiografía del período colonial. Madrid.
Barager, J. R.
    1959 The historiography of the Rio de la Plata area since 1830. Hispanic American Historical Review, 39: 588–642.
Barbosa Lima Sobrinho (Alexandre José).
    n.d. Desde quando somos nacionalistas? Rio de Janeiro, Cadernos do Povo, no. 24.
Basbaum, Leôncio.
    1958 História sincera da República. Rio de Janeiro, Livraria São José.
Bolton, Herbert E.
    1913 Guide to materials for the history of the United States in the principal archives of Mexico. Washington, D.C.
    1939 Wide horizons of American history. New York.
Borba de Moraes, Rubens and William Berrien (Editors).
    1949 Manual bibliográfico de estudos brasileiros. Rio de Janeiro, Gráfica Editôra Souza.
Boxer, Charles R.
    1952 Salvador de Sá and the struggle for Brazil and Angola. London.
    1957 The Dutch in Brazil, 1624–1654. London.
    1962 The golden age of Brazil, 1596–1750. Berkeley, University of California Press.
    1963 Race relations in the Portuguese colonial empire, 1415–1825. London.
Brazil. Ministério da Educação e Cultura.
    1962 Sinopse estatística do ensino superior. Rio de Janeiro.

Carmagni, Marcelo.
1963 El salariado minero en Chile colonial: su desarrollo en una sociedad provincial. El Norte Chico, 1690–1800. Santiago, Chile.
Chaunu, Pierre.
1964a História da América Latina (Portuguese translation). São Paulo.
1964b L'Amérique et les Amériques. Paris.
Chaunu, Pierre, and Huguette Chaunu.
1955–60 Séville et l'Atlantique (1504–1650). Paris. 8 vols.
Facó, Rui.
1963 Cangaceiros e fanáticos: gênese e lutas. Rio de Janeiro, Editôra Civilização Brasileira.
Furtado, Celso.
1959 Formação econômica do Brasil. Rio de Janeiro, Editôra Fundo de Cultura S.A.
Gil Munilla, Ladislao.
1954 Descubrimiento del Marañón. Seville.
Gómez Canedo, Lino.
1961 Los archivos de la historia de América. Período colonial español. Mexico City, Pan American Geographical and Historical Institute. 2 vols.
Góngora, Mario.
1962 Los grupos de conquistadores en tierra firme, 1509–1530; fisionomía histórico-social de un tipo de conquista. Santiago, Chile.
Gordon, Wendell C.
1961 The contribution of foreign investments. A case study of the United States foreign investment history (Offprint). Inter-American Economic Affairs. Summer.
1962 Foreign investment. Business Review. The University of Houston Press. Winter.
n.d. Role of foreign investment in economic development. Southwestern Social Science Association. Annual meeting (mimeographed).
Hamilton, Earl J.
1934 American treasure and the price revolution, 1501–1650. Cambridge, Harvard University Press.
Haring, Clarence H.
1939a El comercio y la navegación entre España y las Indias en la época de los Habsburgos. Paris.
1939b Los bucaneros de las Indias Occidentales en el siglo XVII. Paris.
1947 The Spanish empire in America. New York.
1958 Empire in Brazil. Cambridge, Harvard University Press.
Harrison, John P.
1961 Guide to materials on Latin America in the National Archives. Vol. I. Washington, D.C. The National Archives.
Hill, R. R.
1916 Descriptive catalogue of the documents relating to the history of the United States, *In* Papeles Procedentes de Cuba. Washington, D.C.
Jaguaribe, Helio.
1958 O nacionalismo na atualidade. Rio de Janeiro, Instituto Superior de Estudos Brasileiros, Ministerio da Educação e Cultura.
Kling, Merle.
1959 Contribuição para uma teoria da instabilidade do poder e da política na América Latina. Revista Brasileira de Estudos Políticos. (Jan.)

pp. 7–29. Translated from the Western Political Quarterly, March, 1956: 21–35.

Leite, Seraphim, S.J.
1938–50 História da Companhia de Jesus no Brasil. Lisbôa e Rio de Janeiro. 10 vols.
1956–58 Monumenta Brasiliae, Monumenta Historica Societotis Iesu. Rome. 3 vols.

Lambert, Jacques.
1963 Amérique Latine: structures sociales et institutions politiques. Paris.

Lynch, John.
1958 Spanish colonial administration 1782–1810. London.

Manchester, Alan K.
1933 British preëminence in Brazil. Its rise and decline. Chapel Hill, University of North Carolina Press.

Manning, William R.
1925 Diplomatic correspondence of the United States concerning the independence of the Latin American nations. New York. 3 vols.

Mauro, Frederic.
1960 Le Portugal et l'Atlantique au XVII ème siècle. Paris.
1961 México y Brasil: dos economías coloniales comparadas. Historia Mexicana 10 (April–June): 570–87.

McGann, Thomas F.
1957 Argentina, the United States and the inter-American system, 1880–1914. Cambridge, Harvard University Press.

Mendes de Almeida, Cândido.
1963 Nacionalismo e desenvolvimento. Instituto Brasileiro de Estudos Afro-Asiáticos. Rio de Janeiro.

Morales Padrón, Francisco.
1955 El comercio Canario-Americano. Seville.

Nabuco, Joaquim.
1883 O abolicionismo. London, A. Kindon.

Parry, John H.
1963 The age of reconnaissance. London.

Pérez Embid, Florentino.
1948 Los descubrimientos en el Atlántico hasta el tratado de Tordesillas. Seville.

Poppino, Rollie E.
1953 A century of the Revista do Instituto Histórico e Geográfico Brasileiro (Offprint). From the Hispanic American Historical Review, Vol. XXXIII (2) (May): 307–23.

Potash, Robert A.
1960 The historiography of Mexico since 1821. Hispanic American Historical Review, 40: 383–424.

Prado Jr., Caio.
1945 História econômica do Brasil. São Paulo.

Prebisch, Raúl.
1964 Towards a new trade policy for development. Report of the Secretary General of the United Nations. Conference on Trade and development.

Rodrigues, José Honório.
1957 Teoria da história do Brasil. São Paulo, Companhia Editora Nacional. 1st edition 1949.

1958   La historiografía brasileña y el actual proceso histórico. Anuário de Estudios Americanos, vol. XIV. *Also in* Jornal do Brasil, Rio de Janeiro, August 18, September 7, 14, 22, 1958.

1961   Brasil e África: outro horizonte. Rio de Janeiro. 2nd edition 1964. English translation Brazil and Africa, University of California Press, 1965.

1962a   Uma política externa própria e independente. Jornal do Brasil, Rio de Janeiro, June 10 and 17.

1962b   The foundations of Brazil's foreign policy. International Affairs, July.

1963   Aspirações nacionais. São Paulo, Editôra Fulgor.

1965   Conciliação e reforma no Brasil: um desafio histórico. Rio de Janeiro, Editôra Civilização Brasileíra.

Romein, Jan.

1962   The Asian century. Berkeley, University of California Press.

Shepherd, W. R.

1907   Guide to the materials for the history of the United States in Spanish archives. Washington, D.C., Carnegie Institute.

Stein, Stanley J.

1964   Latin American historiography: status and research opportunities. *In* Social Science Research on Latin America, edited by Charles Wagley. New York, Columbia University Press, pp. 86–124.

Toynbee, Arnold.

1962   Economy of the western hemisphere. London.

Trevelyan, G. M.

1919   The recreations of an historian. London.

Wagley, Charles (Editor).

1964   Social Science Research on Latin America. New York, Columbia University Press.

Webster, Charles.

1938   Britain and the independence of Latin America. London, Oxford University Press. 2 vols.

Werneck Sodré, Nelson.

1962   Formação histórica do Brasil. Rio de Janeiro. Editôra Brasiliense.

1964   História da burguesia brasileira. Rio de Janeiro, Editôra Civilização Brasileira.

Whitaker, Arthur P.

1951   The Americas in the Atlantic triangle. *In* Ensaios sobre la Historia del Nuevo Mundo, E. McInwis, editor. Mexico City.

1961   Latin American history since 1825. Washington, D.C.

9

Anthropology

When I was invited by the Joint Committee on Latin American Studies of the Social Science Research Council to take part in this Conference, the subject I was to cover was determined in advance. I was expected to present first, my view on the development and trends of anthropology in Latin America, and second, my reaction to what recently had been written (Strickon 1964: 125–167) on the subject.

The development of the so-called social sciences has so enlarged their scope and the range of subjects covered by them that, now and then, their system of classification requires evaluation and revision. In the case of the anthropological sciences, which are concerned with that complex concept called culture, there is even greater need for a fresh analysis of their component parts, a new conceptual interpretation and a determination of their paramount trends and tendencies. The present Conference offers us, at the very least, an opportunity to discourse on the nature, contents, and aims of the social sciences in Latin America.

In this connection, the admirable book *Social Science Research on Latin America,* edited by Charles Wagley (1964), offers meaningful replies to some of the problems encountered in our studies; and we hope that the present Conference will furnish additional answers to those eternal questions which loom larger than ever in this twentieth century: Where do we come from? Where are we? Where are we going? Nevertheless, in my opinion, a statement such as the one I was asked to make calls for a brief sketch of the general historical background, and a brief account of the origins and development of anthropology in general. To put it more clearly, it might be said that my subject covers first, the why and wherefore of this science in America; second, a

selective chronological presentation of works, authors, and subjects which are representative of this development in some of the
nations of our continent; third, the reasons for the present state
of development and trends of anthropology in those same countries. Last, I should point out that, because of the limited time at
my disposal, I lay no claim to having dealt thoroughly with the
subject with which we are concerned; what follows is no more
than a rough draft and is intended purely for information
purposes.

General Historical Background

Ideas and Philosophies

If the news of today is the history of tomorrow, the news of
yesterday is the key to what man is and what he does. Herodotus
when traveling, used to ask: Who are you? Where do you come
from? Where do you live? And his reflections led him to ask
himself: Can climate change the character and physical appearance of man? Can these be changed by his way of life and his
nutrition? Is the father or the mother the natural head of the
family? Can different customs arise independently, or must we
seek for a historical connection between them? How much time is
required for the development and spread of different ethnic
groups? These questions are part and parcel of orthodox anthropological ontogeny. We still ask them today, and because of them
Penniman (1935: 26) has called Herodotus the first anthropologist.

But reflecting on man and his culture does not make an anthropologist; nor does mere desire. Such great philosophers of
classic Greece as Hippocrates, Plato, and Aristotle engaged in
deductive analysis in order to form their views on the individual,
culture, society, the republic, the state, and above all on social
and cultural values. In other words, the philosophers expressed
their opinions (thereby creating philosophy) on the supposedly
similar natures and different characteristics of men, and on man's
destiny in the light of individual and group needs and desires.
Their works, with thousands of others in the Library of Alexandria, constituted part of the fountain of wisdom from which the
intelligentsia of the West were to drink.

Under the Roman Empire, Lucretius contributed to the development of the Science of Man by differentiating between three ages, stone, bronze, and iron, in the development of human culture (Penniman 1935: 35). Strabo, Cicero, and Seneca developed other philosophical views on man, his way of thinking, feeling, and doing things (Barnes and Becker: 1945 I, 183–88). Later St. Augustine wrote what amounts to a work of classification and applied anthropology, *De Civitate Dei,* which for centuries dominated Christian thought.

In subsequent centuries, in the same and neighboring territories, anthropological judgments and opinions were strongly influenced by the vision of the world evolved in Arabian philosophy. This hegemony was maintained by Islam's political supremacy, commercial power, scientific insights, and achievements, which combined with a genius for integration. Writings of the Arab chroniclers together with collections of physical objects were housed in the world's first museum at Alexandria. The fluidity of the Arab world and its failure to consolidate its culture favored, however, an East-West encounter, which eventually resulted in European expansion. The Crusaders and the travels of Marco Polo were not only examples of this expansion, but also an interesting source of original ethnographic descriptions (Barnes and Becker 1945: 266–74).

The profits resulting from trade led to an increase in travel and, faced with the overwhelming variety of men's achievements, people developed a wealth of opinion on what men are and what they do. This awakening of interest and the spread of knowledge were facilitated, if only for a restricted elite, by the use of paper and the invention of printing. The stage was set for the great epic of the fifteenth century: the discovery of America, as if it were India or Asia. The remarkable exploits of Portuguese and Spanish sailors cleared up many geographical mysteries; at the same time, however, they increased doubts as to the nature of man and the ways in which society had developed.

Accounts and Chroniclers

In the sixteenth century, space and time—that is to say, geography and history—loom large in the minds of those few who occupied themselves with such matters. Thus, for the newly discovered continent we have the geographical accounts of Martin

Enciso and Joseph de Acosta. In addition, the extremely valuable *Relaciones Geográficas de Indias* and the countless documents preserved in the Archives of Seville and Madrid contain information which makes it possible for us to identify the geographical factors which conditioned the unity and the diversity of American groups. There is also an abundance of natural and moral histories from such renowned authors as Pedro Martín de Anghiera, the first historian of the voyages of discovery, Gonzalo-Fernández de Oviedo, the first critic of the conquest and the conquerors, López de Velasco, a major chronicler of the Indies, Román y Zamora, who wrote comparative interpretations, and Bartolomé de las Casas, that remarkable man. All of them were honest with themselves, and set down for their own times and posterity what they held to be significant and true. Nevertheless, their indiscriminate use of conceptual categories and failure to distinguish between the representative and the illustrative was bound to influence the scholars and critics of their own day as well as of ours.

Within regional limits, referring specifically to Mexico and Central America, the minimum required sources of anthropological information are the great work of Sahagún, the native manuscripts dealing with deities and genealogies, and taxation (Codexes Dresden, Pereciano and Mendoza), the histories of Díaz del Castillo, Diego Durán, Mendieta, and the Toltec-Chíchimec history, the accounts of Landa, Pomar, and Alonso de Zorita, the chronicles of the Popol Vuh, the Books of Chilam Balam, and Tezozomoc, the annals of Cuauhtitlan, and the records of the Cakchiquel Indians. For Colombia, Andagoya, Belalcazar, and Robledo are recommended. The sixteenth century sources on the Andean peoples, following alphabetical order, are Betanzos, Cabello de Balboa, Cieza de León, Estete, Jerez, the Molinas, Polo de Ondegardo, Sámano, and Blas Valera.* These chroniclers, as officers and missionaries, "created" American anthropology. Zealous men, full of unshakeable faith, they wrote down with enthusiasm their impressions and accounts. They were attempting to

* For a selective bibliography on the American Indian cultures, see Comas 1953. Specific bibliographical references for Mexico and Central America are to be found in Jiménez Moreno 1937–1938, Vol. 1: 47–77, 167–97, and 289–421, and Bernal (1962). For Colombia and the Andean regions, Schwab 1936, IX–1: 1–26 and 2: 4–27; and Steward (Editor) 1948, Vol. 4: 570–609.

fill the hiatus between the Catholic scriptures and the spirit of Iberian laws on the one hand, and the existence of a New World and new peoples, on the other.

Along with these works the published or unpublished documents about the discovery, conquest, laws, the colonizing effort, and the organization of the ancient Spanish possessions in America are of extraordinary anthropological importance. If to space and time elements we were to add the social aspect, and use the comparative method for all three, this highly needed undertaking would be quite significant for ethnologists and anthropologists. It would give us the first synthesis of the contact between two cultures, a new situation with distinctive categories, in the long process of the cultural history of indigenous America.

Those tireless travelers and diligent observers of a bygone day, endowed with a serene confidence in their destiny, whether secular or religious, discussed the eternal subject of similarities and differences between men and between their social and cultural worlds. If their pages are permeated with preconceived notions, hasty judgments, and a strong flavor of passion, humility, or childishness, they nevertheless deserve a place of honor on our shelves. We, in the second half of the twentieth century, are not very different from them in subjectivity.

During the seventeenth century, the written accounts, chronicles, and histories do not greatly differ from the works mentioned above. Friars, viceroys, king's envoys, officials of the Crown, and of the governments of the New World (New Spain, Kingdom of New Granada, New Castile, etc.) continued their efforts to hispanize the American native, and to transplant the Spanish state into the West Indies. However, in their zeal for evangelization, colonization, cultural transference, and strong government, churchmen and laymen alike studied aboriginal cultures and societies from the viewpoint of European foreigners. They saw with the eyes of conquerors. There was much improvisation and even more contradiction between philosophy and legislation relating to the Indians and their actual application (Zavala 1944; 1948). Nevertheless, with intelligence and patience, the present-day ethnologists can still analyze these sources and learn much about the results of population policy in similar and different natural environments, compulsory and voluntary associations for purposes of security, the nature, provenance, and distribution of taxes, changes and transformations in the many forms of land tenure, sources and conditions of employment, controls of types and quantities of production, and many other subjects. If we were to classify and catalog these data, making a distinction between the representative and the illustrative, we would identify the bases for the emergence of social groups or classes and of the cultural nuclei or the levels in the process of homogenization or diversification in early Latin America.

This seventeenth century which was one of depression, at least in New Spain (Borah 1951), offers rich material on the cultures and societies of the prehispanic period. Among general works, given in chronological order, the following are to be recommended: the *Dècadas* of Herrera, the history of Gregorio García, the descriptions of Pedro Simón and Vásquez de Espinosa, the *Política indiana* of Solorzano Pereira, and the *Compilation of Laws* of 1680. Sources for Mexico and Central America are Torquemada, Remezal, Gage, the works of the Jesuits Alegre and Pérez de Ribas, the *Teatro Mexicano* by Vetancurt, and the *Recordación Florida* by Fuentes y Guzmán. For Panama there is Requejo Salcedo, and for New Granada, Juan de Castellanos on Antioquía and the Chocó, and Fernández Piedrahita. Last, for Peru or New Castile we have the *Commentarios reales* of the Inca Garcilaso, the history of Morúa, the *Nueva crónica* of Poma de Ayala, the *Relación* of Santa Cruz Pachacuti, the works of the Jesuits Arriaga and Anello Oliva, and those of Calancha, Montesinos, and Father Cobo.*

Scientific Development

Theories and Propositions †

Despite the strenuous efforts made to unify the aboriginal population, most of the ethnic groups continued to be dispersed, and even boundaries and political and territorial divisions of the Spanish colonies were not clearly set. Moreover, the prescribed mode of treatment of the Indians under the white men's control

---

* The reader may find the complete citations in Comas, Jiménez Moreno, Bernal, Schwab, and Steward mentioned above.

† This section is indebted to an article by Hoselitz (1950).

was, in its application, uncertain, changeable, and often highly contradictory. Thus we see on the one hand, extremely rigid legal criteria and the lack of a well-defined practical policy on the other.

In the eighteenth century, the impetus of encyclopedism, the progressive concepts of the enlightenment, and the mercantilist spirit of the age began to penetrate into the small circles of intellectuals and the power-holding elites. Many laws and edicts were modified by them for the good or ill of the Indians and mestizos as they began to discover their own American identity.

But this discovery is not theirs alone. Hobbes, Locke, Voltaire, and Montesquieu make specific references to the American Indians, while Rousseau discourses on the happy savages inhabiting the shores of the Orinoco. The references and descriptions of the American Indians go beyond mere reflections and chronicles. They constitute the first attempt to formulate logical theories and propositions about the Indians based on comparative data. Figures and facts tend to converge; the essential and basic characteristics are separate features; and the overall picture of human culture and society becomes clearer. There is a fresh conception of the unity of man and of the secondary or derived diversity of his works. However, that occurs in Europe. In America, only few avenues toward knowledge are discovered. It is not until the second half of the eighteenth century that we see glimpses of economic and political independence. But these attempts to establish an Americanist identity were isolationist and provincial in character.

The uprisings of Atahualpa and Tupac Amaru in the Andean mountain region represent a peculiar case for we have no scientific data of the causal factors which would give the necessary perspective for anthropological research. Similar social and cultural unknown factors might arise if some analytical research is carried on in order to explain the wherefore of the Mexican Indian and the mestizo, white, and *criollo* institutions of the eighteenth century, despite the studies of Chávez Orozco (1943), Chevalier (1956), Gibson (1964), Miranda (1952), and Zavala. These historical events and sociocultural conditions are of the greatest significance for the proper understanding of much of the subsequent "political independence" movement. Consequently, those of us who pride ourselves on being cultural and social anthropologists must systematically analyze the documents of the national archives. Of special importance are those sections dealing with land grants, bounties, labor, Indians, taxes and town finances, civil administration, domestic and overseas trade, and the sociopolitical role played by the establishment of the *Intendencias* into the provincial structures of New Spain.

In general terms, and particularly for the eighteenth century, the *Relaciones Jesuitas,* an impressive collection of seventy-three volumes, is an assemblage of ethnographic and sociological data which every student must know because of the political influence which these religious corporations, as genuine economic enterprises, had in America. The following are also of interest to the American scholar: Robertson's study of comparative synthesis, *History of America,* Jefferys' work on the French possessions in North and South America, and Boturini's *Catálogo Indiano.* For Mexico, the *Historias* of Clavijero and Antonio de Solis, and Villaseñor's *Teatro americano* are recommended. For Guatemala, there are Villagutierre and Fray Francisco Ximénez; for Colombia, the *Relaciones de mando* are a minimum requirement, and for the Andean peoples, the documents relating to Atahualpa, the *Memorias* of Tupac Amaru, and the *Estado del Perú* by Saharraura Tito Atauchi. Special mention should be made of the work of the Jesuit missionary, Florian Baucke, who concerned himself with the customs of Spaniards, *criollos,* and Indians in the territory of the viceroyalty of Buenos Aires. His work gives a meaningful illustration and a sociological representation of the different economic, social, and cultural groups.

Convergencies and Constructions *

The different theories of society and culture which were formulated in Europe in the eighteenth and nineteenth centuries all have three elements in common: origins, age, and change. Between Saint-Simon, who regards ideas as the force of progress, and Lenin, who is responsible for the ideological expansion of economic determinism, we have a constellation of students pur-

* I have taken these two concepts from Penniman (1935), although they are in relatively infrequent use today.

suing similar themes. They are distinguished by the specific criteria used, terminologies or units of classification, themes or subjects they dealt with, and the ability to compare and confront.

From the analytical information on the history of ethnological theory, and on the American natives, supplied by Lowie (1937), we must draw attention to Adolph Bastian's writings on the independent, yet similar, development of the social and cultural characteristics of the American Indian. His thesis had been used to substantiate the theory of the psychic unity of mankind (1878–89: 30–38). The studies of Bachofen and McLennan, in which new concepts, terminology, and classifications are introduced, make extensive reports on matriarchy, the place assigned to women, the abduction of the bride, marriage, and the laws of exogamy among the Iroquois, Aztecs, Mayas, Incas, and the Indians of the Orinoco, Amazon, and Chaco regions. Morgan observed the customs of the Iroquois and like Bachofen and McLennan was an evolutionist and a follower of cultural parallelism. In his writings, he draws astonishing inferences in order to achieve a comprehensive picture of social institutions. Edward Tylor, regarded as the father of ethnology, but really the godfather since he gave it its name, dealt with such American subjects as the origin of ceramics, myths, games of chance, ancestry, and residence rules of married couples. Among the groups he writes about are the Aztecs, Mayas, Incas, and the Patagonian and Fueguian Indians. Tylor was a creator of terms, concepts, and structural systems, but he was averse to systematization. He is also the author of a book on Mexico and the Mexicans. The erudite Frazer, in *The Golden Bough* deals in an a priori manner, but in great detail, with some aspects of primitive religion.

At the same time, but in open and explicit contrasting ideas, arose the English and German historical and diffusionist schools. Elliot Smith and W.J. Perry maintained that culture arose under exceptionally favorable circumstances, and Egypt must be the source of all higher culture. Thus, Egypt was the cradle from which culture spread to the rest of the world, including Mexico and Peru (Lowie 1937: 161–65). The present author considers Ratzel the leader and the most serious and methodological oriented man among the German diffusionists. Ratzel stressed mankind's essential uninventiveness, and explained the complexity of real history in terms of contact metamorphosis. Using the Toltec, Aztec, Maya, and Quechua as illustrations, Ratzel concluded that cultural similarities were due to the spread of cultural characteristics from a primeval community. Frobenius and Graebner made numerous ethnological comparisons between Africa, Oceania, and the ancient cultures of Peru, Central America, and Mexico with a view of isolating and diagnosing the "foci, circles and the particular system of culture strata." Father Schmidt and Father Koppers, departing somewhat from the earlier writers, emphasized "centers and circles" formed by influxes of different peoples who had respectively different influences on the American cultures.

Last, another group of scholars is formed by the French sociologists. De Tarde postulated certain laws of imitation, giving exaggerated importance to tradition. Le Bon emphasized the power of feelings and emotions as the elements which shaped the character and morals of people. Lévy-Bruhl, as a philosopher, was mainly concerned with the mentality of primitive peoples. Durkheim determined the elementary forms of religious life, the division of labor, the types of society, and some laws on social organization. Marett, dealing with the supernatural and religious phenomena, evolved an instructive theory, the most balanced thus far, on the value system of primitive man. Van Gennep, studying the initiation rites, and Eduard Hahn, mastering some sociological interpretations of economic development, may well belong to this group. Almost all of the last-mentioned writers were concerned with the Incas, Aztecs, Maya, and the primitive tribes of Central Brazil and Tierra del Fuego.

Synthesis: Diversity in Unity

To the above summary must be added the essential and representative fact that all those scholars to a greater or lesser extent dealt with a variety of topics such as utensils, tools, animals, people, houses, languages and dialects, the family, systems of kinship and of blood relationship, moral sentiments, religion, worship, rites, stories, legends, and myths. Nevertheless, their common interest in replies to questions concerning origins, ages, and changes from the simple to the complex forms of sociocultural life, their use of comparative methodology, their desire to see man as a whole, to assign a common origin to all culture, and above all, the attempt to address themselves and their studies to the cultural history of mankind gave the requisite unity to the theories and scientific aims of nineteenth century anthropology. For this reason, many of their works were read and discussed eagerly at the remarkable meetings of the Ethnological Society of Paris, founded in 1839, and at a like society founded in 1843 at London.

In fact, the scientific theories to which we have drawn attention show great diversity, as do many others of collateral or secondary value for this brief account of the development of anthropology in Latin America. At the same time the theories are unified. A few examples from sociology are highly representative of this synthesis, diversity in unity.

The three stages of evolution proclaimed by Auguste Comte, founder and publicizer of sociology, were to have a strong influence on the writings of his contemporaries and successors. It was Morgan's scientific treatise on primitive society, known throughout the world by the writings of Engels and Marx, which gave rise to the radical doctrine of historical materialism. Herbert Spencer, lecturer and popularizer par excellence, discoursed on the stages of savagery, barbarism, and civilization, through which all peoples of the world must pass. Acceptance by the scientific world of Darwin's *Origin of Species* helped promote a similar hypothesis for sociocultural levels.

We now arrive at synthesis and conclusion. The accumulated knowledge of anthropology in the nineteenth century was not strong enough to permit solid classifications and theories. Both evolutionism and diffusionism are mutually complementary doctrines; they are no more irreconcilable than are the products of man's mind and of his hands. Nevertheless, the apparently conflicting viewpoints, the different evaluations of logical sequences, and the contrasting aims of some scholars produced the most fruitful period yet known for the development of ideas on the individual, society, and culture.

There was a time lag before these ideas reached America. An example of convergence and construction, although of another type, is furnished by Humbolt's *Political Essay*. Humboldt, endowed with an encyclopedic intellect, wrote on nearly everything to be found in New Spain. Another example is Rafinesque's comparative treatise, *The American Nations,* and Herriot's book on Canada and regions of North and South America. Less important is Juarros' history of Guatemala. Furthermore, the Repository of Antiquities and the Natural History Collection merged in 1825, and became the National Museum of Mexico. The opening of Mexico's National Archives in 1823 by Lucas Alamán and the gathering and publication of ancient American documents by Dupaix and Lord Kingsborough were constructive works of the highest significance for the subsequent development of anthropology. Last, because of the long historical tradition of American studies, and the positive approach through geographical surveys and natural science research, we must mention the establishment of a good number of societies and academies of history, geography, statistics, and natural sciences (*Unión Panamericana* 1954). In these associations, members and guests read and discussed works which deserved the name of "anthropological studies."

Anthropology in Ibero-America *

Scattering Interests

In the second half of the nineteenth century many historians, naturalists, and travelers concerned themselves with certain regions of the Americas. However, their interests were quite varied, and there was consequently a random accumulation of data.†

It can be stated that John L. Stephens, who "discovered" the Mayas in 1841, initiated archaeological studies in Indo-America.‡ His findings aroused such interest that for more than forty years there is hardly a study on Mayan archaeology which fails to mention him. Next in time, the unreliable Prescott's books on

---

* The term *Ibero-America* might raise reasonable objections. However, in our history the influence and presence of cultural complexes transferred from an Iberian matrix constitute a possible common denominator or essential element in the behavior patterns of more than 80 percent of the people inhabiting Mexico, the West Indies, and Central and South America.

† I used some of the bibliographical information given by the authors mentioned above.

‡ In this section the term Indo-America refers to those portions of the continent which in the second half of the nineteenth century were still inhabited by natives or Indians who had actually reinforced their local and closed cultural behavior supposedly dating to before the sixteenth century.

the conquests of Mexico and Peru, Brasseur de Bourbourg who, while traveling through Mexico and Central America between 1857 and 1864, studied archaeological sites, indigenous languages, aboriginal customs, and some of the physical characteristics of the people, and George Squier (1858 and 1877), whose studies of the Central American countries and Peru contain much of interest to cultural and social anthropologists.

Among those who wrote about prehispanic America there are significant contributions displaying the enthusiasm and the humanistic spirit of their authors. Of general interest are the treatise of Bastian (1878–1889) and Bandelier's works (1877, 1878, and 1879) on the wars and war tactics of ancient Mexicans, the social organization and government of the Aztecs, and on their system of land ownership and inheritance. Other valuable works are Brinton's studies of American myths (1882) and of the Mayan chronicles. Worth mentioning also are Soler's essay (1887) on pre-Colombian America and Bancroft's volumes (1874–1882 and 1883–1888) on the native races of the Pacific States and on Mexico and Central America. Special mention should be made of the inter-American publications of Seler, Stoll (1884), Lumholtz (1900; 1904) and Sapper (1902) who in the closing years of the nineteenth century were representative of what was most notable about the German academic concern with the cultural history of the ancient inhabitants of the Americas. Accordingly, their writings bear the mark of scientific honesty even though both they and the above-mentioned authors understood honesty to mean great erudition with slim proof for their findings. During this time a great man appeared on the American scene. Because of his immense capacity for learning and work, subsequent decades reserved for Paul Rivet a rendezvous with history.

Among the various societies interested in Americanist studies, the following deserve mention: the American Ethnological Society, established in the second half of the nineteenth century, the *Société Américaine de France*, with its *Archives* (1859) and *Actes* (1863), the *Comission Scientifique du Mexique* which published its *Archives* between 1865 and 1867, the *Zeitschrift für Ethnologie* which began publication in 1869, the reports of the American Museum of Natural History, which began to appear in 1870, the Bureau of American Ethnology of the Smithsonian

Institution, founded in 1879, the American Anthropological Association, established in 1888, the *American Historical Review,* first published in 1895, the *Société des Américanistes* (Paris), which dates back to 1896, the *Annual Reports* of the Carnegie Institution since 1902, and the *Papers,* since 1908, of the famous school of American research (Archaeological Institute of America). In addition the *Anales* of the National Museum of Mexico were, by the first decade of the twentieth century, mainly devoted to anthropological subjects; since 1903, data of archaeological and ethnographic interest are to be found in the *Anales* of the National Museum of San Salvador, in historical publications of the Archives of Honduras, the Museum of San José (Costa Rica) and later in Guatemala's review *Central América* (1909).

There was no lack of enthusiastic scholars within each Latin American nation, and their anthropological interests varied widely. In Mexico, any selection would have to include the geographic, historic, and statistical *Atlas* of Ramírez (1858), Edward Tylor's book (1861), the historical studies of native languages made by Orozco y Berra, Garciá Cubas' *Atlas* (1858) and his geographic, statistical, descriptive, and historical table (1884), the histories of Chavero, the treatise of Velasco on geography and statistics (1889–1898), Diguet's ethnographic essays (1889), Lumholtz (1900; 1904), Sapper (1902), Preuss (1910; 1912), McGee (1898), and Starr (1901; 1904), Peñafiel's writings on demographic subjects, Hrdlicka's papers on different subject matters, and the immense work of compilation and editing done by Francisco del Paso y Troncoso (1905 *et seq.*). Regarding Central America, the *Memoria para la Historia del antiguo Reino de Guatemala* by García Pelaez (1854) is very stimulating, the same may be said of the histories and ethnographic descriptions made by Milla y Vidaurre (1879) and Peralta (1883; 1892).

For the Andean nations and regions, the ethnographic and linguistic studies of Ernst (1870–1887) on the Goajiro and Motilon Indians, Villavicencio's geography of Ecuador (1858), the geography of Peru by Paz Soldán (1862), and the geographic and statistical dictionary by another Paz Soldán (1877). Also the studies of Gonzáles Suárez (1878 and 1903) on the natives of Cañaris and the Indians of the Imbabura and Carchi provinces, Bandelier on Bolivia, Uhle on ancient Peru and Chile, the numerous compilations and bibliographies by José Toribio Medina (1882 *et seq.*) on the aborigines of Chile. Last, Codazzi's *Atlas* on geography and history of Colombia (1889), the two Restrepo's work (1892 and 1895, and 1929) on the Quimbaya and Chibcha Indians, and the valuable collections of historical documents edited by Jiménez de la Espada.

Most of the anthropological studies and the works published during the first three decades of the present century should be considered in this section. However, a mere listing of the titles would not justify the chapter subheading; the crucial proof would be in the reading. Thomas and Swanton made a comparative study of languages; Holmes and Joyce, eager United States archeologists, described the ancient Central American cultures; Starr, Hrdlicka, and Nicolas León devoted a great part of their lives to study of the physical anthropology of some Mexican Indians; Tozzer (1907) compared the Mayas and the Lacandon; Paul Radin explored in Mexico and Central America; Recinos and Villacorta dealt with Guatemala; Conzemius (1927–1928 *et seq.*) studied the Paya, Lenca, Sumo, Mosquito, Rama Indians and other native groups of Central America; Salas (1908) had contributed to the ethnography and history of Venezuela and Colombia.

In addition, Nordenskjöld traveled throughout South America and wrote about Peru and Bolivia and about the Cuna Indians and Choco (1929 and 1938) of Panama; Bolinder (1917) studied the Motilon Indians and (1925) the ancient Chibcha; Koenigswald (1908) investigated the Cayúa; while Jijón y Caamaño continued to write on the Indians of Ecuador. Rivet produced even more and better research especially on the linguistics and comparative ethnography of South America. The German group continued to be active. Markham (1911), Bingham (1922), and Means (1931) wrote in literary fashion about the Inca, and Bowman (1915) used the same style on the South American Indians. Ricardo Palma, Tello, and Luis Valcarcel recorded Peruvian traditions, with their pronounced and positive nationalism; Latchman (1909) and Guevara (1913) studied the Araucanians; while Gunsinde and Köppers devoted themselves to thorough research on the aborigines of Tierra del Fuego, and published abundantly. By then, Franz Boas rises over the horizon. A new act was to be opened in the development of anthropology in Ibero-America.

Integration: Men and Works

The great mass of written material on the culture of American aborigines was bound to lead to the first attempts of serious and scientifically evaluated synthesis. Franz Boas made such an attempt, and with success. His varied interests (Lowie, 1937: 128–55, and 1947: Vol.-24: 303–22 and Goldschmidt, editor, 1959) are too well known to be repeated here. Actually, he was the first integrator of anthropology, and the stimulator of Americanist studies. His work as researcher and teacher of anthropology has always been a source of pride for Columbia University: The mark he left on the science of man was deep and broad. He not only criticized many of the old ethnological theories on origins, chronology, and the reasons given for the persistence, change, or disappearance of certain social and cultural forms of human life, but he laid down also the methods and field techniques which should be applied according to different areas and subject matters. This integrative work is perhaps his greatest contribution to anthropology.

In other areas of research, during the first decades of our present century, it should be mentioned that the descriptive and comparative studies of Wissler (1917) referred to the Indians of the New World. Lehmann's *Zentral-Amerika* (1920), Krickeberg's *Amerika* (1922), Spinden (1928), Schultze-Jena (1933, 1935, and 1938), the range of Rivet's work, and the detailed studies of Termer (1930) are part of our anthropological knowledge. Consequently, they too may be listed as integrated works, and at the same time they represent the last pieces of overall views taken by single individuals. From that time on the compiled material led to plurality of interests, to specialization, and to the ascent of research teams; thus, new concepts, methods, and field techniques began to be used.

Turning our attention to Mexico, we must point out that there have always been some scholars concerned with the things of yesteryear. Furthermore, the early dates marking the establishment of the Repository of Antiquities and the National Archives, the founding (1833) of the National Institute of Geography and Statistics, and the opening (1857) of the first public library are indicative of nationalism among the people of Mexico, and a proof of their interest in intellectual matters and their concern with the things of tomorrow.

About 1865, the National Museum, at Moneda Street, housed ancient manuscripts, pottery, old maps, and ethnographic charts, which totaled some 250 items; in 1877 it published its first *Anale;* in 1885 the Federal Government expanded the Inspectorate of Archaeological Monuments; some years later the Museum acquired clothing, work tools, and domestic utensils of various ethnic groups; in 1895 the Eleventh International Congress of American Scholars was held, the first to take place in Ibero-America. Later, the Museum took on another name (Museum of Archaeology, History and Ethnology), cutting itself loose from its old ties with the natural sciences, and published its own *Anales* We are now at 1910, the beginning year of the Mexican Revolution, which marked also a new educational achievement: the establishment of the International School of American Archaeology and Ethnography, the first school of this kind in the world.

On this point, Columbia University can feel justly proud. The plan for the School was drawn up by its President, Nicholas Murray Butler, "in collaboration with representatives of Universities of France, Germany and the United States, and those of the Mexican Government." Seler, Gordon, Boas, Dixon, and others signed the statutes, and Seler, Boas, and Tozzer served successively as directors in the first three years of the life of the school (Comas 1950: 103).

In addition to the "great sages" who laid the foundations of the science of man in Mexico, there now appeared a visionary. Manuel Gamio,* a graduate of Columbia, where he had studied under Boas, fought for the establishment of a Bureau of Anthropology in every Ibero-American country. In his first theoretical and practical treatise, *Forjando patria,* published in 1916, he set down what needed to be done in anthropology: "Approach in an objective and scientific manner the problems of improving the lot of the aborigines, through integral study of their biological and cultural characteristics, that being the only method of ascer-

---

* Most of the data and bibliographical references on Doctor Gamio are taken from Comas (1956: 1–26).

taining their immediate needs and the most effective way of satisfying them." (Is this idea a partial reason for our present conference?) In 1917 he achieved his ambition; in the Mexican Ministry of Agriculture the first Bureau of Anthropology of Ibero-America was created. He then began his comprehensive study on Teotihuacan. Some years later he founded the short-lived review *Ethnos,* of which he was the owner and which was wholly dedicated to American anthropology. He also contributed to *El México Antiguo,* which is required reading to this day, and to *Mexican Folk-Ways,* which appeared from 1925 to 1937.

In his study entitled *La población del valle de Teotihuacán,* he deals with the environment, the archaeology, the ethnic and social evolution during hispanic times, and the colonial society, and suggests ways to improve the lot of the present population.

However, in the author's opinion Manuel Gamio made mistakes both in choosing the area of Teotihuacán, and in selecting some members of his team of collaborators. Regarding the first mistake, the archaeological and historical reconstruction and its supposed correlation with present-day Mexican life could not be scientifically proved; regarding some of his fellow researchers, friendship turned out not to be the proper basis for selecting a working team. Summing up, Gamio's great merit was the power of vision he exercised in an endeavor to merge the results of a number of disciplines (history and science among others) and the attempt to produce an integrated if not an analytical whole. A steady stream of his varied and valuable ideas appeared in different periodicals, and he gave such open proof of moral integrity and civic courage that he had to leave his country. Back again (1925) at Columbia University, he used some grants to explore Guatemalan archaeological sites; later, he wrote two studies (1930; 1931) for the Social Science Research Council on Mexican immigration to the United States, and on the Mexican immigrant.

At this point, Paul Rivet, Alfonso Caso, and Robert Redfield deserve to be mentioned. The first was an experienced ethnologist who integrated his findings; the second was an organizational genius; and the third is important for his great capacity to act as a creator, and transmitter of original and fruitful ideas.

Born in 1876, Rivet devoted himself to anthropology from an early age; he was a member of the *Société Américaine de France,* and founding member of the *Société des Américanistes.* At the turn of the century, he was already working on linguistics, prehistory, archaeology, ethnography, and physical anthropology, for there was hardly any part of the anthropological world with which Rivet was not concerned. His encyclopedic knowledge led him to compare Australia and Oceania with America, and different American ethnic groups among themselves. Starting in 1919, and for over twelve years, his bibliographic compilations on American studies appeared regularly in the *Journal de la Société des Américanistes.* He traveled through nearly all of Indo-America and Ibero-America, doing surveys and research, and giving lectures and courses on anthropology to students and the general public. As we shall see, he was to play an important role later in the formal development of Colombian "nationalist" anthropology.

Alfonso Caso is mentioned here because of his talent for order and composition, his defense of administrative and cultural achievements, and, because it was he who mapped out the course of modern Mexican anthropology. Having undertaken in 1925 the study of Mexico's ancient history, he worked as an archaeologist in the National Museum; from 1930 he explored the archaeological site of Monte Albán, Oaxaca; in 1933 he was appointed Director of the Museum; and some years later he was to discover at Monte Albán burial places containing magnificent jewelry. His subsequent activity in the National Institute of Anthropology and History is one of the cornerstones of Mexican anthropology.

Following other paths than those chosen by Gamio and Caso, although sharing with them their humanist approach and integrationist interest in American anthropology, Robert Redfield concerned himself with the ideal distribution and quality of social and cultural constants, and his work is more original and scientific than Gamio's. He studied a community (Tepoztlán, 1930) and its contemporary culture and society, and he tried to establish the why and wherefore of certain processes. Moreover, taking into account the role and distribution of some sociocultural complexes, he built together a whole which he then separated into its component parts by means of analysis.

Although ethnological research had continued in Indo-America, and a number of Americanists (Gusinde, 1931 and 1937; Hernández de Alba, 1936; Karsten, 1935; Kirchhoff, 1931; Kroeber, 1939; Lothrop, 1937; Métraux, 1936; Radin, 1933; Rivet, 1939; Father Schmidt, 1937; Termer, 1935; and Thompson, 1933) were still concerned with origins and historical correlations, in the 1930s the influence of Boas was increasingly felt among anthropologists, and the methods and techniques used were bound to change.

Nationalist Anthropology *

The Experience of Mexico

It is not in vain that a profound awareness of the ancient cultures permeated the very air breathed by the Mexican people. Their feelings toward the Indians, whether positive or negative, were at all times and everywhere openly expressed. The things of yesteryear had been more important than the looming future as factors of cultural causation in the various social strata of the country. Accordingly, the doctrine proclaimed in the 1930s by General Lázaro Cárdenas in favor of the disinherited (Indians and farmers) and the dispossessed (industrial workers and petty officials) met with maximum response, seeing that it was intended to benefit the majority of the country's inhabitants. His agrarian laws, the redistribution of privately owned idle and cultivated land, and his programs for the economic, social, and cultural betterment of the rural population were received more as gifts of a Messiah than as the consequence of evolution resulting in progress and human justice. This paternalistic attitude gave a new shape to Mexican politics, and influenced even certain professional and intellectual milieus.

This was the moment awaited by Gamio and Caso; a new social value was being given to Mexico and to the Mexicans. Men who were teaching history and anthropology in the old halls of the National Museum joined forces with some instructors of the Universidad Obrera and with others from the then recently es-

---

* Beginning here, bibliographies of many individual writers are not supplied because their work should be known to every professional anthropologist concerned with Indo- and Ibero-America.

tablished (1937) *Instituto Politéchnico* to set up a curriculum of anthropology with two special branches, physical and social anthropology. The aim was to "promote at all costs the effort to achieve the status of independence being made in recent years by a handful of Mexican researchers . . ." (Jiménez Moreno 1948–49: 137). The educational authorities turned a benevolent eye on the project; formal courses were begun in 1938, and D. F. Rubin de la Borbolla, a diligent and enthusiastic promoter, became the coordinator of seven professors and five students! Caso, Kroeber, Mendizábal, Redfield, and Rivet were among the advisors. At the same time, economic assistance was received from the new Department of Indian Affairs. This agency felt the need for specific plans and programs of action for the "natives," and this led to the emergence of the anthropology section of the Department.

A number of facts should be mentioned here to emphasize the establishment of the curriculum of anthropology: It was nothing less than the crystallization of Mexican nationality or, at any rate, of one aspect of it. In September 1935, the Seventh Scientific American Congress was held in Mexico City. In 1936, the first Regional *Indigenista* Congress took place, and the findings of the few Mexican anthropologists and sociologists attending were used to illustrate the so-called indigenist problems. A few months later, the Linguistic Week organized by the National University and the Summer Institute of Linguistics of Arkansas, was held. Papers were presented on indigenous languages (still spoken by millions of persons) and on the need to use them in order that attempts to "integrate the Indian into national life" might be successful. In 1937 and 1938 there were other Indigenist Congresses at which further anthropological studies on Indo-America were presented (Cámara 1961: 35–36). These events, combined with the awakening of a social conscience as a result of the new redistribution of land, the end of the haciendas, the expropriation of the oil properties held by foreign interests, the trade union movement, and the fair treatment of the proletariat, contributed to the emergence of Mexican nationalist anthropology.

There were other developments as well. In 1938, the *Revista de Historia de América* was established. By this time, Pericot's work, *América Indígena* (1936) was already known. Paul Rivet came as the first Visiting Professor to what was to be the National School of Anthropology and History, Jiménez Moreno published the first systematic ethnographical bibliography and Heliodoro Valle attempted a bibliography on the Maya. Students and enthusiastic amateurs went to the field to work in the native, social, physical, and cultural environment. In addition, the University of California (Berkeley and Los Angeles) sent some of its researchers to the Mexican Northwest; the Carnegie Institution, with Kidder and Redfield, had research teams in the Maya area; and members of the National Geographic Society studied the Olmeca area. Furthermore, Zingg studied the Tarahumara and Huichol Indians, Ralph Beals the Mayas Bevan the Chinantec, Soustelle and Mendizábal the Otomi, Parsons the Zapotec, and McQuown the Totonac, while Spicer was among the Yaquis, Swadesh and Jules Henry with the Tarascan, Villa Rojas was beginning to study the Indians of Chiapas, and Boggs published in 1939 his bibliography of Mexican folklore. Directly or indirectly all of them contributed to the theoretical and practical teaching of anthropology in Mexico. The Tarascan and Maya projects resulted, respectively, in the collecting of basic data for experimental applied anthropology designed to solve the economic difficulties of the Indians in Mexico, and a scientific approach to record the processes of change in Yucatán (Cámara, 1961.).

Within the background of all these promising developments, Gamio and Caso were taking constructive actions. The former, while holding important office in the national government (still perhaps the best way for an intellectual to make a decent living in the Ibero-American countries), had been biding his time, waiting for another opportunity. In 1939 the First Assembly of Philologists was held, and there was established the Council of Indian Languages, an organization that took part in literacy programs and campaigns. Furthermore, the twenty-seventh International Congress of Americanists took place, while in 1940 the First Inter-American Indigenist Congress was held. Gamio took part in these three important events for the development of anthropology in Mexico, contributing fresh ideas, his vigor, and his ideal of long standing: *indigenismo*. Two years later, he held another high post, that of director of the Inter-American Indigenist Institute, discharging his duties with loyalty and tenacity. From that position he promoted and coordinated the main features of *indigenismo* in Ibero-America, and was the author of all the unsigned editorials published in the reviews *América Indígena* and *Boletín Indigenista* from 1942 to 1956, the year of his death. In the opinion of the present writer, his best works are *Forjando Patria* and the books on the Mexican immigrants. Gamio's *Hacia un México nuevo: problemas sociales* (1935) is a fine example of intellectualism combined with applied anthropology.

Pursuing other aims, Alfonso Caso founded in 1937 the *Boletín Bibliográfico de Antropología Americana;* in 1939 he was appointed Director of the National Institute of Anthropology and History, and in 1948 Director of the National Indigenist Institute. He can take much of the credit for the up-to-date publication of the *Anales* of the Museum and those of the Institute, of *El México Antiguo,* of the *Revista Mexicana de Estudios Antropológicos* (a publication which was preceded by *Estudios Históricos,* which he founded in 1927), of *Mexican Folk-Ways* and other periodicals. Above all, he deserves credit for the development of the Mexican Society of Anthropology and History, the National School of Anthropology and History, and the establishment of the Coordinating Indigenist Centers.

Similar Experiences Elsewhere

The first successes of the Mexican anthropological movement soon became known abroad. However it was not so much because of the impact of the Mexican experience in effecting economic, social, and cultural change but because of demagogic comments on the "new socialist state in the process of formation." Nevertheless, it may properly be stated that once Mexican theoretical and practical anthropology had received formal recognition, even under succeeding national governments, it continued to develop at such a rate that it influenced similar movements in Guatemala, Colombia, and Peru. We shall discuss these events very briefly, since we lack detailed information.

In Guatemala, the historical-archaeological scene was dominated by the Carnegie Institution and the Middle American Research Institute, although the new series of *Anales* of the

Guatemalan Society of Georgraphy and History began to be published in 1925 as one more step in the long process of the affirmation of nationalism. These publications regularly reported archaeological, historical, and ethnographic subject matters. In addition, the travels and explorations were continued and they were aimed at the reconstruction of prehispanic history. Sapper and Termer maintained their reputations as outstanding academic writers. Meanwhile, Wisdom studied the Chorti, La Farge was at Santa Eulalia, and McBryde in Sololá; Villacorta published his *Geathemala* series (new editions of chronicles and chroniclers), and David Vela and Goubaud were doing field work on the modern Quiches. Added to this, Redfield and his associates (Andrade, Tax, and Wagley) were working on what after some ten years was to be the largest archive on the modern cultural anthropology of Guatemala and its neighboring countries (microfilm collection, 1946–1949). While it is difficult to describe this period as one of nationalist anthropology, in view of the very slight participation of administrative and technical personnel of Guatemala, the influence and the results of these studies created the necessary atmosphere for later achievements with clearly nationalist overtones.

In Colombia it may certainly be said that an academic and national anthropology was created. It is in Colombia that Paul Rivet performed his many exploits in American studies. Full of enthusiastic appreciation for the experience of Mexico, he went to Bogotá to negotiate with high government officials. In June 1941 he succeeded in establishing the National Institute of Ethnology and the beginnings of formal teaching. Moreover, Pérez de Barradas was engaged in archaeology and the *Revista de Indias* was publishing good data on the cultural history of Colombia. At the same time, the National Archaeological Museum was opened. The first number of its review appeared in 1943, and Duque Gómez, the Pinedas, and the Reichel-Dolmatoffs published the results of their field and academic researches. The Choco, Karibs, Motilones, Chimila, Kwaiker, Chamis, Guambian, Guajiros, Kogi, and some jungle Indian tribes were ethnologically reported. The work received the generous assistance of the Rockefeller Foundation, the American Museum of Natural History, and the French Government.

During the same period, Antonio García, an economist, began his struggle for the establishment of the Indigenist Institutes (central and departmental), expending great effort and losing part of his own small capital in these commendable endeavors. His *indigenist* program had to await the appropriate moment, even as Gamio and Caso in Mexico had had to bide their time until the right opportunity. Last, it should be noted that in 1940 the Center for Linguistic and Ethnological Research in Colombian Amazonia, under the intelligent and fruitful direction of Marcelino de Castellví, began very significant work in the Putumayo area.

With reference to the crystallization of Peruvian nationalist anthropology, it should be stated that Palma, Tello, and Valcarcel had for a number of years been writing on the traditions and archaeology of the territory of Peru and on its ancient history. The *Inca*, first published in 1923, had not left a profound influence; nevertheless, Monje's articles on adaptation in the Andes and the books of Castro Pozo, Mariátegui, and Poblete Troncoso on indigenous communities, the "Peruvian reality," and agricultural and mining workers, respectively, had aroused a national political consciousness, both among the peasant and working masses and the Peruvian bureaucratic and intellectual elites. The work of Haya de la Torre, strongly nationalistic and anti-Yankee, made him the leader of *Aprismo*, a political movement which struggled for Peruvian emancipation and the elimination of all foreign influences in Peru.

Regarding cultural science, the National Museum of Lima already had a tradition behind it, and in 1931 it began to publish its journal. The *Boletin Bibliográfico* of the Central Library of the University of San Marcos reported on books and pamphlets dealing with Peru, and similar information about the Andean area, the Amazon zone, and the writings of "eminent national authors." In the Peruvian highlands, there were enthusiastic "historians" and "archaeologists" who formed "groups," and "friends" who published pamphlets. In 1936, the Wenner-Gren Foundation gave them financial assistance, and more serious archaeological explorations were begun, and a review was edited. In 1938 the Magdalena Museum was opened in Lima. Next year, the Seventeenth International Congress of Americanists met there, and the Institute of Andean Research began its important work.

As the reader may well conclude, these events, because of their nature and purposes, constitute positive factors in the emergence of Peruvian anthropology although less coherent and less well organized than that in Mexico.

Contemporary Anthropology

Achievements and Affirmations

Major problems for students of American anthropology were: the origins of the aboriginal cultures, their cultural relationships, and the deduced or inferred chronologies of prehistory, later epochs, and cycles of cultural history.

In Mexico, Guatemala, Colombia, and Peru there emerged a science which was nurtured and developed by nationalist thinking. Nevertheless, at this point two separate interests came together. The economic, administrative, and technical aid given by foreign countries, especially the United States, was motivated as much by their interest in the future well-being of the natives as by their desire to amass fresh and original material in what had traditionally been regarded as an anthropologically important laboratory. Both at the beginning and at the end, the catalyst which integrated anthropology and the attitude which united the anthropologists has been the concept of culture and, above all, the common belief of the anthropologists in the equality and goodness of men.

Thus, since the establishment of Mexico's National School of Anthropology and History, we may well speak of a contemporary anthropology.* The writings of Redfield, Linton, and Herskovits (1936) on acculturation have been decisive. Even works on ancient Mexican history relied on them for fundamental concepts. In the thirties and forties important methodological changes had taken place. The idea of reconstructing the ancient history of Indo-America gave way to an overriding interest in

* Because of the abundant anthropological material amassed during this contemporary phase, we are compelled to carry selection to a point where we may lay ourselves open to criticism for mentioning situations and data which are not quite representative but are illustrative.

direct observation of sociocultural processes and the phenomenon of change. The concepts of culture areas, ages, and distribution of traits and cultural centers of tribal groups were now studied in terms of communities and larger social frameworks, with a view to distinguishing trends in culture change (Steward 1943 and 1949a; 669–772) and in the national American cultures. Interest now centered on Ibero-America.

My point is of twofold nature for it relates both to methodology and concepts. Where methods are concerned, it must be noted that, from being interested in tribal and primitive groups, we were shifting to the study of communities resulting from social contact and cultural interchange between America and Europe. These communities seemed so amply represented and so clearly defined that Beals (1938) wrote of the emergence of a new and distinct culture—the American culture. Regarding the conceptual aspect, anthropologists necessarily began to deal with phenomena (agricultural and handicraft production and distribution, social structures and relations, "moving" into distinct cultural groups or social sectors, ways, and customs of the people, and religious and political thinking and organization) which had previously been the academic heritage of economists, sociologists, and psychologists. Later, our publications began to include statistical data. That was something new for anthropology in general, and especially for American anthropology.

The growth of community studies in Mexico, Guatemala, Peru, and other areas of Ibero-America and publication in the preceding two decades are positive proof that this new genre of research was pioneering and welcomed (Cline, 1952–32: 218–42). Robert Redfield and his methods and objectives became one of the most discussed and highly controversial issues, as is only natural in the case of an innovator and his substantive and deeply thought-out conceptual and methodological scheme. Hundreds of researchers accepted, defended, and applied his ideas while others refuted, condemned, or disdained them. He was criticized for his antihistorical approach, his failure to take national society into account, and it was claimed that his folk-urban continuum was hypothetical and utopian. Nevertheless, if Oscar Lewis (1951) found opposed forms of behavior in Tepoztlán, that was because he had a different scientific approach and wanted to find them; if Redfield failed to study a hacienda or stock-raising farm in Yucatan, that was a deliberate avoidance on his part. Despite these "faults," the community studies represent a rare case of group participation in the field of American studies, an affirmation of a new anthropological trend in Ibero-America, and a highly praised contribution to social theory in general.

In other areas of intellectual activity Julian Steward (1943, 1946, and 1955) suggested new ideas and posed new problems related to research on cultural change in Ibero-America, and proceeded to edit seven encyclopedic volumes as a synthesis of the cultural history of man in South America. The *Handbook of South American Indians* constituted another great anthropological work. The adjustments, additions, new prospects, and criteria proposed by Steward for the study of areas led to fresh achievements and postulates for contemporary American anthropology.

The Second World War caused the United States of America to pay greater attention to all its neighbors south of the Rio Grande. The founding of the Institute of Social Anthropology in the Smithsonian Institution brought together a scholarly, trained group of anthropologists who traveled in some Ibero-American regions and who were officially associated with local scholars and administrative personnel in their anthropological research. Students and teachers of the schools of anthropology in Mexico, Peru, and Brazil participated enthusiastically in that work, and their findings resulted in the formation of new postulates of Ibero-American anthropology. Those of us who in one form or another collaborated on the community studies, on the *Handbook of South American Indians,* and on the studies of the Institute of Social Anthropology were always aware of the dichotomy and the apparent contradiction between the different approaches; nevertheless, this may well have been due to the immaturity of our own knowledge at that time. The present writer found it truly bewildering, but extremely profitable, to work on community studies with Sol Tax, to help Kirchhoff on the indigenous history of Central America for the *Handbook,* and to receive guidance from Beals, Brand, and Foster of the Institute of Social Anthropology. In addition, the writer traveled in South America for two years (1945 and 1946) obtaining first hand knowledge of the research done for the *Handbook,* and of the work carried on by local anthropologists. Further enlightenment came when engaged in sociological studies in the highlands of Boyacá, Colombia, and ethnographic studies among the Quechuas of Ecuador and Peru, and later helping Antonio García establish indigenist institutes in Colombia and Ecuador.

To sum up, the achievements and affirmations of anthropology in America have resulted in shifting the center of gravity from Indo-Americanism to Ibero-Americanism. The scientific findings are evidenced by the copious bibliography on community studies from Mexico, Central and South America, and by the studies suggested, produced, and perfected by the Committee on World Area Research, of the Social Science Research Council (Hall 1947, Wagley 1948, Tax *et al.* 1949, and Steward, 1955).

Publications and Teaching

In the preceding sections we have mentioned some of the more significant works, either generally representative or illustrating some particular feature, related to anthropology and to its development in Indo-America and, subsequently, in Ibero-America. Nevertheless, we must ask ourselves this crucial question: Has sufficient use been made of this work? Our answer, although we will have to substantiate it, is in the negative.

The purpose of the organization and operation of any institution is to preserve a part of an existing social order and, at the same time, to organize and control any desired changes by setting up the necessary machinery for efficient adaptation and adjustment. That is the very nature and essence of institutional forms of behavior. The science with which we are concerned, anthropology in America, has never really been a vital component of society and culture; consequently, its institutionalization is yet to be brought about. As noted above, it is not enough for a person to become an anthropologist just to ponder on Man or want to study him, understand him, and help him. Even the efforts to establish a national anthropology were not, to tell the truth, institutionalized, although they did provide the motivations for exploration, scientific achievements, numerous publications, and the establishment of formal teaching centers.

But who directed these activities and how many learned from them? On the one hand, there was a very small intellectual elite, representing a composite of men of vision, organizers, administrators, researchers, popularizers, and teachers; on the other hand were the students, emotionally or rationally oriented, who assimilated the expressly stated and obvious ideas without bringing to them a mature critical sense resulting from comparative analysis, substantive evaluation, and scientific synthesis. Thus, valuable as were the bibliographical lists of Schwab, Pericot, Jiménez Moreno, Steward, Comas, Bernal, and others, and the lists of anthropological publications compiled by Beals, Bennett, Métraux, Redfield, *et al.,* they reached a limited number of individuals and seldom resulted in group motivations. To give another illustration, who among Ibero-Americans has followd the suggestions of Beals, Redfield, and Tax (1943) on anthropological problems relating to the peoples of Mexico and Guatemala, or those posed by Steward regarding South America? In fact, only a handful. The general picture was one of isolation, inadequate intercommunication, and very little teamwork. It may be that the United States scientists who did research in Ibero-America or in Indo-America have read more of these publications and with greater profit; if so, they did not have the necessary breadth of approach: Their specialization and one-sided attitude held them in iron bonds.

A representative example of other institutional agencies set up for the purpose of dissemination of knowledge is the Pan American Union. Its many and varied informative publications, monographs, technical handbooks, and special studies represent a great and invaluable effort by its Office of Social Studies; yet very few professionals have the studies on their shelves and, what is worse, our libraries are short of many issues. Incredible as it may seem, even the specialized centers and national offices of the Organization of American States and other inter-American organisms do not have all these publications on hand. This inaccessibility of published material applies also to the volumes of the *Handbook of Latin American Studies,* and materials issued by the Pan American Institute of Geography and History, the National Institute of Anthropology and History of Mexico, the Inter-American Indigenist Institute and the national indigenist institutes, the Proceedings of the international Congresses of Americanists (Comas 1954), the Indigenist Bibliography of

Mexico and Central America (Parra and Jiménez Moreno 1954), and the Bibliography of Archaeology and Ethnography by Bernal. As other examples of publications which are poorly distributed and scarcely used, we may mention *Las dimensiones de la cultura* (Erasmus 1953), the articles edited by Kroeber in *Anthropology Today* and by Thomas in *Current Anthropology*, the tremendous collection of translations, reprints, and original works of the *Seminario de Integración Social Guatemalteca* (1956–1959), of the *Revista Colombiana de Antropología*, and of *Perú Indígena*.

In our opinion, the scarcity of these excellent publications and their limited use and application is due mainly to poorly organized distribution by the responsible offices and to lack of interest on the part of the "scholars" in what is happening and what is being done in our contemporary American anthropology. Fortunately, at this very moment, we are receiving a great deal of information on the development of the social sciences in Ibero-America. Perhaps, gatherings like this Conference, at least where we are concerned, will bridge the gap between the periodical or occasional publications and the purposes they are supposed to serve.

As we all know, where the teaching of anthropology is concerned prior to the middle of the past century, both in Europe and in America, only a few courses and informal lectures were offered on ethnology and ethnography. These were, moreover, either very general or extremely specialized, viewing primitive man and the American Indian as astronomers view the distant stars through powerful telescopes. Now, a hundred years later, our ethnology and cultural and social anthropology in most cases view the American primitives and their nonprimitive descendants as units and laboratory elements, making use of high precision instruments which could be likened to microscopes, and resulting in excessive specialization. Consequently, the aims of anthropology and the teaching programs are completely different. I shall attempt to illustrate this situation in both quantitative and qualitative terms.

My first example is the National School of Anthropology and History in Mexico, with which I am familiar. Present teaching consists of three levels of curricula. First, there is a series of ten courses which must be taken by every student. These teach him historical anthropology in general and four of its subbranches: physical anthropology, archaeology, ethnology, and linguistics; second, the student is given another group of ten fundamental courses which impart to him appreciation and knowledge of the particular branch of anthropology he wishes to pursue; and, last, he is given a total of eight assignments of a specialized, regional or local, character relating to that particular subbranch. The graduate program should be completed in four years, the fourth year being devoted to field or laboratory work to assemble the necessary material for a dissertation or thesis. The faculty is composed of forty-eight instructors, each of whom has from three to eight hours of classwork a week. No tuition fees have ever been charged, since our school is under the administration of the Ministry of Public Education.

In the twenty-seven years of its existence, our school has admitted more than 1,000 students, of whom only 92 graduated; we have had students from 14 different countries, the United States and the Central and South American nations being prominent among them, but Mexico has always been the main supplier. Despite the small number of graduates in proportion to enrolled students, our work is highly commendable and unique.

Critical analysis, however, brings to light some negative aspects: first, an inadequate background of general culture on the part of the entering students; second, an extremely high percentage of dropouts, owing to various factors, including bewilderment apparently brought about by lack of a clear understanding of what the profession of anthropoligist really is; third, a general resistance to studying anthropological works written in foreign languages (especially English), attributable to "nationalist sentiments," which makes it difficult indeed to acquire basic knowledge; fourth, insufficient theoretical training stemming from lack of practice in formulating abstract ideas; fifth, confusion and even despair arising from the great disparity between the traditional curriculum with its historical approach and the public demand for a new type of knowledge and of specialists in the social sciences; and sixth, the part-time and scattered activities of the instructors which do not offer an opportunity for a close teacher-student relationship.

Other centers which teach anthropology at the university level exist at Bogotá and Medellín, Colombia, and at the Ethnological Institute of the University of San Marcos in Lima. We have no specific or statistical information on the subject; nevertheless, we hazard the guess that their deficiencies are caused by factors similar to those operating in Mexico.

Attention may be drawn, by way of comparison, to a few very important facts regarding students of anthropology in the United States, since they are bound to exercise a decisive influence in Ibero-America. At the moment, over 800 professionals, for the most part Ph.D.'s in anthropology, are teaching and doing research work in some 100 departments, schools, and faculties of the many universities which offer advanced degrees. In all these centers in which anthropology is taught, there is an annual average of 2,000 students working for a master's or doctor's degree. Where courses and programs are concerned, the departments offer one course in American anthropology at the very least, and more than 25 now have in addition two or three courses on Latin America, while special programs exist in 14 universities for study and work in Indo-America or Ibero-America. Last, of the 344 Ph.D.'s conferred by 64 universities in the period 1959–1963, 77 dissertations were written on Indo-America and Ibero-America, and these may be broken down as follows: 36 related to Mexico, 14 to Central America, and the rest to South America, with a majority on Peru.*

The Future of Anthropology in Ibero–America

Any attempt to sum up the cultural and social anthropology which we have created in Mexico would require us to refer to the studies of the cultural and social characteristics of certain Indian and mestizo groups for purposes of historical reconstruction or description of situations and conditions which exist, especially on the study of communities today. This is the core of our anthropology and the information obtained has been utilized, *inter alia*, for: first, publicizing subjects of historical interest; second,

* Sources: *Guide to Graduate Departments of Anthropology*, for the Years 1962–63, 1963–64, and 1964–65, published by the American Anthropological Association, Washington, D.C.

publication of sociological monographs; third, evaluation of projects and execution of programs intended to integrate into the national culture some half-million individuals regarded as indigenous; fourth, active collaboration in the literacy campaigns of the Federal Government; fifth, formulation of effective operational standards for the Social Rural Welfare Centers; sixth, analysis of cultural and social aspects of the planning and construction of roads and highways; seventh, contributing to the growth of tourism through the preparation of guides and of descriptive literature; eighth, working for the establishment and maintenance of the various regional anthropological institutes and museums in the country; ninth, participation in congresses, round tables, discussion committees, and conferences, held in or out of Mexico; and, tenth, training future generations of anthropologists, both in our National School and in the specialized study centers of some of the provincial universities.

The nature and character of the anthropological activities described above are fully comprehensible and justified if we take into account the origins and *raison d'être* of our School of Anthropology and History and of the other Mexican academic and administrative institutions. It will be recalled that there has always been in Mexico an interest in her ancient and traditional cultures, as well as a desire to bring social justice to dispossessed or disinherited groups. The movement toward change as reflected in the industrialization and modernization of the Mexican nation, although in apparent contradiction with the general philosophy of most of the country's inhabitants, was in fact not incongruent but rather complementary, and advantageous. A new sociocultural synthesis was attempted in Mexico; the roots of the traditional cultures provided the nourishment for the affirmation and consolidation of a unique industrial society which is simultaneously singular and universal in character.

Regarding the present situation and condition of cultural and social anthropology in the other countries of Central and South America with which we are concerned in this essay,* there are very few professional anthropologists. Nevertheless, there is an eager desire to study and learn about the behavior of their vari-

---

* We remind the reader that in this paper we have dealt almost exclusively with the development of anthropology in Mexico, Guatemala, and parts of Colombia and the Andean nations.

ous ethnic groups and national subgroups and, above all, to make practical use, wherever appropriate, of the foresighted and progressive teachings of applied anthropology, more, however, as a matter of bureaucracy and current fashion than as a system of thought and action. Emotion and dilettantism prevail over reason and scientific objectivity. But then, how could our outlook on life have been different? It has been shaped by political bossism, and internal and external exploitation (colonialism in the economic and the cultural spheres in the past and in our own day) coupled with the refusal to reform and reorient the anachronistic, misunderstood, and misapplied Monroe Doctrine.

The facts to which I have drawn attention are not peculiar to Ibero-America. In various nations of Asia and Africa, similar lines of evolution and development appear to have led to like motivations and objectives regarding study and research and their immediate applications to the "solution of concrete problems." The work of our departments or institutes of Indian affairs and also our teaching and research centers must be evaluated bearing in mind this factor which, while it is in no way justified, is readily understandable when subjected to historical anaylsis.

The above-mentioned agencies are fighting desperately to make their voices heard in high-level governmental decision-making. Alfonso Caso's tenacious efforts to centralize anthropological work in Mexico and the determination with which Davalos Hurtado, the present Director of the National Institute of Anthropology and History, has sought to protect this institution from the onslaughts of opportunists and petty politicians, furnish adequate proof of how difficult it is for us, when we are left to ourselves, to carry out an integral, dynamic, and progressive scientific undertaking. But the general picture at present is encouraging. We have human resources—people—imbued with an enterprising spirit. Our centers of anthropological research have done meritorious work, and the indigenist centers are promoting applied anthropology, although still rather one-sidedly, cautiously, and on too small a scale.*

* The National Institute of Anthropology and History of Mexico has published over fifty works in the last ten years on subjects of social history and cultural and social anthropology. Regarding the National Indigenist Institute, its publications (memoranda, pamphlets of the *Acción Indigenista*, and a few reports and books) are very good of their kind.

In Guatemala, the hazardous and disturbing career of its National Indigenist Institute is well known; the abandonment of its National Institute of Anthropology and History for lack of economic resources, and the fact that both institutes were short of full-time specialized technical personnel, have resulted in very limited achievements. In El Salvador, a single man, Marroquín, who has good training in anthropology, calls his works (1959 and 1964) sociological research. He makes us reconsider conceptual and methodological polarizations and think both about the need to classify theoretical schemes and research problems, and about the adoption of more accurate terms and units of classification. In Panama, Reina Torres and a group of students have been doing good ethnographic work among the Cunas, and Mireya Suárez of the Bureau of Planning of the National Government, has been contemplating serious and profound anthropological and sociological research. In Colombia, Arboleda (1959) has written on the present state of the social sciences; there has been work by the Reichel-Dolmatoffs and the Pinedas, and we know Orlando Fals Borda has been making desperate efforts to hoist the pennant of science at the National University. In Peru, we know that the Anthropology Department of the University of San Marcos has been encountering difficulties similar to those of the School of Anthropology in Mexico, although to a lesser extent, due to the limited number of professionals and of achievements. In Cuzco, community development programs have been initiated, and Cornell University is continuing its applied anthropology project.

We must mention the useful contributions, which regrettably reached a small number of readers, of the fine group of researchers whose work was edited by the Council on Foreign Relations (1960). This group, which included distinguished Americanists, has sketched generalized data on certain social aspects of change in Ibero-America, but they have shown themselves, in our opinion, as being both naive and prejudiced.

What Can and What Should Be Done?

I must warn the reader that I have no intention of engaging in codification or in normative philosophy. I wish merely to offer a few ideas on certain structures, content-objectives, and lines of research which are capable of realization, and which we as professionals responsive to social problems have a certain moral obligation to pursue. I might add that my suggestions are highly selective. In the book, *Social Science Research on Latin America* [Wagley, (ed.) 1964], almost all of the contributors presented both general and specific ideas on these things. What I have to say is, therefore, supplemental, although I venture to think it original.

In my view, the era of the thinkers (philosophers and speculative theorists) in American anthropology is drawing to an end. Let us give it the coup de grâce. It is our duty, at the very least, to fill the vast gaps in our basic knowledge, to make the necessary syntheses, and to pose the problems of fields of study, methodologies, and techniques relating to the new questions which contemporary man in America is asking himself.

In the light of the foregoing, I should like to suggest that it would be desirable to reexamine, for example, Kirchhoff's ideas and proofs (1943) concerning *Mesoamérica* and those of Willey and Phillips (1955) on method and theory in American archaeology. To what extent would it be possible to identify certain related cultural regularities in the different systems and at different levels of pre-Columbian cultural development? If this is possible we should proceed, using documentary sources, to try and discover the same or other cultural regularities in the socially differentiated structures and social and economic sectors which persisted or emerged after the native groups made contact with the Europeans. The research methods and techniques used by such noted social historians as Chamberlain, Donoso, Jiménez Moreno, Kubler, José Miranda, Picon Salas, Roys, Scholes, Elman Service, and Zavala could be extremely helpful in showing us how to acquire this knowledge, which is authentically American and which we so greatly need. We could then proceed to the period of independent America. A group of researchers utilizing the techniques which Cosío Villegas provided for the study of the history of Mexico could achieve surprising results. Ethnologists and cultural and social anthropologists could pool their knowledge and efforts to plan and map out the search for these related cultural regularities. They would concentrate on certain sociocultural aspects characteristic of different ethnic groups (Indians, *mestizos, criollos*) or on different vital manifestations (economy, social structure, religious, and/or political behavior and sentiments) of similar ethnic groups, following approaches, methodologies, and techniques of an historical, cultural, or sociological nature. In short, I would suggest a great salvage operation on cogent anthropological research which would enable us to determine the basic theses, with the aim of arriving at a synthesis both analytical and integrational, of the historical equations and sociocultural processes of Indo-America and Ibero-America (Tax 1952; Gillin 1947 and 1955; Foster 1960; and Cámara 1964).

Bearing in mind that nearly everywhere in Indo-America the Indians or indigenous nuclei or groups are in the midst of economic, social, and cultural change, the suggested approach would merge the knowledge of the various specialists in the social sciences. The desired interdisciplinary program and its joint or collaborative execution would present a very strong challenge, and the results would constitute the essence and the groundwork of studies of Indo- and/or Ibero-Americanism. Past, present, and future would be presented both in their separate features and as a coherent whole; ancient and modern cultural profiles and social portraits would be seen as causal aspects of the emergence of our national cultures, and the identification of some common denominators in the sociocultural panorama of our America would lay the foundations for another monumental achievement: a new and genuine Pan-Americanism.

But the task is an arduous one. We must begin by clarifying concepts, classificatory terms, units of measurement, semantics, and hundreds of phrases whose nonuniform use by social scientists has caused more harm to the development of our branches of knowledge than even the fact that they have not been widely practiced. The strategy of an historical-anthropological salvage operation would also require us to become acquainted with the cultural and social development of Spain, that abundant source from which we all sprang, and to learn much more about other Mediterranean societies and cultures. It is through such study that we can become aware both of our uniqueness and of our universality. To sum up, the salvage operation would answer the questions: Where do we come from? Where are we? Where are we going?

At other levels and using other methodological approaches, new analyses and syntheses will have to be made, first of all, with regard to the various cultural, social, economic, and psychological classifications relating to Indo-America and Ibero-America, in accordance with the classificatory index or descrete measurable unit that may be selected as guiding factor.

Communities, Indians, *mestizos, ladinos, criollos,* peasants, rural, rur-urban, centripetal, centrifugal, lower and middle class, closed groups, open society, plural, segmental, etc., are only a few of the extremely imprecise terms we have been using. According to the sociocultural elements that have been used as indicators or components, or dependent upon the methodology employed or the objectives sought, these terms have been utilized to identify in a particular way, and sometimes even in generalizations, which are mostly vague, haphazard, and insufficiently empirical, only a part of history and a part of reality. Total reality could be grasped by means of the historical salvage operation and through the interpretation of cultural and social processes. We therefore suggest that *ad hoc* committees should discuss and ponder social and cultural components or indicators and their planned and programed utilization in a properly scientific methodology and perspective. Similarly, the various anthropology-teaching centers in Ibero-America will have to analyze and face their incongruities, contradictions, and deficiencies, and the difference between what is interpreted, what is taught, what is learned, and what is actually done. That would offer an opportunity for the final crystallization and emergence of a new type of researcher-teacher, who is sorely needed in Ibero-America, who would diagnose and expound with scientific responsibility Ibero-America's capacity to establish its national and American identity.

REFERENCES

Adams, Richard N.
  1956   Cultural components in Central America. American Anthropologist, 58–5: 881–907.
  1957   Cultural surveys of Panama, Nicaragua, Costa Rica, Guatemala. . . . Washington, D.C., Pan American Sanitary Bureau.
Arboleda, José Rafael, S. J.
  1959   Las ciencias sociales en Colombia. Rio de Janeiro, Centro Latino Americano de Pesquisas em Ciências Sociais, No. 7.

280 *The Social Sciences*

Bancroft, Hubert H.
1874–82 The native races of the Pacific States of North America. San Francisco, A. L. Bancroft and Co. 5 vols.
1883–88 History of Mexico. San Francisco, A. L. Bancroft and Co. 6 vols. (Also in one volume, New York, 1914.)
Bandelier, A. F.
1877 On the art of war and the mode of warfare of the ancient Mexicans. Salem, Mass.
1878 On the distribution and tenure of lands, and the customs with respect to inheritance among the ancient Mexicans. Salem, Mass.
1879 On the social organization and mode of government of the ancient Mexicans. Salem, Mass.
Barnes, H. E., and H. Becker.
1945 Historia del pensamiento social. México, Fondo de Cultura Económica. 2 vols.
Bastian, Adolph.
1878–89 Die kulturländer des alten Amerika. Berlin. 3 vols.
Beals, Ralph L.
1938 The emergence of an American culture. *In* The Civilization of the Americas. Berkeley, University of California Press.
Beals, Ralph L., Robert Redfield, and Sol Tax.
1943 Anthropological research problems with reference to the contemporary peoples of Mexico and Guatemala. American Anthropologist, 45(1): 1–21.
Bernal, Ignacio.
1962 Bibliografía de arqueología y etnografía: Mesoamérica y Norte de México: 1514–1960. Memoria VII del Instituto Nacional de Antropología e Historia. México.
Bingham, Hiram.
1922 Inca Land. Boston.
Boas, Franz.
1912 The history of the American race. New York Academy of Sciences, Annals, XXI: 177–83. New York.
Bolinder, Gustaf.
1917 Einiges über die Motilon-Indianer der Sierra de Perijaa. (Kolumbien, Südamerika.) Zeit. Ethnol., vol. 49: 21–51. Berlin.
1925 Die Indianer der tropichen schneegebirge; forschungen im nördlischten Südamerika. Stuttgart.
Borah, Woodrow.
1951 New Spain's century of depression. Iberoamericana 35, Berkeley.
Bowman, Isaiah.
1915 South America. Chicago, Rand, McNally and Co.
Brinton, Daniel G.
1882 American hero myths. Philadelphia.
Cámara, Fernando.
1961 Algunos antecedentes del orígen y desarrollo de la Escuela Nacional de Antropología e Historia. *In* Homenaje a William Cameron Townsend en el XXV aniversario del Instituto Lingüístico de Verano. México.
1964 El mestizaje en México. Revista de Indias, XXIX(95–96): 27–86. Instituto Fernández de Oviedo.

Chávez Orozco, Luis.
1943 Las instituciones democráticas de los indígenas mexicanos en la época Colonial: América Indígena, III (Jan.): 73–82; (April): 161–71 (July): 265–76; (October): 365–82. México.
Chevalier, François.
1956 La formación de los grandes latifundios en México (Tierra y Sociedad en los Siglos XVI y XVII). In Problemas Agrícolas e Industriales de México, VII-I (Jan.–March). México. Original French edition: Institut d'Ethnologie, Paris, 1952; English edition: Land and society in colonial Mexico, Berkeley, University of California Press, 1963.
Cline, Howard F.
1952 Mexican community studies. Hispanic American Historical Review, 32: 212–42.
Codazzi, Agustin.
1889 Atlas geográfico e histórico de la República de Colombia. Maps by Manuel M. Pas and text by Dr. Felipe Pérez. Paris.
Comas, Juan.
1950 Bosquejo histórico de la antropología en México. Revista Mexicana de Estudios Antropológicos, vol. XI. México.
1953 Bibliografía selectiva de las culturas indígenas de América. Instituto Panamericano de Geografía e Historia. México.
1954 Proceedings of the International Congresses of Americanists. In Instituto Indigenista Interamericano. Ediciones Especiales, no. 11. México.
1956 La vida y la obra de Manuel Gamio. In Estudios Antropológicos publicados en Homenaje al Dr. Manuel Gamio. Universidad Nacional Autónoma de México. Sociedad Mexicana de Antropología. México.
Council on Foreign Relations.
1960 Social change in Latin America today: its implications for United States policy. New York, Vintage Books.
Conzemius, Eduard.
1927–28 Los Indios Payas de Honduras. Journal de la Societé des Américanistes, n.s. XIX: 245–302; XX: 253–360. Paris.
1932 Ethnographical survey of the Moskito and Sumu Indians of Honduras and Nicaragua. Bulletin, Bureau American Ethnology, no. 106. Smithsonian Institution, Washington, D.C.
Diguet, Leon.
1889 Contribution à l'étude ethnographique des races primitives du Mexique; la Sierra de Nayarit et ses indigènes. (Extrait des Nouvelles Archives de Missions Scientifiques, vol. IX.) Paris.
Erasmus, Charles.
1953 Las dimensiones de la cultura. Historia de la etnología en los Estados Unidos entre 1900 y 1950. Bogotá, Colombia, Editorial Iqueima.
Ernst, A.
1870 Die Goajiro-Indianer. Zeit. fur Ethnologie, vol. 2: 328–36. Berlin.
1887 Die ethnographische stellung der Guajiro-Indianer. Zeit. fur Ethnologie, vol. 19: 425–44. Berlin.
Faron, Louis.
1959 See Steward, Julian. 1959.
Foster, George M.
1960 Culture and conquest: America's Spanish heritage. Viking Fund Publications in Anthropology, no. 27. New York.

Gamio, Manuel.
1916　Forjando patria (Pro-nacionalismo). México, Porrúa Hermanos.
1922　La población del Valle de Teotihuacán. México, Talleres Gráficos, 2 vols. in 3.
1930　Mexican immigration to the United States; a study of human migration and adjustment. Chicago, The University of Chicago Press.
1931　The Mexican immigrant, his life-story; autobiographic documents. Chicago, The University of Chicago Press.
1935　Hacia un México nuevo: Problemas sociales. México.
García Cubas, Antonio.
1858　Atlas geográfico, estadístico e histórico de la República Mexicana. México.
1884　Cuadro geográfico, estadístico, descriptivo e histórico de los Estados Unidos Mexicanos. México.
García Pelaez, Fco. P.
1854　Memoria para la historia del antiguo reino de Guatemala. Guatemala.
Gibson, Charles.
1964　The Aztecs under Spanish rule: a history of the Indians of the valley of Mexico, 1519–1810. Stanford, Cal., Stanford University Press.
Gillin, John.
1947　Modern Latin American culture. *In* Social Forces, 25: 243–48.
1949　*See* Tax, Sol, *et al.*
1955　Ethos components in Latin American culture. American Anthropologist, 57(3), part 1: 488–500.
Goldschmidt, Walter (Editor).
1959　The anthropology of Franz Boas. Memoir No. 89 of the American Anthropological Association, vol. 61, no. 5, part 2. Also published by The University of California Press, Los Angeles, 1959.
Gonzales Suárez, F.
1878　Estudio histórico sobre los Cañaris. Quito.
1903　Los aborígenes de Imbabura y del Carchi. Quito.
Guevara Silva, Tomás.
1913　Las últimas familias i costumbres araucanas. Anales de la Universidad de Chile, Vol. CXXX, Year 70, pp. 215–342 and 411–64; Vol. CXXXI, pp. 877–940. Santiago, Chile.
Gusinde, Martin.
1931　Die Feuerland-Indianer Vol. I. Die Selk'nam. Mödling bei Wien.
1937　Die Feuerland-Indianer. Vol. 2. Die Yamana. Mödling bei Wien.
Hall, Robert B.
1947　Area studies: with special reference to their implications for research in the social sciences. Social Science Research Council, Pamphlet 3, New York.
Harris, Marvin (*See* Wagley, Charles, 1955).
Hernández de Alba, G.
1936　Etnología guajira. Bogotá.
Herskovits, Melville J. (*See* Redfield *et al.*, 1936).
Hoselitz, Bert F.
1950　The social sciences in the last two hundred years. *In* The Journal of General Education. The University of Chicago Press. Vol. IV(2), January.
Jiménez Moreno, Wigberto.
1937–38　Materiales para una bibliografía etnográfica de la América Latina.

In Boletín Bibliográfico de Antropología Americana. Instituto Panamericano de Geografía e Historia. México, D.F.

1948–49 Origen y desarrollo de la Escuela Nacional de Antropología e Historia. *In* Revista Mexicana de Estudios Antropológicos. Vol. X. México.

1954 (*See* Parra, M. G., and M. W. Jiménez. 1954.)

Karsten, Rafael.
1935 The headhunters of Western Amazonas. The life and culture of the Jibaro Indians of Eastern Ecuador and Peru. Societas-Scientiarum Fennica, Commentationes Humanarum Litterarum, vol. 7, no. 1. Helsingfors.

Kirchhoff, Paul.
1931 Die verwandtschaftsorganisation der Urwaldstämme Südamerikas. Zeit. fur Ethnologie, vol. 63: 85–193. Berlin.

1943 Mesoamérica. *In* Acta Americana I: 92–107. Journal of the Sociedad Interamericana de Antropología y Geografía (also in Heritage of Conquest, edited by Sol Tax, The Free Press, Glencoe, Ill. 1952).

Koenigswald, Gustav von.
1908 Die Cayuás. *In* Globus, vol. 93: 376–81. Ausland.

Krickeberg, Walter.
1922 Amerika. *In* Illustrierte Völkerkund, published by Georg Buschan. I: 52–427. Stuttgart.

Kroeber, Alfred L.
1939 Cultural and natural areas of native North America. University of California Publications in American Archaeology and Ethnology, vol. 38: 1–242. Berkeley.

Latchman, Ricardo.
1909 Ethnology of the Araucanos. Journal of the Royal Anthropological Institute, vol. 39: 334–70. London.

Lehmann, Walter.
1920 Zentral-Amerika. Berlin. 2 vols.

Lewis, Oscar.
1951 Life in a Mexican village; Tepoztlan restudied. Urbana, Ill., The University of Illinois Press.

1956 Comparisons in cultural anthropology. *In* William L. Thomas (editor), Current Anthropology, a Supplement of Anthropology Today. Chicago, The University of Chicago Press.

Linton, Ralph (*See* Redfield *et al.*, 1936).

Lothrop, Samuel.
1937 Coclé an archaeological study of central Panama. Pt. I, Historical background. Excavations at the Sitio Conte. Artifacts and Ornaments. Memoirs of the Peabody Museum of Archaeology and Ethnology. Harvard University, vol. 7: 1–327. Cambridge, Mass.

Lowie, Robert H.
1937 The history of ethnological theory. New York, Rinehart & Co. (Spanish translation: Historia de la Etnología. Fondo de Cultura Económica, Mexico City, 1946.)

1947 Biographical memoir of Franz Boas 1858–1942. *In* National Academy of Sciences, vol. 24, 9th Memoir. Washington, D.C.

Lumholtz, Carl.
1900 Symbolism of the Huichol Indians. *In* Memoirs of the American Natural History Museum, vol. III(1): 1–228. New York.

284 *The Social Sciences*

1904 El México desconocido. New York.

Markham, Sir Clemens.
1911 The Incas of Peru. London.

Marroquín, Alejandro D.
1959 Panchimalco. Investigación sociológica. San Salvador, El Salvador, Editora Universitaria.
1964 San Pedro Nonualco. San Salvador, El Salvador, Editora Universitaria.

McGee, W. J.
1898 The Seri Indians. Report. Bureau of American Ethnology. Washington, D.C.

Means, Philip A.
1931 Ancient civilizations of the Andes. New York.

Medina, José Toribio.
1882 Los aborígines de Chile. Santiago.

Métraux, Alfred.
1936 Les Indiens Uro-Cipaya de Caranges: la civilization matérielle. Journal de la Société des Américanistes, vol. 28: pp. 120. Paris.

Microfilm Collection.
1946–49 Microfilm collection of manuscripts on Middle American Cultural Anthropology. Nos. 1–26. The University of Chicago Libraries.

Milla y Vidaurre, José.
1879–1919 Historia de la América Central. Guatemala.

Miranda, José.
1952 Las ideas y las instituciones políticas mexicanas. (Primera parte 1521–1820.) Instituto de Derecho Comparado, Universidad Nacional Autónoma de México. México, D.F.

Nordenskjöld, Erland.
1929 Les rapports entre l'art, la réligion et la magie chez les Indiens Cuna et Chocó. *In* Journal de la Société des Americanistes, n.s. vol. 21: 141–58. Paris.
1938 An historical and ethnological survey of the Cuna Indians. H. Wassem, editor. *In* Comp. Ethnogr. Studier, vol. 10. Göteborg.

Pan American Union.
1953 Notas e informaciones de ciencias sociales. Vol. IV (October) No. 23. Oficina de Ciencias Sociales, Departamento de Asuntos Culturales. Pan American Union, Washington, D.C.

Parra, M. G., and M. W. Jiménez.
1954 Bibliografía indigenista de México y Centro América. Memoria IV. Instituto Nacional Indigenista, México.

Paso y Troncoso, Francisco del.
1905–36 Papeles de Nueva España, publicados de orden y con fondos del Gobierno Mexicano, por Paso Y Troncoso. First Series: Vols. I and II. Second Series: Vols. II, IV, V, VI, and VII. Third Series: Vols. I, II, and III. Madrid.

Paz Soldán, Mariano.
1877 Diccionario geográfico y estadístico del Perú. Lima.

Paz Soldán, Mateo.
1862 Geografía del Perú. Lima.

Penniman, T. K.
1935 A hundred years of anthropology. London, Duckworth.

Peralta, Manuel María de.
1883 Costa-Rica, Nicaragua y Panamá en el Siglo XVI; su historia y sus

límites, según los documentos del Archivo de Indias de Sevilla, del de Simancas, etc. Recogidos y publicados con notas y aclaraciones históricas y geográficas. Madrid and Paris.
1892 Etnología centro-americana. Apuntes para un libro sobre los aborígenes de Costa Rica. Madrid.
Pericot García, Luis.
1936 América indigena. (Vol. I of the Series: Historia de América y de los pueblos americanos. . . .) Barcelona.
Preuss, K. T.
1910 Das Fest des Erwachens (Weinfest) bei den Cora-Indianern (Actas del XXI Congreso Internacional de Americanistas 1909), pp. 489–512. Vienna.
1912 Die Nayarit-Expedition I. Die religion der Cora-Indianer. Leipzig.
Radin, Paul.
1933 Mixe text. Journal de la Société des Américanistes, vol. XXV: 40–64. Paris.
Ramirez, José F.
1858 Atlas geográfico, histórico y estadístico de la República Mexicana. México.
Redfield, Robert.
1930 Tepoztlan: A Mexican village. Chicago, The University of Chicago Press.
1941 The folk culture of Yucatan. Chicago, The University of Chicago Press.
1943 (*See* Beals, Ralph, 1943.)
1947 The folk society. American Journal of Sociology, LII: 293–308.
Redfield, Robert, Ralph Linton, and Melville Herskovits.
1936 Memorandum for the study of acculturation. American Anthropologist, 38(1): 149–52.
Restrepo, Vicente.
1892 Estudios sobre aborígenes de Colombia. Bogotá.
1895 Los Chibchas antes de la conquista Española. Bogotá.
Restrepo Tirado, Ernesto.
1929 Ensayo etnográfico y arqueológico de la Provincia de los Quimbayas en el Nuevo Reino de Granada (Revised edition). Sevilla.
Rivet, Paul.
1939 El hombre en América. *In* Boletín de la Academia Nacional de la Historia del Ecuador, vol. XVIII(54): 15–37. Quito.
Salas, Julio C.
1908 Tierra-firma (Venezuela y Colombia). Estudios sobre etnología e historia. Mérida, Venezuela.
Sapper, Karl.
1902 Mittelamerikanische reisen: un studien aus den jahren 1888 bis 1900. Braunschweig:
Schmidt, Wilhelm.
1937 Das Eigentum auf den ätltesten Stufen der Menschheit. Münster.
Schwab, Federico.
1936 Bibliografía de etnología peruana. *In* Boletin, Universidad Mayor de San Marcos. Lima.
Schultze-Jena, L.
1933 Indiana. I. Leben, glaube und sprache der Quiche von Guatemala. Jena.

1935   Indiana. II. Mythen in der muttersprache der Pilpil von Izalco in El Salvador. Jena.
1938   Indiana. III. Bei den Azteken, Mixteken und Tlapaneken der Sierra Madre del Sur von Mexiko. Jena.
Seminario de Integración Social Guatemalteca.
1956–59   Publicaciones y Cuadernos. Editorial del Ministerio de Educación Pública. Guatemala.
Soler, M.
1887   América precolombina. Ensayo etnológico, basado en las investigaciones arqueológicas y etnográficas de las tradiciones monumentos y antigüedades de la América Indígena. Montevideo.
Spinden, Herbert J.
1928   Ancient civilization of Mexico and Central America. American Museum of Natural History, Historical Series, no. 3. New York.
Squier, E. G.
1858   The states of Central America. New York.
1877   Peru. Incidents of travel and exploration in the land of the Incas. New York.
Starr, Frederick.
1901   Notes upon the ethnography of Southern Mexico. Davenport Academy of Sciences, Proceedings: VIII: 102–98.
1904   Notes upon the ethnology of Southern Mexico. Davenport Academy of Sciences, Proceedings: IX: 62–172.
Steward, Julian.
1943   Acculturation studies in Latin America. Some needs and problems. American Anthropologist, 45(2): 198–204.
1955   Teoría y práctica del estudio de areas. Manuales Técnicos, II. Unión Panamericana, Washington, D.C.
Steward, Julian (Editor).
1946–59   Handbook of South American Indians. Bureau of American Ethnology, Bulletin 143, vols. 1–7. Smithsonian Institution, Washington, D.C.
1948   Bibliography. *In* Handbook of South American Indians. Vol. 4: 570–609.
1949   Bibliography. *In* Handbook of South American Indians. Vol. 5: 787–818.
1949a   South American cultures: an interpretative summary. *In* Handbook of South American Indians. Vol. 5: 669–772.
Steward, Julian H., and Louis Faron.
1959   Native peoples of South America. New York.
Stoll, Otto.
1884   Zur ethnographie der Republik Guatemala. Zurich.
Strickon, Arnold.
1964   Anthropology in Latin America. *In* Social science research on Latin America, edited by Charles Wagley. New York, Columbia University Press, pp. 125–67.
Tylor, E. B.
1861   Anahuac: or Mexico and the Mexicans, ancient and modern. London.
Tax, Sol.
1943   (*See* Beals, Ralph, 1943.)

Tax, Sol (Editor).
1952 Heritage of conquest. The ethnology of Middle America. Glencoe, Ill., The Free Press.
Tax, Sol, Charles Wagley, and John Gillin.
1949 Research needs in the field of modern Latin American culture. American Anthropologist, 51(1): 149–54.
Termer, Franz.
1930 Zur ethnologie and ethnographie des nördlichen Mittelamerikas. Iberoamerikanisches Archiv., IV (3): 301–492.
Thomas, Cyrus, and John R. Swanton.
1911 Indian languages of Mexico and Central America and their geographical distribution. Smithsonian Institution, Bureau of American Ethnology, Bulletin 44.
Thompson, J. Erich.
1933 Mexico before Cortes. New York.
Tozzer, Alfred M.
1907 A comparative study of the Mayas and the Lacandones. New York.
Unión Panamericana.
1954 Guía de instituciones y sociedades en el campo de las ciencias sociales. Segunda edición corregida y aumentada. Segunda parte: América Latina. Publicaciones de la Oficina de Ciencias Sociales, Departamento de Asuntos Culturales, Washington, D.C.
Velasco, Alfonso Luis.
1889–98 Geografía y estadística de la República Mexicana. México, D.F. 7 vols.
Villavicencio, M.
1858 Geografía de la República del Ecuador. New York.
Wagley, Charles.
1948 Area research and training: a conference report on the study of world areas. Social Science Research Council, Pamphlet 6. New York.
1949 (See Tax, Sol, 1949.)
Wagley, Charles, and Marvin Harris.
1955 Typology of Latin American subcultures. American Anthropologist, 57(3): 428–51.
Wagley, Charles (Editor).
1964 Social science research on Latin America. New York, Columbia University Press.
Willey, Gordon, and P. Phillips.
1955 Method and theory in American archaeology II: historical developmental interpretation. American Anthropologist, 57(4): 723–819.
Wissler, Clark.
1917 The American Indian. An introduction to anthropology of the New World. New York.
Zavala, Silvio.
1944 Ensayos sobre la colonización española en América. Buenos Aires.
1948 Estudios Indianos. El Colegio Nacional (Ed.) México.

JOSÉ MARÍA FRANCO

10

Latin American Law and Legal Institutions

To be quite candid, it is no easy matter to analyze, comment on, and criticize a specific piece of work by a competent professor of law, who is concerned and acquainted with the legal institutions and the law in Latin America; nor can one feel confident that his thinking has been fully understood on the basis of a study designed for information and guidance purposes, and hence inevitably less extensive and less well documented than it would necessarily be under other circumstances. At best the writer can only commend it, or amplify, rectify, or amend small details, on the strength of his experience as a lawyer whose principles, practice, and experience ought, theoretically at least, to be akin to Professor Karst's (1964a: 290–330).

Methodology

The paper by Professor Karst is concerned primarily with an approach to the problem of practical law, and as such it goes into the question of what already exists, what has already been done, and what ought to be done; and he makes a number of excellent suggestions which we might do well to follow, not only in our eagerness to agree that many things are worth striving for, but also to discover how we can attain them as soon as possible in the general interest of the community and of legal practice and research, and to bring theory in line with practice.

When in 1959 the representatives of 54 law schools, or 62,245 law students* or, to put it another way, the representatives of 2,043 teachers in 49 law schools (one for every 28 students) met

* Compare these figures with the 54,433 students in 157 law schools in the United States during 1963 (Ritchie 1964: 177).

in Mexico City (UNA, Mexico 1959), the meeting did not include spokesman for all the 97 law schools which existed at that time in Latin America; but the number was certainly sufficient to give a good account of the present status of legal science south of the Rio Grande, of the work done in the last few years, and of the steadily growing tendency to include practical training in the study of law. Particulars were given of no less than 80 law institutes, 30 seminars dealing with various legal subjects, and 10 centers, academies, or advisory services for forensic or professional practice or legal workshops, as well as no less than 70 reviews, yearbooks, or legal bulletins.

Although much of the analytical work done in the study of the law has been of the deductive type, this has not been true to such an extent as to neglect jurisprudence, which, where necessary, can be studied through the splendid collections published regularly by all the national supreme courts (in Buenos Aires they run into hundreds of volumes). Thus it cannot be said that adequate source materials do not exist in jurisprudence compilations, nor that civilian training pays little attention to the decisions of courts.

Latin American law, whose links with Iberian law (see José Castán Tobenas 1964) go back to the Latin (France, Italy, Spain, and Portugal) Christian Roman law of western culture, and whose objective and ethical ideal exalts the human person and aspires to bend the law to the realities of human life* rather than to conform to a logical pattern may be studied from the point of view of its principles, but not as regards the situation of each individual country, since the countries differ one from another on points of positive law, in the same way as the various states of the United States.

On the other hand, one cannot but appreciate the tremendous value for western culture of the works and treatises on law by eminent jurists which, in the world of the future, when the systems of common law and civil law have been brought together, will constitute milestones of cultivated and civilized thought (Salvat 1958, Spota 1947–50, Lafaille 1947–50, Baldana 1947,

---

* For information on the origin and inspiration of the various Latin American civil codes, see the work on the subject by José Castán Tobenas (1964), present President of the Spanish Supreme Court, in the bibliography at the end of this paper.

Rivarola 1938, Cossio 1944, Alessandri and Somarriva 1945, Bevilacqua 1958–59, Alves 1957, Wald 1962, Reale 1960, Muñoz 1946, Pina 1956–61, Rojina Villegas 1945–47, García Maynez 1963, Valencia Zea 1960).*

Before we continue with the discussion, it would be well to ascertain Professor Karst's aim, and what is our own aim in studying this particular social science; and we must define and distinguish three important phases essential to the study of law, if we are to remain within our own times, when the law must serve a world which is constantly developing and in the throes of continuous change.

The study of jurisprudence is becoming increasingly important, inasmuch as it interprets the juridical principles embodied in the laws, where formal change is a very slow process. But while positive law presupposes an initial stage or phase in the civil law countries, and jurisprudence presupposes a second phase in which through the efforts of the judge a lawful or unlawful social act is subsumed under a rule of law, the study and investigation of the social environment in which this rule operates, with a view to discovering how the rule works in the society for which it is enacted, or how different circumstances (constant development and continual change) cause it to be modified or discarded, is a task for the modern researcher. The researcher must be equipped with a proper legal training and will have to apply the new techniques, which are of positive value for the sociologist, the anthropologist, the economist, and others and will be equally so for the jurist, especially if he works in interdisciplinary cooperation with other scholars. He will thus be more productive and a more useful member of the community to which he belongs.

In other words, the theoretical and practical teaching of law, carried out at the present time in many law schools as a necessity of modern times, and supplemented by institutes, seminars, academies of forensic practice, and legal workshops, has now to be reinforced by means of research into what some American

* Anyone wishing to become acquainted with the considerable bibliography of juridical science produced in Latin America should consult Alberto Villalón-Galdames: *Una introducción a la bibliografía jurídica latinoamericana* (1963). Although this is not altogether complete, any more than the bibliography of Bayitch (1961), it may be used by Spanish-speaking jurists just as the latter is used by those who speak English.

teachers of law call "law-in-action," involving the technique of the questionnaire, the study of juridical dossiers and notaries' files, statistics, censuses, surveys, and public and private archives of all kinds. Modern research cannot be confined to the study of the books in a law library, because the life of the law is not in books but in society, and it is to living society that the law researcher must turn to find the just, positive, and beneficial principles on which laws are promulgated, reformed, or repealed in accordance with the realities of life.

Research Opportunities: The Legislative, Executive, and Judiciary and Other Institutional Topics Demanding Further Research

The Autonomous National University of Mexico offers, as one of its second year subjects for the degree of Doctor of Law, a course entitled "Methodology of Law." This course not only covers the conceptual study of various aspects of law [natural law, historical, teleological approaches, the French school of exegesis or the school of free scientific research (Geny), the critical theory of law (Stammler), the pure theory of Kelsen, juridical sociologism or realism, irrationalism, phenomenology, and the jurisprudence of the sentiments]; it also goes into the "making of the law," methods for relevant research, and its application especially for teaching.

However, if we want to know how laws are made, or who makes them, or how codes are modified and decrees are promulgated, it is well to turn to the constitutions and the regulations derived from them. These give the answer to many questions. Other answers are to be found in the treatises by theoretical writers on the subject (Linares Quintana 1953–63, González Calderón 1930, F. S. Pérez 1962, Pontes de Miranda 1960, Gil Fortoul 1962, Ruggieri Parra 1949, Andueza 1955, Tena Ramírez 1963, Lanz Duret 1947). Nevertheless, not one of these works reflects the situation completely.

Regarding administrative power (Bielsa 1955, 1964; Cavalcanti, 1960, Gabino Fraga 1960, Serra Rojas 1961, Sayagués Laso 1962, Brewer Carias 1964), there is no doubt that this has seen more development than any other sector in the modern state, indeed there has been a tremendous hypertrophy in all its organs. The study and investigation of many facets of administration, and the execution of the task of improving and reforming it and making it more efficient, will provide society with desirable benefits in regard to rights to liberty, equality, and the pursuit of happiness. The present trend towards gradual socialization or state control in the most advanced Western countries gives a hint as to the general outlook over the next few years in the civilized world. Hence any detailed and exhaustive research into principles, means, aims, financing, results, and practical experience gained by any government institute which administers national property or a public undertaking or service is of the utmost interest, inasmuch as industrial and commercial undertakings have been responsible for the progress and development of modern society, especially where, as in many countries, the state is the major business employer. At the present time, government programs are many and various, autonomous institutes and agencies are becoming more and more numerous, whether for economic development, industrial or agricultural promotion, agrarian reform, social security, or of the old public utility and policy type; and in many instances it is the government which takes the lead at the business level because of some structural inadequacy or lack of capital in the private sector, insufficient financial resources, or inadequate leadership, the result being that the government assumes the role of employer either in competition with private business, or in the absence of competition.

Thus any research into a governmental program, the administration of public property, i.e. community matters or economic development, is of the utmost importance.

The work done by international organizations such as FAO, IADB, ECLA, ILO, is as a rule general in character, and their recommendations are made to governments generally, without normally giving concrete details of specific cases. Nevertheless, pilot studies on a regional scale, made more or less sporadically without following a systematic general plan, are many and varied; and there is no ministry dealing with the promotion of production, industry, or communications which cannot boast a large number of them. The problem is to select the background material, to relate it to laws currently in force, and to search the countries' economies, budgets, and balance sheets, to discover what there has been on the credit or debit side, what is worth recommending, and how presumed benefits are likely to be obtainable in the light of the background and experience gained.

It is not true to say that civilian training has paid little attention to the decisions of the courts, or that most judicial opinions are never published, or that the part played by judges, even during dictatorships, has been so insignificant that one might think it did not exist, or again that the judiciary, as an institution, is not independent. On the contrary, the safeguards of the judicial power are laid down in constitutions, organic laws and regulations, and the judiciary has at all times been exceedingly jealous of its prerogatives and the defense of its rights and duties (Hernández Colón 1963, Dana Montano 1958, 1960).

At the tenth and eleventh Inter-American Conferences of Jurists, held at Buenos Aires in 1957 and at Miami in 1959, respectively, the agenda included the question of specific safeguards for the independence of the judiciary. The work of the former judge, Dr. Dana Montano (1960), in which he adopted the method of a survey, based on a detailed questionnaire, among the majority of the judges throughout the Latin American continent may be regarded as one of the most comprehensive studies on the independence and tenure of judges and judicial officers, as well as on the system of selection and appointment and the financial status of judges.

No one can maintain, of course, that graft, whether political or economic, does not exist, or deny that the decisions handed down in certain countries tend to be overcategorical, whether through indolence, incompetence, or malice, and that the noble profession of the judiciary tends to be brought into discredit; but there are reasons for all this, and they can be investigated, demonstrated, and hence rectified. The social engineer ought therefore to undertake this task and carry it out to the best of his abilities for the good of the community.

Another highly important subject for research is the effective or ineffective protection given by the state to the poor and to the indigenous populations of certain countries, the way in which the legal provisions of the civil codes operate in regard to legal aid for the poor, the extent to which the poor avail themselves of this social right to free legal advice, and the way in which the present lack of confidence on the part of the public could be overcome or corrected by ensuring that equal justice is available for all persons and that it is administered honestly, without delay or excuse (Alcalá-Zamora 1947, 1957; Cunha 1936; Alsina 1956; Couture 1938, 1958; Pina 1951, and Cuenca 1956).

One aspect of justice in which there has always been a perfect integration between law and sociology is penal or criminal law. Interdisciplinary studies on this subject have been carried on for a long time, and many excellent works have been produced, even including studies of society insofar as it affects the state of the law (Gómez 1939–42, Jiménez de Asúa 1943, 1946, 1963; Menéndez 1942; Tabio 1949; Bernaldo de Quirós 1948–49; Carrancá 1950; López Rey 1964; Quiróz Cuarón 1957; Ruis Funes 1948, 1960; Mendoza 1957). Modern sciences such as penitentiary law, penology, police science, and pathology in relation to prisons and jails have developed under the influence of the hard facts of social life, where the juridical phenomenon, as far as sociology is concerned, is an aspect of human existence, and is studied as such.

Labor legislation (Cesarino 1963; Russomano 1962–63; Cardozo 1953; Caldera 1960; Cueva 1949: Cordova 1957) is concerned to a considerable degree with relations between employer and employee in a developing society. In the same way, in mercantile or commercial law (Rivarola 1938; Nuñez 1938; Satanowsky 1957; Wald 1959; Goldschmidt 1958, 1962, 1964; González Miranda 1958; Moles Caubet 1958), or in the economics of Central or Latin American integration [Haas and Schmitter 1964; Pincus 1963; Campo Salas 1960; Urquidi 1962; Mikesell 1961; Prebisch 1962; Inter-American Development Bank (Venezuela) 1964; Lauterbach 1963; Banco de Comercio Exterior, México, 1963] focus is placed on the problem of the burgeoning of economic and commercial activity, where the lawyer contributes his knowledge toward improving the structure, flexibility, and reform of national and supranational institutions. Also of major importance is the study and reform of tax systems with a view to discovering uniform incentives for private industrial and agricultural investment, the question of treatment of foreign capital

(Washington Foreign Law Society 1959, Charter of Punta del Este 1961, Adams and others 1963), banking and financial institutions. Side by side with these quasitheoretical studies, practical research has been done (Baez Finol 1961, Cann 1964) and international meetings have been held to seek solutions for the problems of devaluation of currency, e.g., the Chilean-Uruguayan seminars on comparative law (*Revista de la Facultad de Derecho y Ciencias Sociales,* Montevideo, 1959) and on tax law, where the autonomy of local governments in regard to the imposition of taxes, and the question of international double taxation, have been throughly reviewed (*Revista de la Facultad de Derecho y Ciencias Sociales,* Montevideo, 1957).

The Study, Practice, and Investigation of Law as a Social Science

It may be said, in very general terms, that common law is of judicial origin, the source of its rules being judgments handed down by other judges in similar cases in virtue of the principle of *stare decisis* applied dynamically, and the general rules extracted from precedent being adjusted, polished, and modified constantly in the light of the changing situation without the vexations resulting from the conceptual rigidity of code law (Cueto Rua 1957, Couture 1955).

Roscoe Pound, one of the leading figures of sociological jurisprudence (Recaséns Siches 1956, 1957), recognizing that the real life of law is the outcome not of logic but of experience, as Holmes put it, formulated and developed a program of research into the social effects of juridical institutions and doctrines. The sociological study of life today is important as a background for the formulation of laws, and psychological and ideal factors operate in the creation of law, as a valuable means of making juridical principles effective (Pound 1911–12, 1923, 1935, 1950).

How then, is law taught in the United States (Association of American Schools 1949–50) so as to ensure that on the basis of a comparison of the various systems, the student of civil law can improve the system, if this is possible, by collating experiences and stimulating constructive criticism aimed at overcoming present limitations (Cueto Rua 1957: 289 *et seq.*)?

North American universities are sensitive to the slightest social need, and are organized to cope with contingencies as and when they appear. They are linked with ancillary organizations which have an active influence and with the great philanthropic or welfare bodies, and to a large extent they are financed privately and organized in the form of corporations and thus properly fitted to take up the major challenges constantly arising in the complex and paradoxical society of the United States.

When Christopher C. Langdell established the case method at Harvard University in 1870, he explained in the preface to his first book of selected cases (Langdell 1871) that he would like to see students work in conjunction with the teacher so as to get the greatest and most lasting advantage from the study. He was of the opinion that it was preferable for the student to attend courses rather than devote the equivalent amount of time to private study. Since documentary material for such a method was lacking, he prepared and published a selection of cases suitable for the purpose. Keener introduced the same method at Columbia, Wambaugh at Iowa, and Wigmore at Northwestern University. This method based on the elucidation of juridical truth, and combining the case system with the socratic method, makes use of class discussion and the case book system so that when the time of the examination comes along, it is not the memory of the pupil that is tested, but his capacity to reason and understand the phenomenon of law. This is all very well; the student learns to reason, but he does not acquire an adequate knowledge of the normative structure which the system involves; he is not given adequate information on the theory of law; the system trains "litigant attorneys" rather than consultants; the system is not suitable for the teaching of statute law which is becoming more and more extensive;* and the system is unsuitable for first-year students who are constantly faced with a technique which is difficult even for the most able students, as Cueto shows (Cueto Rua 1957: 333 *passim*).

Thus, since the social situation as it is calls for theoretical studies of sociology, psychology, economics, and politics, which cannot be learned by the case method, a variety of solutions have

* Felix Frankfurter states in "Some Reflections on the Reading of Statutes" (1947: 527) that in 1875 more than 40 percent of the controversies before the Supreme Court were common law litigations; fifty years later only 5 percent were of this type, while today, cases not resting on statutes are reduced almost to zero.

been suggested by distinguished jurists. For example, Pound, Carlton, and Griswold propose the improvement of the cultural background; Brown and Morstein Marx, training for a type suitable for public officials, Lasswell and MacDougal, training with a view to determining and evaluating social conduct and the maintenance and development of democracy. Other suggestions are adaptations of the case method, stressing the formation of skills (American Law Schools 1944), the problem method, and the institutional method, the Frank proposal (Frank argued that the reading of two properly chosen briefs, supplemented by texts, would be more valuable than twenty casebooks in two years), including the suggestion for juridical clinics or legal dispensaries operated by teachers for the training of students. Auxiliary techniques such as law reviews, moot courts—both already in existence—legal aid clinics (advocated by Bradway to ensure that the practice of law goes hand in hand with teaching), and audiovisual aids, are other suggestions put forward. These are the auxiliary techniques which have been most successful up to the present, and they can be safely recommended to law schools which teach the civil law system and which for one reason or another have not adopted them in their recent educational reforms.

All this suggests how the approach should be made to a system of teaching in which theory, practice, and research are clearly delineated; and just as the Latin American school can give guidance and instruction to the college or law school in the United States regarding the teaching of a body of principles clearly established in relation to statutory norms or the general theory of law, so the Latin university needs to give far more emphasis to these auxiliary techniques of the American law school, as advocated by Eduardo B. Carlos in his book *Clínica jurídica y enseñanza práctica* (1959).

There have certainly been strong advocates of practical teaching, especially in Argentina (Abdala 1957, Araya 1928, Baiocco 1930, Bascuñán 1957, Becena 1925, 1928; Bendicente 1933, Bielsa 1957, Buonocore 1957, Colmo 1919, Damianovich 1935, Goldschmidt 1935, Lafaille 1928, Lewis 1935, Lo Valvo 1933, Muratti 1931–37, Giner de los Ríos (no date), Ortega y Gasset 1936, Ramón y Cajal 1935, Palacios 1924, Quiroga 1933, Torino 1935, Prunell 1957), and although seminars, courses in forensic practice, practical training, and juridical workshops have recently been set up in many universities, along with a large number of research institutes, Argentina has to be given the credit for being the first country to concern itself with this matter.

Carlos distinguishes first of all the chair of law, where principles are transmitted by means of oral exposition, in dogmatic manner, with explanatory comments on the codes, the pupil playing a passive role. This method has undergone a profound transformation.* Next comes the seminar, where the students learn the methods of scientific research,† and practical work, which involves direct intervention in the expounding, development, and solution of cases in all their complexity of themes.‡ He makes a distinction that differentiates these institutes from the so-called "clinic," which he favors, the seminar being under the direction of the professor of the subject, whereas the clinic is a kind of synthesis of all the work carried out in the faculty, and may be regarded as a sort of forensic clerkship or apprenticeship in professional routine and adaptation. Here the case system is the most appropriate technique; it is left to the institutes, which already exist in most of the faculties, to impart knowledge and build up a scientific outlook.

It is in this last-named branch of research that technique is likely to undergo further evolution in the field of law and will have to be combined with methods from other sciences with a view to fusing a great many of them together.

The study of statistics, economics, psychology, and anthropology is of great interest inasmuch as it is related to law, and in the investigation of a given situation having juridical effects, all these disciplines must be integrated while the technique to be applied must be a combined one if more efficient results are to be achieved.

Contemporary law is faced with first, problems of technological

* Professor Roberto Goldschmidt, who has traveled throughout the American continent as a teacher in various university faculties, calculates that for the last twenty years or so the system has been gradually abandoned in this part of the world (letter to the author, Feb. 8, 1965).

† The Institute of Practical Teaching of the Faculty of Law of the University of Buenos Aires was set up by Order No. 51 of October 20, 1922 and inaugurated on May 16, 1924.

‡ The Order governing the Seminar of the Faculty of Law of the University of Buenos Aires was approved on May 9, 1938. That of the University of La Plata was promulgated on September 14, 1920.

and economic risks; second, the definition and protection of the position of the individual in relation to the state; third, state intervention in economic life and judicial control; fourth, the development of the most suitable framework for private international business; fifth, the development of a system of international law, similar to national systems, making for stability and peaceful change.* Hence it is of the utmost importance to understand the research techniques and to apply the coordinated knowledge of various sciences so as to promote the social purposes and welfare of peoples in the most satisfactory way possible.

At the Second Conference of Latin American Law Faculties held at Lima in 1961, of the five recommendations approved, one has to do with apprenticeship through the seminar system, and another with practical teaching of law, with the help of courts, law offices, and juridical clinics.

Practical Methods of Research on Law-in-Action

The experience of the United States

The social scientist, whether he is a sociologist, a jurist, an anthropologist, or an economist, has to seek out and become acquainted with the social phenomena from which the law is derived or for which the law is enacted, and has to ascertain the real efficacy of the legal institutions set up by society. His task is not so much to acquaint himself with the abstract content of the law as to discover how the laws operate in the actual social situation, since as institutions they are subject to continual change and can be improved.

It is a novel approach to collect data and evaluate the rule of law in everyday life with a view to ascertaining which laws function and which do not, and to proceed accordingly. Implicit in this is the flight from libraries, the reduction of reliance on books, and the emergence from the isolation of law in an ivory tower. Concern will develop for the practical techniques of re-

* Item 8 (d), of the Declaration of Principles on the Teaching of Law in Latin America, submitted by Professor Dennis Martínez Irizarry, Dean of the Faculty of Law of Puerto Rico, to the first Conference of Latin American Law Schools and Faculties, held at Mexico City in 1959 (Mayda 1960: 407 *et seq.*).

search, the tasks of collecting and compiling data, classifying them, with the help of other social scientists, and studying the underlying economic problems in the national community.

Ehrlich in Europe and Pound in America were the advocates of this approach as early as the beginning of this century, and in the 1920s they asked the first questions in the United States on the role of the rule of law in the crystallization of legal decisions on the basis of judicial briefs, legal files, and registers of documents. Thus they gave a new focus to research, enlisting the backing of ancillary sciences and enhancing the significance of law-in-action.

The integration of law and economics has been a later and more continuous effort (Harris 1958, 1960; Ellis 1954; Timmons 1955, 1959; Beuscher 1955, 1959, 1962, 1964; Byrne 1955; Chryst 1959; Raup 1959). In 1920 Holmes made a remark to the effect that for the rational study of law, the man of letters may be the man of the present, but the man of the future is the one who has mastered statistics and economics (Holmes 1920: 174).

At the University of Illinois, under the auspices of the legal subcommittee of the North Central Land Tenure Research Committee, a symposium was held in 1958 with a view to first, discovering the theoretical philosophical reasons on which economic and legal research can be based; second, evaluating the methods used in economic and legal studies; third, considering ways and means of making the results of this research effective, and fourth, exploring the problems arising out of specific situations and exchanging ideas on current research projects.

Regarding the first point (Chryst 1959), it was specified that because of the interdependence of law and economics, the cases which regularly come before the law courts and legislatures almost invariably have to do with matters involving economic values. There appear to be three types of problems of interest to the economic and legal researcher: the problem that costs and yields cannot be brought into proper association if there are legal impediments to the mobility of resources; the problem of restrictions in certain types of industries, and the problem of uncertainty as reflected in economic and legal relationships such as farming contracts.

Regarding the methodological problems of economic and legal

research (Timmons 1959), the lack of integration between theoretical knowledge and practical work is proved by the fact that these are handled by separate academic departments, and the occupational disease of watertight compartments—as reflected in the terminology used—is not eliminated. To cope with this problem, it is recommended that the professional training of research workers should include interdisciplinary studies during the postgraduate period. In this way law studies can provide the means of achieving economic objectives giving the highest yield by providing reliable bases on which alternative economic decisions can be made, since what is sought in this type of integration is a way of solving fundamental human problems, which cannot be dealt with, let alone studied, through a single discipline.

The task of making the result of economic and legal research effective (Beuscher 1959), and this undoubtedly presupposes lobbying work in the parliamentary corridors, implies the drafting of recommendations of the legislature, with a view to facilitating the attainment of the economic targets involved. This has been going on for some time, witness the series of new legal institutions previously nonexistent—city green belts, rural zoning, state highways, urban growth districts, family trusts, future advance mortgages, contract farming, and vertical integration.

Last, new problems create new types of economic and legal research (Raup 1959), in line with Western economic principles and American law.

Another field, that of commercial transactions within the family and the question of transfer of ownership of family agricultural holdings from one generation to another, has been investigated in thirteen states of the north central region of the United States (Beuscher 1962) by the system of personal interview, reports on cases, direct observation, and the empirical use of registers and statistical data with a view to ascertaining in real life what verbal or written agreements are used by farmowners as a basis for partnership with their children in the family holding. Other aspects of law-in-action have also been advocated as valuable for the all-around training of the social-scientist—attorney, acquainting him with the way in which the theory, principles, and legal precepts are applied in actual cases to supplement or rectify rules of law that have not been accepted by the community and hence have clearly been enacted in error.

Suggestion Concerning Research Technique

Library research, which has produced excellent scholars in the Anglo-Saxon and continental systems, calls for mastery of a technique (Pollack 1962, Price and Bitner 1953), considerable intellectual ability, and steady effort and dedication. But research of the law-in-action type which we advocate as a more advanced phase, though experience here is still in the initial stages, calls for other techniques that require equal skill for mastery. These can be borrowed from another social science to which law is closely related, namely sociology. Here the training technique has been continuous and extensive during the last thirty years (Jahoda, *et al.* 1951, Goode and Hatt 1952). The researcher can prove, or fail to prove, general assumptions, study the way in which established rules are applied or not applied, assess the value of these rules in the community for or through which they exist, or consider the advisability of amendments. For this purpose methods are being tried out for proving hypotheses, drawing up questionnaires, conducting interviews, making sample surveys and calculating probabilities, studying scales, problems of quality, and analysis of cases, data processing, and the technique of drawing up reports.

Frequent use has been made of such techniques on a partial scale, with a greater or lesser degree of precision and competence, where juridical institutions and organs in need of reform have carried out surveys, consultations, or other types of investigation; but they have never been carried out with the realization that these methods are the most suitable and effective, and that this type of technical and painstaking operation is scientifically the most suitable, indeed the ideal and most vital method of consolidating and supplementing library research.*

* The law division of the Instituto de Ciências do Homem of the University of Recife, founded in 1963 (it has also sociology, psychology, and history divisions) claims to train researchers and to carry out social and juridical research in the manner advocated in this paper. See Association of American Law Schools, Foreign Exchange Bulletin, vol. VI, issue No. 2, St. Louis University Law School.

Emphasis on Vital Research

The Center for Development Studies of the Central University of Venezuela has recently initiated a comprehensive teaching and research scheme including courses in economics, sociology, law, and other sciences, for the purpose of giving professional training to postgraduate students in the most up-to-date techniques of research and programing; at the same time, it carries out study projects on social change in Venezuela and on development or economic change strategy.

This type of research center set up in various parts of the continent would be ideal for investigating specific aspects of law-in-action, as a basis for policies to be followed and reforms to be carried out, with a view to discussion at international congresses of jurists or congresses of comparative law such as are frequently held in the New World.

In view of the situation in Latin America in regard to development, rapid economic change, and industrialization, topics concerned with commercial law can be extremely interesting to the extent that they have to do with the action of the law as it evolves, in other words, law research of the most useful type in relation to growth and social change.

This type of research has proved its value and will continue to do so:

1. as a basis for legislation ably drafted and important for economic and social change;

2. as a means of testing periodically the effectiveness of legislative programs and their administration, the extent to which they attain the targets established or fail to reach those targets;

3. as a method of testing and improving the administration of justice, particularly at the level of the man in the street;

4. as a means of discovering the correlation between economic and social forces and the law; the role of custom and the rule of law which differs from the social role;

5. as a method of discovering items of vital importance for the teaching of law and the training of jurists so that the latter may play a more effective part in a developing economy where there are rapid changes of social structure.

Also of capital importance is the study of the rules of law

referring to the family, its formation, composition and decomposition, stability, union, legitimacy and illegitimacy, welfare, separation, divorce, concubinage, adultery, and polygamy (First International Congress of Comparative Law of the International Association of Juridical Science 1957).

The social study of divorce in the United States, where there are 400,000 cases a year, has produced an immense literature, and this subject can be studied as a partial means of ascertaining the evils which lenient legislation can cause in regard to the breakdown of the family. We hear phrases like "divorce begets divorce" or "the impossiblity or excessive difficulty of obtaining a divorce leads to desertion, adultery, or concubinage," but no one has been able to produce conclusive evidence to prove either proposition. The factors influencing the stability of marriage would appear to be infinite in number, the state of industrialization and urbanization of a given society, the status of women, the moral and religious atmosphere, the state of education and housing, attitudes towards prostitution and desertion of the home, laws governing rentals, employment, social security, and succession. The obstacles to research would appear to be formidable and immense, but they make the work exciting and an ideal field for collaboration by a team of sociologists, anthropologists, psychologists, and jurists, i.e. social scientists, in a comprehensive type of research of paramount interest to any country.

With this idea in mind, Professor Max Rheinstein carried out a study in the Comparative Law Research Center of the University of Chicago, and the background material and experience gained are of the utmost interest for this type of work.*

The Law and Agrarian Reform

The question of agrarian reform has gradually become, in theory at least, the point of fusion for research strategies outlined by all types of social engineers. If we listen to an economist on

* Professor Rheinstein drew up a long questionnaire on juridical methods of promoting the stability of the family and legislation on the subject, with a view to placing his findings before the international congress already referred to, held in Spain in 1956. Excellent reports were forthcoming from Belgium, France, and Switzerland, and they can be regarded as model contributions to the subject.

the subject (Massad 1964), he has a great deal to say about research on land tenure, distribution, expropriation, loans, and taxes, which has also been said by the sociologists (See the basic bibliography of the Fifteenth National Congress on Sociology, Sociology of Agrarian Reform, IIS, UNAM, 1964); and indeed the jurists are also working along the same lines (Price 1964). But although in this last respect there are some excellent treatises on agrarian law (Padilla 1954, Pérez Llana 1964, Flores Moncayo 1956, Maldonado 1956, Cardozo 1953, Linhares de Lacerda 1960, Mendieta y Núñez 1964, Caso 1950, Aguilera 1962), up to the present the interdisciplinary research urged by many social scientists would appear to be little more than a pious wish; for even though there has been a certain measure of integration at the time of planning of agrarian reform and the preparation of draft legislation on the subject (*Comisión de Reforma Agraria,* Venezuela 1959),* little or nothing has been done with regard to team research at a subsequent stage, except that the study of what remains to be done has continued (*Curso de capacitación de profesionales en reforma agraria* 1963), frequently with very valuable contributions by individual research workers, e.g., the members of the University of Wisconsin Land Tenure Center sent to various regions of Latin America. A notable feature of their work is the primary emphasis they place on the present development of rural economy and sociology (LTC Newsletter 1962–64).†

The sociological slant which Professor Karst imparts to a whole series of legal research opportunities in regard to agrarian reform is brilliant and penetrating, and there is certainly little to be said except to endorse heartily this fascinating approach, which only an academic jurist of the old school could criticize. Actually, in

* A specimen study of the preparation of draft legislation, in which committees of economists, sociologists, lawyers, and agricultural experts were set up to study the problem exhaustively.

† This Center is in an ideal position to attempt to carry out a long-term project of comprehensive research into topics connected with agrarian reform, since it has both Latin American and United States personnel at its disposal. For this reason it ought to send out, systematically and not sporadically, teams of research workers of different educational background, so that when they are faced with a given situation they can study it from every angle. The Center's contribution would thus be enhanced, and it would render a further valuable service to science.

the last five years, during which a series of agrarian reform laws has been promulgated in Latin America (we are, after all, in the decade of agrarian reform), it would be difficult to find a professional researcher, or a state organization directly concerned with such matters, or a university research institute that has not made a contribution in writing to the elucidation of most of the points raised by Professor Karst. This can be demonstrated by a mere glance at any bibliographical list on the subject (Delgado 1962, Centro Latinoamericano de Investigaciones en Ciencias Sociales 1963, Carroll 1962, LTC University of Wisconsin 1964, *Instituto de Investigaciones Sociales* of UNAM 1964). In fact, his own most recent work, *Latin American Land Reform: The Uses of Confiscation* (Karst 1964), has all the features of an excellent library study.

Nevertheless there are aspects of the subject which have been exploited very little on a regional scale, e.g., the study of water rights in connection with agrarian reform as a means of implementation of agricultural development,* the plight of the *minifundio* in the entire continent south of the Río Grande (Franco 1965), registers of agricultural property in relation to the security of ownership, agrarian loans and inheritance (Thome 1964), the role of rural unionization in the formation and reform of the law (Price 1963, Powell 1964, etc.). All of these merit intense effort in the near future.

With regard to theoretical studies of land tenure, the contribution of agrarian reform to agriculture and economic develop-

---

* The Land Tenure Center of the University of Wisconsin has two research workers, Joseph Thome, an attorney, and Dale Adams, an economist, studying the Coella and Soldana irrigation schemes in the Department of Tolima in Colombia. The former previously made a study of the irrigation works of the Cauca Valley Corporation in Cali. At the same time another attorney, Daniel Stewart, and an agricultural economist, Peter Dorner, are making a similar study in Chile. The two jurists began their work on the relevant codes and administrative regulations, spending a good deal of time on the study of the historic roots of water rights and various aspects of the development of the law in each country. After that they laid their books aside and interviewed administrators concerned with the distribution and use of water for irrigation, at various levels—national, regional, and local. They studied in detail the functioning of the canal network in Chile and of the water supply schemes in the valleys of the Cauca and Sopa respectively. Finally they contacted individual farmers to find out how the system works in practice. Their work will be published shortly.

ment, and these same subjects specifically as a field for comprehensive research, prominent scholars in the United States have done useful work, and their suggestions and experience must be counted as a disinterested contribution to the promotion of science and social welfare policies (Schickele 1952; Raup 1962, 1963; Thorbecke 1962; Parsons 1962).*

The Trend and Evaluation of Agrarian Reform in Relation to the Interaction of its Political, Economic, and Social Aims

If we consider the agrarian reforms carried out in Europe in fourteen countries between 1917 (in Russia) and 1922 (in Finland), and the last reform carried out prior to the Second World War (Spain 1932), it cannot be said that they were successes *qua* reforms, and in some instances it is quite clear even today that they were economically a failure, as in Russia.

Regarding the reforms now being carried out in Latin America, in spite of the fact that they have the European precedent behind them, it would seem that they are likely to go the same way with the exception of the agrarian reform scheme in Mexico; possibly in this case because the reforms are a combination of Roman law principles of exclusive ownership of the land tempered by communal indigenous customs cleverly retained within the framework of the medieval Castilian institution of common lands (*ejido*), brought to New Spain by its first governors, and other institutions set up by the government.

In the opinion of Carlos Carranza (*Reforma agraria en América* 1961), the mistaken policy which is responsible for the failure of agrarian reforms stems from the fact that they are based on agronomic and juridical techniques instead of economic and social techniques embracing the whole of the national territory and not a mere part of it, and that they promote the formation of small holdings and favor one social class only, the peasants or land workers, whereas these are not the only exploited classes. Up

---

* We must also refer here to an intriguing questionnaire, useful for studies on problems of agrarian reform and for its value as an intellectual stimulus, drafted in 1959 by the secretariat of the Pan American Union to specify the scope and extent of reforms, at the time of the meeting of the special committee of experts for the study of the financial requirements for the execution of the plans involved, and reported by Lucio Mendieta y Núñez in 'La reforma agraria de la América Latina en Washington' (1960: 36–38).

to the present a healthy agrarian situation has been found only in countries which have wide open spaces suitable for settlement by a growing population, e.g., the United States, Canada, Argentina, Australia, and South Africa; or countries where effective and intensive state intervention by way of minimum wages, social welfare levies, high taxes, and extension of leases (e.g. Western Europe), has reduced the inequality in land distribution.*

This is a question of principles, and Carranza bases them on Ricardo's law of differentiated economic rent; the rent paid for the use of a given piece of land represents the difference in productivity between one plot of land and another of equal size but of the poorest quality, assuming that the same effort is expended on both:

The manner of organizing the occupation and use of land in accordance with the natural order is to stipulate that the individual occupier shall hand over to the community that part of the production which is due to the community's effort, and keep for himself that part which is attributable to his own effort (Carranza 1961: 191).

Thus the share in production or profit which is attributable to the joint efforts of both cannot be handed over to an absentee landlord who because of the mere passage of time, without the slightest effort or investment of capital but simply and solely through the progress and development brought about by the effort of the community, sees the value of his property enhanced out of all proportion. Such absentee landlords still exist over the greater part of the South American continent, in spite of all the fuss about agrarian reform, which has not been carried through to any appreciable degree except in a few areas, making use of certain specific *latifundios* scattered about the national territory. There has merely been a political distribution of the

* In the natural or physiocratic order there are three principles, according to Carranza—freedom, equality, and justice—which determine the question of access to land and its exploitation, the legitimate right by which no person shall be prevented from freely exercising his productive activities, and the right of every man to the complete ownership of the product of his labor. According to Carranza, the monopoly established by the Roman law principle of ownership which prevails in the Western Latin American society, where the modern concept of social purpose has not yet been put into practice on any great scale, will never allow for long-term success for agrarian reform.

land as a concession to social pressure by particular groups. And at the same time, there have been many failures.

The question arises whether the state is fully aware of what it is doing. At any rate it is significant that state intervention has been purely on a formal level, designed to vest with a semblance of legality, situations which are fiercely debated in the majority of cases; and compromise has been arrived at without any real sense of being effective. Where pressure of public opinion is violent, an *ad hoc* solution may be found, without adequate moral backing or real will to achieve reform on the part of the administrators, who in many instances are the landowners themselves (Delgado 1963).

Conclusion

In commenting on the paper by Professor Kenneth L. Karst, the author considers that apart from emphasizing the many positive points in it and correcting small details here and there, Karst's contribution would have additional value if he rounded off certain points in the paper which might cause perplexity to a Latin American jurist. With this in mind we have urged practical training and legal research methods, describing experiments carried out in the United States and placing the major emphasis on certain aspects of law in which exploration and concordance with the facts call for an immediate survey.

Thus we feel that the following steps are essential:

1. There should be a new approach that would place greater stress on research methods.

2. A distinction should be made between the research done up to the present and that suggested or planned by Professor Karst, the argument being that research relating to economic development (administration of autonomous institutions, legal control of inflation, legal incentives to investment, international double taxation, systems of taxation, agrarian reform, and supranational legal agreements) and to family stability (entail, divorce, separation, property rights, concubinage, relations between parents and children, illegitimacy, and succession) is of primary importance for the improvement of public health and welfare.

3. A comparative study should be made of problems in various countries designed to reveal points of similarity and dissimilarity

in their respective laws and social situations, with the object of ascertaining how the legal rules of law have developed in the light of social pressures.

4. There is an urgent need for convening regional meetings, of at least three weeks' duration, where short courses of training would be given in methods of research and empirical analysis of law-in-action, if possible with the participation of colleagues specializing in social sciences and some teachers from the United States law schools. These meetings would also provide a useful opportunity for imparting information on projects being carried out, and for proposing specific projects on which significant research might be initiated.

REFERENCES

Abdala, Washington.
  1957 Sentido y fines de la universidad. *In* Estudios Jurídicos en memoria de Eduardo J. Couture. Montevideo, p. 4.
Adams, Mildred, and others.
  1963 Latin America: evolution or explosion. Council on World Tensions. New York, Dodd, Mead & Co.
Aguilera Camacho, A.
  1962 Derecho agrario colombiano. Bogotá, Ediciones Tercer Mundo.
Alcalá-Zamora, Niceto.
  1947 Proceso, autocomposición y autodefensa. Mexico City. Imprenta Universidad.
  1957 Causas y efectos sociales del derecho procesal (civil y penal). *In* Estudios Sociológicos, Eighth National Congress on Sociology, held at Durango, U.N.A.M., I.I.S. Mexico City, vol. II, pp. 171-94.
Alessandri, A., and M. Somarriva.
  1945 Curso de derecho civil. Santiago, Chile.
Alsina, Hugo.
  1956 Tratado teórico-práctico de derecho procesal, civil y comercial. Buenos Aires. Second edition, 6 vols.
Alves, João Luiz.
  1957 Código civil da República dos Estados Unidos do Brasil. Rio de Janeiro, Borsoi. Third edition, 5 vols.
Andueza, José G.
  1955 La jurisdicción constitucional en el derecho venezolano. Caracas, Universidad Central.
Araya, Rafael.
  1928 Función social de la universidad moderna. Rosario, Argentina.
Association of American Law Schools, Committee on curriculum.
  1944 Report. Handbook of the Association of American Law Schools.

Association of American Law Schools, Committee on Teaching and Methods.
1949–50   How to teach law. (An outline and bibliography.)
Association of American Law Schools.
1964   Foreign Exchange Bulletin. Vol. VI(2). St. Louis University (editor).
Baez Finol, Vicenzio.
1961   El impuesto predial rural. Su institución en Venezuela. Consejo del Bienestar Rural, Caracas.
Baiocco, Pedro J.
1930   Función social de la universidad moderna. Rosario, Argentina.
Baldana, Juan.
1947   Derecho notarial argentino. La Facultad, Buenos Aires. 12 vols.
Banco de Comercio Exterior.
1963   La integración económica latinoamericana. Mexico City.
Banco Interamericano de Desarrollo.
1964   Posibilidades de integración de las zonas fronterizas colombo-venezolanas. Washington (unpublished).
Bascuñán, Aníbal.
1957   Los seminarios de derecho. *In* Temas de Pedagogía Universitária. Universidad Nacional del Litoral, Rosario, Santa Fé, p. 217.
Bayitch, Stojan A.
1961   Latin America: a bibliographical guide to economy, history, law, politics and society. Coral Gables, Florida, University of Miami Press.
Becena, Francisco.
1925   Casos de derecho procesal civil (Para uso de estudiantes). Madrid.
1928   Magistratura y justicia. Madrid.
Bendicente, Francisco C.
1933   El método en la investigación y exposición de las materias económicas. Rosario, Sante Fé, Imprenta de la Universidad.
Bernaldo de Quirós, Constancio.
1948–49   Derecho penal, edited by J. M. Cajica. Puebla. 2 vols.
Beuscher, Jacob M.
1955   Making land laws serve economic ends. Journal of Farm Economics, vol. 37: 1143.
1959   Changing law to make the results of legal-economic research effective. *In* Legal-economic Research, Agricultural Law Center, State University of Iowa. Iowa City, p. 41.
1962   Law-in-action research in rural areas of the United States. *In* Atti della prima assamblea dell'Instituto di Diritto Agrario Internazionale e Comparato, held at Florence in 1960. Milan, Dott. A. Giuffrè Editore, vol. 2, p. 75.
1964   Agriculture in a multi-state world, a plea for empirical comparative legal studies. *In* Atti della seconda assamblea dell'Instituto di Diritto Agrario Internazionale e Comparato, held at Florence in 1963. Milan, Dott. A. Giuffrè Editore, vol. 1, p. 469.
Bevilacqua, Clovis.
1958–59   Código civil dos Estados Unidos do Brasil comentado. Rio de Janeiro, Livraria Francisco Alves. 6 vols.
Bielsa, Rafael.
1955   Ciencia de la administración. Buenos Aires, Dapalma.
1957   Los cursos de seminario. *In* Temas de Pedagogía Universitaria. Santa Fé, p. 217.

1964 Derecho administrativo. Buenos Aires, Abeledo Perrot. 5 vols. Sixth edition.

Brewer Carías, Allan-Randolph.
1964 Las instituciones fundamentales del derecho administrativo y la jurisprudencia venezolana. Caracas, Universidad Central de Venezuela.

Buonocore, Domingo.
1957 Temas de pedagagía universitaria: selección, prólogo, notas y bibliografía. Santa Fé.

Caldera, Rafael.
1960 Derecho del trabajo (venezolano). Buenos Aires.

Campo Salas, O.
1960 Comercio interlatinoamericano e integracíon regional. *In* Ciencias Políticas y Sociales, 6th year (19): 39 *et seq.*

Cann, Kenneth T.
1964 The structure of local government finance in Brazil, with comments on its relationship to community development. The Land Tenure Center, University of Wisconsin (mimeographed).

Carlos, Eduardo B.
1959 Clínica jurídica y enseñanza práctica. Buenos Aires, Ediciones Jurídicas Europa-América. Second edition.

Cardozo, Francisco Malta.
1953–56 Tratado de direito rural brasileiro. São Paulo, Edição Saraiva. 3 vols.

Carrancá y Trujillo, Raul.
1950 Derecho penal mexicano. Mexico City, Antigua Librería Robledo. 3rd edition.

Carranza, Carlos.
1961 Reforma agraria en América. Buenos Aires, Associación Argentina por la libertad de la cultura.

Carroll, Thomas.
1962 Land tenure and land reform in Latin America: a selected, annotated bibliography. Washington, D.C., Inter-American Development Bank (Preliminary version, mimeographed).

Caso, Angel.
1950 Derecho agrario. Mexico City, Editorial Porrúa.

Castán Tobenas, José.
1964 Los sistemas jurídicos contemporáneos del mundo occidental. Comparative Juridical Review, vol. 1. Coral Gables, Florida.

Cavalcanti, Temistocles Brandão.
1960 Tratado de direito administrativo. Rio de Janeiro, Livraria Freitas Bastos. 4 vols. Fourth edition.

Centro Latinoamericano de Investigaciones en Ciencias Sociales.
1963 Bibliografía sobre la reforma agraria en América Latina (mimeographed).

Cesarino, A. F.
1963 Direito social brasileiro. Rio de Janeiro, Livraria Freitas Bastos. 2 vols. Fifth edition.

Chryst, Walter E.
1959 Some general considerations of the theoretical foundations of legal-economic research. College of Law, State University of Iowa, Iowa City, p. 11.

Colmo, Alfredo.
1919 La cultura jurídica y la facultad de derecho. Buenos Aires.
I Congreso Internacional de Derecho Comparado de la Asociación Internacional de Ciencias Jurídicas.
1957 Tema IV: Estudio comparado de los medios jurídicos, directos o indirectos, de asegurar la estabilidad de la familia. Revista del Instituto de Derecho Comparado, nos. 8–9, Barcelona.
Cordova, Efren.
1957 Derecho laboral cubano. Havana. 2 vols.
Cossio, Carlos.
1939 La plenitud del orden jurídico y la interpretación de la ley. Buenos Aires, Losado.
1944 La teoría egológica del derecho y el concepto jurídico de la libertad. Buenos Aires, Losado.
1945 El derecho en el derecho judicial. Buenos Aires, Losado.
Couture, Eduardo J.
1938 El deber de decir verdad en juicio civil. Montevideo.
1955 Algunas observaciones preliminares sobre la enseñanza del derecho en los Estados Unidos. Montevideo.
1958 Fundamentos de derecho procesal civil. Buenos Aires, Depalma. Third edition.
Cuenca, Humberto.
1956 El derecho procesal en Venezuela. Caracas, Universidad Central de Venezuela.
Cueto Rua, Julio.
1957 El "Common law." Buenos Aires, Editorial La Ley.
Cueva, Mario de la.
1949 Derecho mexicano del trabajo. Mexico City. 2 vols.
Cunha, Oscar da.
1936 O dolo e o direito judiciário civil. Rio de Janeiro.
Curso de Capacitación de Profesionales en Reforma Agraria.
1963 Informe. Tomo I, La reforma agraria y el desarrollo económico y social de los países latinoamericanos; Tomo II, Aspectos jurídicos e institucionales de la reforma agraria; Tomo III, La reforma agraria y sus medidas complementarias; Tomo IV, Elaboración de proyectos específicos de reforma agraria; Tomo V, Estrategia y táctica de la reforma agraria y otros seminarios desarrollados durante el curso. Santiago, Chile.
Damianovich, Horacio.
1935 Ideas directrices del nuevo estatuto de la Universidad del Litoral, Universidad, No. 1, Santa Fé.
Dana Montano, Salvador M.
1958 La importancia de la independencia del poder judicial y de la inamovibilidad de los jueses como garantíba de la misma. Buenos Aires, La Ley.
1960 Las garantías específicas de la independencia del poder judicial. Boletín de la Biblioteca del Congreso de la Nación. Buenos Aires, pp. 13 *et seq.*
Delgado, Oscar.
1962 Bibliografía latinoamericana sobre reforma agraria y tenencia de la tierra. Mexico City (mimeographed).

1963 Revolución, reforma y conservatismo como tipos de políticas agrarias en Latinoamérica. Revista de la Universidad Libre, 4a. época, No. XV. Bogotá.

Ellis, Harold H.
1954 Collaboration between law and agriculture, 7 Journal of Legal Education 65.

Flores Moncayo, José.
1956 Derecho agrario boliviano. Sante Fé. Fourth edition.

Fraga, Gabino.
1962 Derecho administrativo. Mexico City. Ninth edition.

Franco, José María.
1965 Minifundia and land consolidation in Venezuela and Colombia. University of Wisconsin.

Frankfurter, Felix.
1947 Some reflections on the reading of statutes. Columbia Law Review 47: 527–46 (May).

García Maynez, Eduardo.
1944 Introducción al estudio del derecho. Mexico City, Editorial Porrúa.

Gil Fortoul, J.
1962 Historia constitucional de Venezuela. Caracas.

Giner de los Ríos, Francisco.
1916–28 Obras completas. 19 vols. Madrid. Vol. X: Pedagogía universitaria.

Goldschmidt, James.
1935 Metodologia jurídico-penal; cursillo dado en la Universidad de Madrid.

Goldschmidt, Roberto.
1958 Estudios de derecho comparado. Universidad Central de Venezuela. Caracas.
1962 Nuevos estudios de derecho comparado. Universidad Central de Venezuela. Caracas.
1964 Curso de derecho mercantil. Universidad Central de Venezuela. Caracas.

Gómez, Eusebio.
1939–42 Tratado de derecho penal. Buenos Aires. 6 vols.

Gonzáles Calderón, Juan A.
1930–31 Derecho constitucional argentino. Buenos Aires. 3 vols. Third edition.

Gonzáles Miranda, R.
1958 Estudios acerca del régimen legal del petróleo en Venezuela. Universidad Central, Caracas.

Goode, William J., and Paul K. Hatt.
1952 Methods in social research. New York, McGraw-Hill.

Haas, Ernst B., and Philippe C. Schmitter.
1964 Economics and differential patterns of political integration: projections about unity in Latin America. International Organization, vol. XVIII(4): 4 *et seq*.

Harris, Marshall.
1958 Legal-economic interdisciplinary research. Journal of Legal Education, vol. 10.
1960 Facilitating agrarian reform through the integration of law and economics: agrarian reform and economic growth in developing

countries. Washington, D.C., U.S. Department of Agriculture, p. 41 *et seq.*

Hernández Colón, Rafael.
1963   Sobre la selección de la judicatura. Revista de Derecho Puertorriqueno, No. 8. Universidad Católica de Puerto Rico, Ponce.

Holmes, O. W.
1920   The path of the law. Collected legal papers. New York, Harcourt, Brace and Co., p. 174.

Inter-American Development Bank. IADB.
1964   *See* Banco Interamericano de Desarrollo.

Jahoda, Marie, Morton Deutsch, and Stuart W. Cook.
1951   Research methods in social relations with special reference to prejudice. New York, Dryden.

Jiménez de Asúa, Luís.
1943   El Criminalista. Buenos Aires, La Ley.
1946   Libertad de amar y derecho de morir. Buenos Aires, Losada. Sixth edition.
1963   Estudios de derecho procesal y criminología. Buenos Aires. 2 vols.
1964   Tratado de derecho penal. Buenos Aires, Losada. 7 vols. Second edition.

Jiménez de Asúa, Luís, and others.
1929   Casos de derecho penal. Para uso de estudiantes. Madrid. Second edition.

Karst, Kenneth L.
1964a   The study of Latin American law and legal institutions. *In* Social Science Research on Latin America, edited by Charles Wagley. New York, Columbia University Press, pp. 290–333.
1964b   Latin American land reform: The uses of confiscation, Michigan Law Review, vol. 63(2).

Lafaille, Hector.
1928   Inaugural address to the Instituto de Enseñanza Práctica, given on May 16, 1924. Informes y antecedentes del Instituto de Enseñanza Práctica, Buenos Aires.
1947–50   Derecho civil. Buenos Aires. 5 vols.

LTC (Land Tenure Center). University of Wisconsin.
1962–64   Newsletter, nos. 1–18.
1964   Bibliography: Agrarian reform and tenure, with special sections on agricultural finance, taxation and agriculture, agricultural statistics, and bibliographical sources. University of Wisconsin (mimeographed).

Langdell, Christopher C.
1871   Selection of cases on the law of contracts. Boston, Little, Brown and Co.

Lanz Duret, Miguel.
1947   Derecho constitucional mexicano y consideraciones sobre la realidad política de nuestro régimen. Mexico City. Fourth edition.

Lauterbach, Albert.
1963   Objetivos de la administración de las empresas y requerimientos de desarrollo en la América Latina. Revista de Economía Latinoamericana, 3rd year, No. 9, p. 119 *et seq.*

Lazo, Oscar.
1962   Código civil concordado y anotado de acuerdo con la legislación nacional y la jurisprudencia de casación y de instancia. Caracas. Second edition.

Lewis, Juan T.
1935 Objeto y fin de la universidad. Universidad, No. 1, Santa Fé, p. 37.
Linares Quintana, Segundo.
1953–63 Tratado de la ciencia del derecho constitucional argentino y comparado. Buenos Aires. 9 vols.
Linhares de Lacerda, M.
1960 Tratado das terras do Brasil. Rio de Janeiro, Editóra Alba. 2 vols.
López Rey, Manuel.
1964 El delito de aborto en España y en América Latina. Boletín del Instituto de Derecho Comparado de México, XVII(49): 31 et seq.
Lo Valvo, José.
1933 El problema universitario del profesionalismo y la investigación. Santa Fé.
Maldonado, Abraham.
1956 Derecho agrario, historia, doctrina, y legislación. La Paz, Imprenta Nacional.
Massad, Carlos.
1964 Economic research in Latin America. In Social Science Research on Latin America, edited by Charles Wagley. New York, Columbia University Press, pp. 214–42.
Mayda, Jaro.
1960 Problems of legal education in Latin America. Journal of Legal Education, vol. 12(3): 407 et seq.
Mendieta y Núñez, Lucio.
1960 La reforma agraria de la América Latina en Washington. Mexico, Instituto de Investigaciones Sociales de la Universidad Nacional Autónoma de México, pp. 36–38.
1964 El problema agrario de México. Mexico City, Editorial Porrúa. Eighth edition.
Mendoza, José Rafael.
1957 Curso de derecho penal venezolano. Caracas, El Cojo.
Menéndez, J.
1942 Principios de derecho criminal. Havana, Jesús Montero.
Mikesell, Raymond F.
1961 The movement toward regional trading groups in Latin America. In Latin American Issues: Essays and Comments, edited by A. O. Hirschman. New York, The Twentieth Century Fund, pp. 125–51.
Moles Caubet, Antonio.
1958 La organización del registro inmobiliario en Venezuela. Revista de la Facultad de Derecho, no. 16. Caracas.
Muñoz, Luís.
1946 Comentarios al código civil para el distrito y territorios federales. Mexico City, Lex.
Muratti, Natalio.
1931–37 Prólogos, trabajos de seminario. Rosario. Vols. V to XI.
Núñez y Núñez, Eduardo Rafael.
1938–39 Código de comercio. Habana, Cultural S.A., 2 vols. Vol. I, 1938; Vol. II, 1939.
O'Byrne, John C.
1955 Discussion: Economic-legal approach to agricultural problems. Journal of Farm Economics, vol. 37: 1157.
Ortega y Gasset, José.
1936 Misión de la universidad. Madrid.

Ortega Torres, Jorge.
　1961　Código civil, con notas, concordancias, jurisprudencia de la Corte Suprema y normas legales complementarias. Bogotá, Ed. Temis. Fifth edition.
Osorio, Joaquim Luiz.
　1948　Direito rural. Rio de Janeiro, Ed. José Konfino.
Padilla, Francisco E.
　1954　Derecho agrario. Facultad de Derecho y Ciencias Sociales. Tucumán,
Palacios, Alfredo.
　1924　Los nuevos métodos. Universidad de La Plata. Revista de Ciencias Jurídicas y Sociales. La Plata.
Parsons, Kenneth H.
　1962　Agrarian reform policy as a field of research; Agrarian reform and economic growth in developing countries. Papers from a seminar on research perspectives. U.S. Department of Agriculture, Washington, D.C.
Pérez, F. S.
　1962　La constitución nacional y la Corte Suprema, con la jurisprudencia sobre los artículos de la carta política. Buenos Aires. 3 vols.
Pérez Llana, Eduardo A.
　1964　Derecho agrario. Santa Fé. Fourth edition.
Pina, Rafael.
　1951　Temas de derecho procesal civil. Mexico City.
　1956–61　Elementos de derecho civil mexicano. Mexico City, Editorial Porrúa. 4 vols.
Pincus, Joseph.
　1963　El mercado centroamericano. Oficina Regional para Asuntos de Centroamérica y Panamá. Guatemala.
Pollack, Erwin.
　1962　Fundamentals of legal research. Brooklyn, Foundation Press.
Pontes de Miranda, Francisco C.
　1960　Comentários à constituíção de 1946. Rio de Janeiro, Borsoi. Third edition, 7 vols.
Pound, Roscoe.
　1911–12　The scope and purpose of sociological jurisprudence. Harvard Law Review, 24: 591; 25: 140.
　1923　Interpretation of modern legal history. Cambridge, Mass.
　1935　Sociology of law and sociological jurisprudence. University of Toronto Law Journal.
　1950　An introduction to the philosophy of law. New Haven, Yale University Press. Eighth edition.
Powell, John D.
　1964　Preliminary report on the Federación Campesina de Venezuela. Land Tenure Center, University of Wisconsin (mimeographed).
Prebisch, Raúl.
　1962　The economic development of Latin America and its principal problems. Economic Bulletin for Latin America, United Nations, New York, vol. 7, no. 7.
Price, Miles O., and H. Bitner.
　1953　Effective legal research. New York, Prentice-Hall.

Price, Robert E.
1963 Rural unionization in Brazil. Land Tenure Center, University of Wisconsin (mimeographed).
1964 Selective bibliography on the legal aspects of agrarian reform in Latin America. Land Tenure Center, University of Wisconsin (mimeographed).

Prunell, Antonio J.
1957 Contribución al estudio de la práctica y didáctica del derecho. Estudios jurídicos en memoria de Eduardo J. Couture. Montevideo, p. 567.

Quiroga, Pedro R.
1933 El método de la investigación jurídica, Anales de la Facultad de Ciencias Jurídicas y Sociales de la Universidad de La Plata, p. 588 *et seq.*

Quiróz Cuarón, Alfonso.
1957 Un aspecto de la sociopatología del derecho en México: la impunidad. Estudios sociológicos del 80 Congreso Nacional de Sociología, Instituto de Investigaciones Sociales, Universidad Nacional Autónoma de México, tomo II, p. 219 *et seq.*

Ramón y Cajal, Santiago.
1935 Reglas y consejos sobre investigación científica. Madrid. Seventh edition.

Raup, Philip M.
1959 Tailoring legal-economic research to emerging problems. *In* Legal-economic Research, Agricultural Law Center, State University of Iowa, p. 55 *et seq.*
1962 The role of research in agrarian reform; Agrarian reform and economic growth in developing countries. Papers from a seminar on research perspectives, U.S. Department of Agriculture, Washington, D.C.
1963 The contribution of land reforms to agricultural development: An analytical framework. Economic Development and Cultural Change, vol. XII(1), Chicago.

Reale, Miguel.
1953 Filosofia do direito. São Paulo, Edição Saraiva. 2 vols.
1960 Teoria do direito e do estado. São Paulo, Livraria Martins Editôra. Second edition.

Recaséns Siches, Luís.
1952 Vida humana, sociología y derecho. México. Second edition.
1956 Tratado general de sociología. Mexico City, Editorial Porrúa.
1957 Las relaciones entre sociólogos y juristas. Jurisprudencia sociológica y sociología del derecho. Estudios sociológicos del 80 Congreso Nacional de Sociología, Instituto de Investigaciones Sociales de la Universidad Nacional Autónoma de México, Mexico City, vol. I, p. 141 *et seq.*
1961 Tratado general de filosofía del derecho. Mexico City, Editorial Porrúa. Second edition.

Revista de la Facultad de Derecho y Ciencias Sociales. Montevideo.
1957 and 1959.

Ritchie, John.
1964 Legal education in the United States, Washington and Lee Law Review, vol. XXI: 177.

Rivarola, Mario A.
  1938   Tratado de derecho comercial argentino. Buenos Aires. Cía. Argentina de Editores. 6 vols.
  1941   Instituciones de derecho civil argentino. Buenos Aires. 2 vols.
Rojina Villegas, Rafael.
  1945–47   Derecho civil. Mexico City, Editorial Jús. 11 vols.
Ruggieri Parra, P.
  1949   Política y constitución de Venezuela. Universidad Central, Caracas.
Ruiz Funes, Mariana.
  1948   La peligrosidad y sus experiencias legales. Havana.
Russomano, Mozart V.
  1962–63   Comentarios à consolidação das leis do trabalho. Rio de Janeiro, J. Konfino, Sixth edition, 5 vols.
Salvat, Raymondo M.
  1958   Tratado de derecho civil argentino. Buenos Aires. Tenth edition, 6 vols.
Satanowsky, Marco.
  1957   Tratado de derecho comercial. Buenos Aires. 3 vols.
Sayagués Laso, Enrique.
  1959–63   Tratado de derecho administrativo. Montevideo, Editorial Porrúa. 2 vols.
Schickele, Raimer.
  1952   Theories concerning land tenure. Journal of Farm Economics, Proceedings, The American Farm Economic Association, vol. XXXIV(5).
Serra Rojas, Andrés.
  1961   Derecho administrativo. Mexico City, Editorial Porrúa. Second edition.
Spota, Alberto.
  1947–50   Tratado de derecho civil. Buenos Aires. 5 vols.
Stead, William H.
  1963   El desarrollo económico de Puerto Rico. Mexico City, Libreros Mexicanos Reunidos.
Tabio, Evelio.
  1949   Comentarios al código de defensa social. Havana, Jesús Montero. 8 vols.
Tena Ramírez, Felipe.
  1963   Derecho constitucional mexicano. Mexico City, Editorial Porrúa. Sixth edition.
Thome, Joseph R.
  1964   Title insecurity in Colombia. Land Tenure Center, University of Wisconsin (mimeographed).
Thorbecke, Erik.
  1962   Agrarian reform as a conditioning influence in economic growth; Agrarian reform and economic growth in developing countries. Papers from a seminar on research perspectives and problems, U.S. Department of Agriculture, Washington, D.C.
Timmons, John F.
  1955   Integration of law and economics in analyzing agricultural land use problems. Journal of Farm Economics, 37: 1126.
  1959   Methodological problems in legal-economic research. Agricultural Law Center, State University of Iowa, p. 23 *et seq.*

Torino, Enrique.
   1935   Informe elevado a la Facultad de Ciencias Jurídicas y Sociales de la
          Universidad de Buenos Aires. Boletín menusal del Seminario de
          Ciencias Jurídicas y Sociales, Buenos Aires, p. 1654 *et seq.*
Universidad Nacional Autónoma de México.
   1959   Primera Conferencia de las Facultades y Escuelas Latinoamericanas de
          Derecho. Mexico City.
UNAM (Universidad Nacional Autónoma de México). Instituto de Investiga-
          ciones Sociales.
   1964   Bibliografiá mínima del decimoquinto congreso nacional de sociolo-
          gía, sociología de la reforma agraria. Mexico City (mimeographed).
Urquidi, Victor L.
   1962   Free trade and economic integration in Latin America. Berkeley,
          California, University of California Press.
Valencia Zea, A.
   1960   Derecho civil. Bogotá, Editorial Temis.
Villalón-Galdames, Alberto.
   1963   Una introducción a la bibliografía jurídica latinoamericana. Uni-
          versity Microfilms Inc., Ann Arbor, Michigan.
Venezuela. Ministerio de Agricultura y Cría. Comisión de Reforma Agraria.
   1959   Reforma agraria. Caracas. 4 vols.
Wald, Arnold.
   1959   A cláusula de escala móvel: um meio de defesa contra a depreciação
          monetária. Rio de Janerio, Editôra Nacional do Direito. Second
          Edition.
   1962   Direito Civil brasileiro. Rio de Janeiro, Editôra Lux. 5 vols.
The Washington Foreign Law Society.
   1959   A symposium on the law of Latin America, held at the George
          Washington University Law School, 1955–56. Washington, D.C.

BRYCE WOOD

Notes on Conference Proceedings

This report of discussions at the Conference deals indirectly with the papers and is intended primarily to bring out some of the principal features of the discussions, to supplement the Introduction by Manuel Diégues Júnior, and to present some suggestions that both complement and differ from the formal presentations of the papers.

In holding this conference, the Joint Committee on Latin American Studies hoped to further communication not only between social scientists in the United States and Latin America, but also among Latin American social scientists, to assess attitudes toward social science research, and to explore ways of mutual cooperation in scholarly activities.

The title of this volume has been chosen advisedly, for it would be inaccurate to speak of "social sciences" as organized disciplines in all branches and in all twenty countries of Latin America. There are social scientists, however, in all disciplines if not in all countries, and a substantial number of them are full-time professionals engaged in teaching, contract research, and advisory or other affiliations with central banks and other governmental agencies. A high proportion of the leading social scientists have received at least part of their graduate training in the United States or Western Europe, particularly France and England.

The Milieu

For Latin American social scientists, as scholars and as citizens, the great problem is their relationships to the processes of economic and social development. How can the special skills of social scientists contribute to meeting the issues presented by demands for rapid and fundamental social change, often in circumstances of acute political tension?

As a political scientist said:

In the United States, social scientists work in a relatively stable social situation, while we are going through a permanent crisis, with insistent demands for far-reaching changes in a short time. . . . This forces us to develop a critical and dialectical type of social science to understand the social problems of Latin America.

A colleague added: "We have received an inflow of sociology from all over the world—from Marx, Weber, Parsons, Gurvtch and others—and with a selection of their ideas we are tying to do macroanalyses of national societies."

An urgent concern is felt for the development of scientific thought "to explain present reality" and to "transform the existing social structure." Social scientists cannot avoid being involved in the all-encompassing processes they are observing. They cannot be neutral:

The social scientists in Latin America have a critical attitude toward the established order; they have, on the whole, decided to help bring about transformations, and they have chosen planning as their instrument. . . . Research by social scientists must match requirements for planning and development. Otherwise, people will say professors are talking about nonexistent problems.

If social scientists cannot be politically neutral, it was thought that they should make every attempt to be professionally objective, and an economist suggested some alternative research topics that brought to the surface notable differences of opinion. The economist's views were that instead of agrarian reform, the proper subject of study would be the role played by agriculture in economic development; similarly, "tax reform is not the basic problem but, rather, the role of the public sector in economic development." And also, economic integration of Latin American countries is not as fundamental a question as industrialization, or the factors shaping industry in Latin America as a whole. This opinion reflected patience and the long view and a greater emphasis on research than that giving precedence to transformation through planning.

The differences suggested by these comments are important and far-reaching. Concerning development, it was suggested by a sociologist that there is need to formulate patterns of research in which social sciences may contribute through macroanalysis "so we may look at social processes and the whole time in which we live." An economist suggested, however, that "it is not yet possible to have an integrated development policy for a country," and another added that "in Latin America we do not know how the national economies function; consequently there is an appearance of improvisation in economic policies, and decisions are usually based on political and not on economic analysis."

Although there is general recognition that development cannot be explained solely by economic factors, there is also a concern on the part of economists about "dangers" resulting from "the invasion of the field of economics" by other social scientists who may be unaware of the economic implications of their own recommendations. While good economists and good sociologists might work together effectively, it was thought that efforts at interdisciplinary research had thus far been largely unsuccessful. There was hope, however, that progress might be made gradually, based primarily on an increase in numbers of more rigorously trained social scientists. Furthermore, interdisciplinary research should be attempted on small and limited problems: "We should not spend our time on integrating theories, but try only to work on the small scope of specific hunches on noneconomic factors such as how fast groups can move from one set of resources to another." Such a problem approach, combined with teamwork by sociologists and economists modeled on the experience of the Economic Commission for Latin America (ECLA), appeared to offer more promise for the present than efforts at comprehensive theoretical agreement. The position was also taken, however, that Latin America is enjoying a flowering of social sciences because many of its countries are making the transition from traditional to modern societies: "Social sciences are born in crisis, and we are forced to consider this problem of over-all scientific thinking since we are faced with some of the same problems faced by the founders of the social sciences."

The status of different disciplines varies from country to country. In general, economists are in great demand both by government and industry. As a sociologist admiringly said: "The economists are making the history of our countries as no other social scientists are." Economists were given a remarkable opportunity for disciplinary advancement with the formation of ECLA in 1948 by the Economic and Social Council of the United Nations. ECLA was given vigorous direction by a strong Latin American staff of economists, and it became the chief spokesman for Latin America on domestic and international problems of development, if any single agency may be said to be able to play that part.

In addition, ECLA, according to one economist, "has taught us the need for economic research to be done on the basis of teamwork; we cannot use the traditional individual research methods any longer." ECLA has thus been a training institution, as well as the principal source of economic theory, policy, and data relevant to Latin America's place in the world economy for the past decade and a half. ECLA has also had important internal effects since it provided concepts that were applied for a time in the Brazilian Northeast through the development organization SUDENE.

The growth of anthropology has been notable chiefly in Brazil and in Mexico where, in the 1930s, the initiation of serious research was contemporaneous with the establishment of national unity and the intensification of national feeling. Emphasizing the new synthesis that has emerged in their country, Mexican anthropologists prefer the term "Ibero-American" to "Latin American"; the former suggests only geographical origins of human resources, while the latter implies a cultural dominance that is viewed sympathetically neither by Mexican anthropologists nor Mexican nationalists. The measure of public appreciation of the role of anthropology in social development may be gauged through contemplation of the magnificent Museum of Anthropology in Mexico City, opened at the end of 1964.

While some economists are firmly established in central banks and some anthropologists in national museums as well as in planning agencies and action programs, historians, political scientists, and sociologists lack comparable recognition and support outside the universities.

Geography is in a special position. There are military-geographic institutes in some Latin American countries, whose work is principally map-making and traditional military history. Still generally regarded as a natural science, geography is just beginning to show a few signs of emerging from cartographic concentration and to show an interest in ecology. Human geography is largely neglected in Latin America, and geographers have not contributed much to the efforts to overcome natural obstacles to agricultural development. There is little field research except in Brazil and Chile, and geographers have given little attention to problems of resource conservation. Scholars in other disciplines would welcome contributions that human geographers might make to regional and urban planning.

On the whole, historians in Latin America have not done work relevant to modern problems of development and do not appear to want to commit themselves to such work: "In Brazil, political history does not exist, and the story is not much better with respect to economic history. In Chile, history is a deplorable collection of facts and dates that does not help to understand the functioning of Chilean society." There is perhaps greatest appreciation of historical research in Mexico, where a half-century's experience with one revolution and under one constitution has established a tradition that is vigorously expanding, and that Mexicans view with justifiable pride.

Sociologists and political scientists have neither the demonstrably applicable methodological equipment of the economist nor the identification with national unity of the anthropologist —at least, the Mexican anthropologist. As a sociologist said:

Latin American sociologists must at present be considered as men desiring the development of science rather than as trying to enlarge special frontiers of scientific knowledge. It is necessary to establish the institutional requisites that make possible the development of science. Application has its place, but we are trying to create conditions that allow institutions to work autonomously, and with vitality and continuity. The democratization of power in most of Latin America has not yet advanced sufficiently to allow complete freedom for research and for the expression of the scientific mentality.

Several participants observed that it is a serious matter when social scientists run the risk of persecution, deprivation of political rights, and even exile in some Latin American countries, just at the time when social and political problems are extremely acute and objective analyses of them are most needed. At the same time, it was pointed out, social scientists should avoid martyrdom and should try to survive and work without losing their perspectives; they have the professional privilege of living in a period when it is not necessary to imagine artificial conditions of structural changes for real ones are knocking on the doors. When social scientists as intellectuals feel a deep sense of social responsibility, the topics, methods, and controversiality of their research are bound to be examined critically and publicly. Furthermore, if their research problems are framed in terms of reforms in fundamental social structures, then there are political risks to be run; and some who have become administrators of development programs fostered by one regime have become exiles when their work was repudiated by a successor regime. There are many nuances of timing, emphasis, and involvement, and with rapid political and other changes, it is not difficult for a social scientist to make political errors if he undertakes research on important issues, even if the issues are associated with action in pursuance of the officially approved Alliance for Progress. Those who go further than research and are seen as attacking accepted values through participation in planning agencies or through social theory make still more hazardous choices, if they wish to maintain their professional positions at home. These problems arise, of course, in those countries where modernization is most advanced, research opportunities most open, and social scientists most free to develop their disciplines. There will for a while be some attrition on the front lines, but happily, exiled social scientists usually appear to find outlets for their talents in more hospitable environments elsewhere in Latin America, the United States, or an international secretariat.

As recognition is gradually given to the need for development of the social science disciplines as part of overall national development or modernization, the social science frontier will become quieter; squatters may become homesteaders and then form cooperatives.

Transnational Relationships of Social Scientists

Regarding the contents of *Social Science Research on Latin America,* edited by Charles Wagley, it was noted that Latin America, to United States social scientists, is only a subject of study to be observed from afar, but "for Latin American social scientists, Latin America is not only the object of study—this is where we live." This means that there is a lack of symmetry in the reality faced by scholars from the two areas, and no fully satisfactory reconciliation is available because the differences of approach have not themselves been studied. However, the great gap is not between Latin American and United States social scientists, but between Latin American social scientists and their own societies. It was suggested that in the United States perhaps the late C. Wright Mills was in a position roughly equivalent to that of Latin American sociologists.

A principal omission in the book edited by Charles Wagley was that of a chapter on population, including population structure and technical characteristics of the various demographic strata. The chapter on history evoked the comment that economists considered the lack of satisfactory work in economic history to be a gap that should be closed this is a field between economics as an applied science and history and since underdeveloped countries are more interested in applied work, historians do not get much support. Because of their lack of knowledge of economic history economists do not have full acquaintance with "the realities of our economies."

A second important omission in the book was discussion of inter-American relations, particularly the nature of the influences exerted by the United States on the countries of Latin America. The hope was expressed that a later conference might be called, aiming at a scholarly exploration of this field of research. In this connection interest was expressed in the suggestion that, on an informal and private basis, scholars might make a cooperative effort to improve the accessibility of archival sources for students of economic, political, and diplomatic history.

The chapter on sociology gave rise to comments by Latin Americans that the distinction between quantitative and qualitative was too sharply drawn:

The periodization of sociology is questionable, notably the assertion that scientific sociology began only as late as 1945. There is a cumulative process of development of scientific thinking. . . . Statistics should be a part of the training of sociologists; it aids research on immediate and practical problems, but this should not be the foundation of sociological knowledge. We have a concern also with subjective reality which may be important to other social sciences as well. . . . Economics and sociology must be part of an overall truth.

Furthermore, "Latin American social phenomena are not accompanied by sufficiently organized data so that foreigners may gain a precise understanding of them. Refined quantitative techniques cannot be used, and it is not possible to appreciate them when they are viewed from outside, as laboratory problems."

An objection of a similar sort was made to the traditional-modern dichotomy presented in the chapter on political science. Latin American scholars did not consider this distinction to be applicable in their countries where there was a continuous process of growth of social sciences. It was suggested that the difference might be clearly defined in the United States where fairly stable social conditions had been experienced for a long period of time. A broader view supporting this position was also offered:

Progress is not just empirical, descriptive and pragmatic. There is also theoretical progress by way of explanation of models with which we work despite the difficulty of lack of human and material resources. . . . We combine European and American traditions and look forward to making original contributions by adding to them the results of the study of Latin American societies.

Cooperation among social scientists as professionals has a number of aspects. It was suggested that "an unconscious scientific colonialism" on the part of United States social scientists might result in actions that could destroy much of the work of recent sociology in Latin America: "We are less interested in work on our problems by United States sociologists than in discussions of general social science with our colleagues. There is a crisis in Latin America with respect to research by foreign scholars."

The most promising cooperation among social scientists now would appear to be collaborative field research on applied problems, selected by Latin American scholars, with colleagues from abroad whose interests are compatible. Joint research efforts can improve communication and minimize the "outsider-insider" problem referred to earlier. Field research on applied problems would minimize arguments about disciplinary boundaries and focus attention on trying to solve problems which have feasible solutions and costs that can be measured with reasonable accuracy. Textbooks on sociology in the United States:

... classify social problems, but in our countries, where planning is being done, we are more interested in studying other fields more in line with social reality. If there were more TVA's in the United States, and if they had been studied we would have had a greater contribution toward what we mean by applied sociology—the conditions of intervention in social reality.

As a specific example, it was noted that useful interdisciplinary collaboration had been secured in the membership of planning committees in the development programs of the Brazilian northeast. It was found that community development programs would be useless to initiate unless, concomitantly, stable institutions were established capable of responding to demands and of undertaking tasks of political socialization after the first organization effort had reached a plateau.

To the extent that Latin Americans define the problems, the crisis of research by foreigners would be mitigated, and the intrusion of outsiders would be reduced if they participated as members of local institutes. Such collaboration is difficult to arrange, but it may well be worth trying, not only to augment the limited number of qualified social scientists, but also to learn more about applied sociology. Latin Americans consider that they need to augment research projects using quantitative methods, but that they still have a different type of sociology that does not use the full kit of tools available elsewhere, partly because more advanced techniques may be rejected in some countries or in some sectors of society in Latin America, and partly because these techniques are not adequate for studying problems in Latin America which differ from those elsewhere.

With respect to training, it was noted that the assistance of first-class social scientists from abroad is needed. Recent Chilean experience with so-called "ambassadors of science" as visiting professors was regarded with satisfaction in the field of economics, but there remained certain systemic difficulties in the educational systems making it difficult for optimum use to be made of foreign scholars. One of these difficulties was the hamstringing of the development of social sciences because of the impossibility for part-time students, taught by part-time professors, to receive intensive training.

The results of field research in the applied sciences, it was noted, do not act by themselves. The work of social scientists must be institutionalized, and this task is often in the hands of lawyers, since "the law is the training for top leadership in Latin America." Until now, legal education has concentrated on the classification of legal rules and principles relating to abstract man and with the creation of abstract theories. This implies a static conception of law, and men so trained are, as a group, one of the most conservative elements in the universities. There are other views, one of which is that of law as social engineering: There is need for cooperation between social scientists and lawyers if this view is to gain significant acceptance. If, as a sociologist said, "in our societies in these times of rapid change, we have to know the trends so that they may be organized," organization is likely to be the job of lawyers, whose education should, to a greater degree than at present, inform them about the societies in which they live. Lawyers are not, it was observed, going to stick to dry formalism, and social scientists should find ways to work with those lawyers most interested in the organization of change.

Contributors

MANUEL DIÉGUES, JÚNIOR is Director of the Centro Latinoamericano de Pesquisas em Cêncas Sociais, Rio de Janeiro. One of his most recent works is *Imigração, urbanização, industrialização: estudos sôbre alguns aspectos da contribuição cultural do imigrante no Brasil* (Rio de Janeiro, Centro Brasileiro de Pesquisas Educacionais, 1964).

FLORESTAN FERNANDES is Professor of Sociology at the University of São Paulo. In addition to the publications mentioned in the bibliography accompanying his essay, his book on Negro integration in Brazil has been translated into English and will be published by the Columbia University Press in the near future.

LUIS ESCOBAR CERDA is the author of several books and articles on economics and education. He is a former dean of the Faculty of Economics, University of Chile, and a former minister of economy for Chile. At present he is an executive director of the International Monetary Fund and a member of the Inter-American Committee of the Alliance for Progress (CIAP).

JOSÉ NUN is Visiting Lecturer, Department of Political Science, and Associate Researcher, Institute of International Studies, University of California, Berkeley. He was appointed late in 1966 as director of a research project on political marginality in Latin America, sponsored by the Instituto Latinoamericano de Planificación Económica y Social (ILPES) and the Centro Para el Estudio del Desarrollo Económico y Social de América Latina (DESAL). An Argentine by birth and early training, he has published articles on Latin American politics, notably several dealing with political instability and military coups.

DANIEL COSÍO VILLEGAS is a member of El Colegio Nacional and former president of El Colegio de México. He is the general editor of *Historia moderna de México*. *American Extremes* is a collection of his essays, translated by Américo Paredes (University of Texas Press, 1964).

VÍCTOR L. URQUIDI is President of El Colegio de México and director of its Economic and Demographic Research Program. He is the author of *Free Trade and Economic Integration in Latin America* (University of California Press, 1962) and *The Challenge of Development in Latin America* (New York, Praeger, 1964) as well as numerous articles and essays on economic development issues. He has directed research programs for the Banco de México, the Mexican Ministry of Finance, and the Economic Commission for Latin America.

VICTOR FLORES OLEA is a professor at the School of Social and Political Science of the National University of Mexico. He holds a law degree from the National University and has done graduate work in political science at the University of Rome and the University of Paris. His publications include *Política y Dialéctica* (Ed. UNAM, México, 1964) ; and *Marxismo y Democracia Socialista* (Buenos Aires, Ed. Jorge Alvarez, 1965), as well as numerous essays and articles.

OCTAVIO IANNI is associate professor of sociology at the University of São Paulo. His most recent books include *Industrializacão e Desenvolvimento Social no Brasil, Estado e Capitalismo (Estrutura Social e Industrializacão no Brasil)*, and *Raças e Classes Sociais na Brasil,* In progress is a study on the political models of Brazilian economic development.

JOSÉ HONORIO RODRIGUES is a Brazilian historian, formerly director of the National Archives, and presently a member of the faculty of the Instituto Rio Branco. His publications include *Brazil and Africa* (University of California Press, 1965).

FERNANDO CÁMARA BARBACHANO is curator of the ethnographic section in the new National Museum of Anthropology, Mexico City. He holds degrees both from the National School of Anthropology and History of Mexico, and the University of Chicago, and has engaged in field research in Mexico and Peru, and in applied anthropological studies of urban problems in Mexico City and other places. He headed the Housing Development Project in 1961–64 at Ciudad Sahagún (Hidalgo) Mexico. His most recent monograph is *Persistencia y cambio cultural entre Tzeltales de los Altos de Chiapas: Estudio comparativo de las instituciones religiosas y políticas de los Municipios de Tenejapa y Oxchuc* (México, Escuela Nacional de Antropología e Historia, 1966).

JOSÉ MARÍA FRANCO has received law degrees from universities in Spain, Venezuela, and the United States. He is presently practicing law and teaching in Caracas. His articles on legal subjects include "Cadastral Surveying, Title Registration and Land Taxation as Interdependent Tools of Development: Their Application to Venezuela" (in preparation); and "La Investigación Integral Agraria en los Estados Unidos" (Revista de la Facultad de Derecho, Universidad de los Andes, Mérida, Venezuela, 1965) .

BRYCE WOOD has taught at Reed and Swarthmore Colleges and at Columbia University, and is an Executive Associate of the Social Science Research Council. He is author of *The Making of the Good Neighbor Policy* and *The United States and Latin American Wars, 1932–1942* (Columbia University Press, 1961, 1966).

PARTICIPANTS IN THE CONFERENCE
ON LATIN AMERICAN STUDIES

The following, in addition to the authors of papers and members of the Joint Committee, participated in the Conference:

George L. Bach, Carnegie Institute of Technology
Reynold E. Carlson, The Ford Foundation
Orlando Carvalho, University of Minas Gerais
Jean Casimir, Latin American Center for Research in the Social Sciences
Luis A. Costa Pinto, University of Rio de Janeiro
Ary França, University of São Paulo
Joseph Grunwald, The Brookings Institution
Rex D. Hopper, Brooklyn College
Bertram Hutchinson, Latin American Center for Research in the Social Sciences
Kenneth L. Karst, University of California, Los Angeles
Enrique Oteiza, Instituto Torcuato Di Tella
Luis Ratinoff, National University of Colombia
Robert E. Scott, University of Illinois
Rodolfo Stavenhagen, Latin American Center for Research in the Social Sciences
Stanley J. Stein, Princeton University
Arnold Strickon, Brandeis University
John Thompson, University of Illinois
Charles Wagley, Columbia University